IMPROVING THE QUALITY OF LIBRARY SERVICES FOR STUDENTS WITH DISABILITIES

IMPROVING THE QUALITY OF LIBRARY SERVICES FOR STUDENTS WITH DISABILITIES

EDITED BY PETER HERNON
AND PHILIP CALVERT

A Member of the Greenwood Publishing Group

Westport, Connecticut • London

Library of Congress Cataloging-in-Publication Data

Improving the quality of library services for students with disabilities / edited by Peter Hernon and Philip Calvert.

   p. cm.

   Includes bibliographical references and index.

   ISBN 1–59158–300–4 (alk. paper)

   1. Academic libraries—Services to people with disabilities. 2. Academic libraries—Services to people with disabilities—United States. 3. Academic libraries—Services to people with disabilities—New Zealand. I. Hernon, Peter. II. Calvert, Philip J., 1949– . III. Title.

Z711.92.P5I47 2006

027.6'63—dc22   2005030261

British Library Cataloguing in Publication Data is available.

Library of Congress Catalog Card Number: 2005030261

ISBN: 1–59158–300–4

First published in 2006

Libraries Unlimited, 88 Post Road West, Westport, CT 06881

A Member of the Greenwood Publishing Group, Inc.

www.lu.com

Printed in the United States of America

The paper used in this book complies with the
Permanent Paper Standard issued by the National
Information Standards Organization (Z39.48–1984).

10 9 8 7 6 5 4 3 2 1

The authors and publisher gratefully acknowledge permission for use of the following materials:

   From Chapter 7. Terry G. Vavra, *Improving Your Measurement of Customer Satisfaction: A Guide to Creating, Conducting, Analyzing, and Reporting Customer Satisfaction.* Milwaukee, WI: ASQ Quality Press, 1997. ISBN: 0–87389–405–7.

   From Chapter 12. Reprinted from *The Internet and Higher Education,* 7, Sheryl Burgstahler, Bill Corrigan, and Joan McCarter, "Making Distance Learning Courses Accessible to Students and Instructors with Disabilities: A Case Study," 233–246, 2004, with permission from Elsevier.

   Figure 12.1, "Supplementary Set of Statements." Reprinted from *The Journal of Academic Librarianship,* 26, Danuta A. Nitecki and Peter Hernon, "Measuring Service Quality at Yale University's Libraries," 270–271, 2000, with permission from Elsevier; and reprinted from *Library & Information Science Research,* 27, Peter Hernon and Philip Calvert, "E-Service Quality in Libraries: Exploring Its Features and Dimensions," 377–404, 2005, with permission from Elsevier.

   Every reasonable effort has been made to trace the owners of copyright materials in this book, but in some instances this has proven impossible. The author and publisher will be glad to receive information leading to more complete acknowledgments in subsequent printings of this book and in the meantime extend their apologies for any omissions.

CONTENTS

Illustrations   ix

Preface   xi

1   Students with Disabilities in Higher Education,
      by Peter Hernon and Philip Calvert   1
    Definitions   2
    The Picture in Other Countries   5
    Issues   7
    Trends   10
    Conclusion   10
    Notes   11

2   Context, by Peter Hernon   15
    Examples   16
    Enforcement   18
    Some Relevant Associations, Organizations, and
      Government Agencies   20
    Conclusion   21
    Appendix: Examples of Relevant Associations,
      Organizations, and Government Agencies   22
    Notes   26

3 Legal Context within the United States,
    by Kathleen Rogers   31
    What Is the ADA and Section 504?   33
    Who Is Protected under Section 504 and the ADA?   34
    What Is a "Reasonable Accommodation?"   37
    Accommodating Psychological Disabilities   38
    Students Who May Pose a Direct Threat   40
    Conclusion   41
    Notes   43

4 An Increasingly Diverse Student Population:
    A Rationale for Consideration of Universal Access at
    Postsecondary Institutions, by Todd K. Herriott   45
    Legislative Initiatives   46
    Social Consciousness   48
    Educational Response   49
    Universal Design Movement   50
    Application to Libraries   52
    Conclusion   54
    Notes   54

5 Disability Support Services, Victoria University of
    Wellington, by Ava Gibson   57
    How DSS Works   57
    The Students with Whom We Work   58
    Relations with the University Library   60
    Library Services—What Is Important?   61
    What Does DSS Want to Know about Library Services?   64
    Conclusion   65
    Notes   65

6 Perspective of Library Directors   67
    Kearney State University Library   68
    University of Pittsburgh Library System   69
    Gallaudet University Library   70
    Landmark College Library   72
    University of Auckland Library   80
    University of Canterbury Library   81
    Massey University Library   82
    Conclusion   84
    Appendix: Library Policies: Services for Users with Disabilities   85
    Notes   89

7   Literature Review, by Peter Hernon   93
    Some General Writings   94
    Overview   95
    Adaptive Technologies   97
    Accessible Web Page Design   98
    General User/Use Studies   100
    Service Quality   102
    Satisfaction   107
    Some Survey Instruments and the Rationale for
        a Localized Approach   108
    Conclusion   110
    Notes   111

8   Developing and Testing an Instrument:
        New Zealand, by Philip Calvert and Peter Hernon   117
    Instrument Development   118
    Findings   120
    Conclusion   133
    Appendix: Service Quality: Potential
        Statements and Dimensions   133
    Notes   138

9   Refinement of the Data Collection Instrument,
        by Peter Hernon and Jennifer Lann   139
    Review of the Data Collection Instrument   140
    The Pretest   141
    Findings   145
    Conclusion   150
    Appendix: Service Quality: Library Collections and
        Services for Those with Disabilities   151
    Notes   156

10 Conducting Your Own Study, by Philip Calvert   159
    The First Step   159
    Target Population and Distributing the Survey   161
    Incentives   162
    The Survey Instrument   163
    Detailed Form Design   164
    Printed Form   165
    Web-based and E-mail Surveys   166
    Piloting and Testing   168
    Supplementary Data Collection   169

	Conclusion	169
	Notes	170
11	Reporting and Using the Results, by Philip Calvert	173
	The Software	174
	Data Entry and Analysis	175
	Presenting the Data	181
	Reporting the Results	184
	Conclusion	186
	Notes	186
12	Continuing to Improve Service Quality for Students, by Peter Hernon and Philip Calvert	187
	Information Literacy	188
	Our Variation of a Data Collection Instrument for Gauging Service Quality	192
	Management's Knowledge of Student Expectations	200
	Research Agenda	202
	Conclusion	204
	Notes	205
Bibliography		207
Index		223
About the Editors and Contributors		231

ILLUSTRATIONS

Figures

8.1 Depiction of Quadrants (in Quadrant Analysis)   126
11.1 Graphical Representation of Data (taken from Table 11.2) 182
12.1 Supplementary Set of Statements   193

Tables

8.1 The Largest Gaps between Service
Expectations and Service Performance   121

8.2 The Lowest Gaps between Service
Expectations and Service Performance   123

8.3 Highest Mean Scores for Service
Performance by the Library   124

8.4 Ranking of the Eleven Dimensions   128

8.5 Ranked List of Dimensions   129

8.6 The Revised Set of Statements (Section A)   132

9.1 Promotion of the Survey   142

9.2 Possible Reasons for Low Response   144

11.1 Hypothetical Expectations Data   177

11.2 Hypothetical Performance Data   178

11.3 Gaps Scores (Calculated from the Previous Tables)   180

PREFACE

"Delivering great service is difficult. If it were easy, it would be more common."[1]

Academic libraries are service organizations that, within the context of the institutional mission, meet the information needs of the populations they serve and develop the information literacy abilities of students whom, it is hoped, among other things, become life-long learners who are able to locate, retrieve, evaluate, and apply information as they convert it into knowledge. As service organizations, libraries are concerned about service quality and its impact on current and future users of library collections and services.

The literature of library and information science (LIS) discusses the need for libraries to interact with their communities and to convert more of the populations served into dedicated, delighted users. In essence, the goal is no member of the populations covered by the institutional mission "left behind"—adoption of the U.S. Department of Education's popular name for the 2001 public law dealing with "no child left behind." Yet, discussion of the role of libraries in meeting information needs tends to focus on general populations—faculty, students, and staff—and not some of the so-called special ones (e.g., students needing remedial studies, international students who are disadvantaged in their ability to communicate in English both orally and in written form, and students with disabilities). This book addresses one of these populations—students with disabilities—and encourages greater inclusion of data collected in the planning and delivery of library services. Disabled students' needs, aspirations, and expectations should not be assumed; rather, as for anyone, their needs and expectations merit investigation. Furthermore, the services provided to them should not be narrowly interpreted—just conform to the laws of the land.

Improving the Quality of Library Services for Students with Disabilities incorporates research into the design of a data-collection process to ascertain the library-related expectations (service quality and, to some extent, satisfaction) of students with disabilities. It also shares the perspectives of library directors, campus-wide disability officers, and a college attorney who specializes in the area. This project originated while I was on sabbatical leave and teaching at Victoria University of Wellington (New Zealand). A strength of the work therefore is that it has a two-country and international perspective. Clearly, the content of this book has implications for library services and the education of students worldwide.

The intended audience for this book includes academic librarians, students in LIS programs preparing for their professional careers, members of boards of trustees, and disability officers maintaining a partnership with libraries. Although the focus is on academic librarianship, the issues and data-collection process developed here are relevant to public libraries and their oversight boards.

Working in a partnership with disability services, librarians can see that, when using library resources and services—either on-site or remotely—people with special needs do not feel isolated and sensitive to the perception that they are different. One of the challenges facing the LIS profession is inclusiveness: reaching out to the entire populations served and meeting the information needs and expectation of all faculty, staff, and students who need the intellectual atmosphere and content of libraries. We need to stop making assumptions about different members of populations, listen to their needs and expectations, and factor the results of that listening into the development and improvement of services and their delivery.

Students with disabilities are not a problem; they are an opportunity. Like all other students they are individuals who have potential, and the academic library has a role to unleash and develop that potential.

Peter Hernon
June, 2005

NOTE

1. Leonard L. Berry, *On Great Service: A Framework for Action* (New York: The Free Press, 1995), 267.

1

STUDENTS WITH DISABILITIES IN HIGHER EDUCATION

Peter Hernon and Philip Calvert

Individuals with disabilities are a valuable resource.[1]

In a *Census Brief* released in 1997, the U.S. Bureau of the Census estimated that "about 1 in 5 Americans have some kind of a disability, and 1 in 10 have a severe disability. And, with the population aging and the likelihood of having a disability increasing with age, the growth of the number of people with disabilities can be expected to accelerate in the coming decades."[2] More recently, the 2000 census of population and housing showed that 49,746,248 people of at least five years of age declared a disability; that number represents 19.3 percent of the U.S. population—close to the one in five statistic.[3] As Thomas R. Wolanin and Patricia E. Steele note,

Among children and youth under age 21, the percentage receiving federally mandated education services for students with disabilities has steadily risen to 13 percent or 6 million students in 2000. Students with LD [learning disabilities] constitute the largest single group and range in various studies from 46 percent to 61 percent of all students with disabilities. The percentage of students with disabilities who have completed high school has increased from 61 percent in 1986 to 78 percent in 2001. These students increasingly graduate with standard diplomas and are academically qualified to attend higher education. About 9 percent of all undergraduates in higher education report having a disability, a percentage that has tripled in the last two decades. This amounts to about 1.3 million students.[4]

Focusing on students with learning disabilities, Wolanin and Steel mention that the number of these students is "large, rapidly growing" and that there is a "new group of students … whose disability is 'invisible' [meaning not apparent from looking at someone], and who are disproportionately from affluent families."[5]

Discussing students in higher education, they note that "approximately 10 percent of the total student population had some kind of disability, and of those with disabilities roughly half have more than one disability." Furthermore, "minority students (other than Asians) and low-income students are more likely to have disability than other groups."[6] The National Center for Education Statistics places the percent of college students with disabilities at 9 percent in 1999/2000—up from under 3 percent in 1978. Moreover,

About half of these students were enrolled at public 2-year institutions, and another 26 percent were enrolled at public 4-year institutions. The percentage of students with disabilities was higher at public 2-year and private for-profit institutions than at public and private not-for-profit 4-year institutions. Among students with disabilities, 26 percent reported receiving disability-related services or accommodations. However, 22 percent of students with disabilities reported not receiving the services or accommodations they needed. At private for-profit institutions, 11 percent of students with disabilities reported not receiving the services or accommodations they needed, compared with 21 to 24 percent of their counterparts at other types of institutions.

Of the students with disabilities, 29 percent had an orthopedic or mobility impairment; 17 percent mental illness or depression; 15 percent a health impairment; 12 percent a visual or hearing impairment; 11 percent a learning disability or Attention Deficit Disorder (ADD); and 15 percent had some other type of disability. Students with a learning disability or ADD were more likely than students with other types of disabilities to report receiving services. . . . Nevertheless, 32 percent of students with a learning disability or ADD reported not receiving the services or accommodations they needed.[7]

The National Center for Education Statistics also noted that

The Americans with Disabilities [ADA] Act of 1990 and Section 504 of the Rehabilitation Act of 1973 require postsecondary institutions to make education accessible for students with disabilities. At the postsecondary level, disability-related services and accommodations might include, for example, alternative examination formats, readers, interpreters, or ramps for wheelchair access.[8]

Completing the profile, Cathy Henderson presents a profile of college freshmen who have disabilities. Her report is part of the Cooperative Institutional Research Program, which is an ongoing national survey of a sample of full-time freshmen at four-year institutions.[9]

DEFINITIONS

Naturally there are different definitions of disabilities within and across countries, and academic institutions vary in their ability to provide comparable levels of assistance. If eligibility criteria determine which students are accepted and identified as being disabled, then those criteria influence the number and types of individuals identified; still policies set by government apply to the equity of the selection. Furthermore, as institutions vary in the degree of academic resources they can provide, students with disabilities receive different levels of support. Such observations underscore the importance of the legal framework to define terms and set standards for all institutions to meet.

Section 504 and the Americans with Disabilities Act (ADA) of 1990 cover students:

- With attention-deficit disorder (ADD) or attention-deficit/hyperactivity disorder (ADHD);
- With learning disabilities who do not manifest a significant discrepancy between intellectual ability and achievement;
- Who are transitioned out of special education programs;
- Who are considered to be socially maladjusted;
- Who have a history of drug and alcohol abuse;
- With health needs; and
- With communicable diseases, such as AIDS.

To provide a framework for subsequent chapters, this section defines some key terms, namely:

- Disability, which, according to Section 504 of the 1973 Rehabilitation Act, refers to a person who has a physical or mental impairment that "substantially limits" one or more major life activities, has a record of such impairment, or is regarded as having such an impairment. Section 504 states that "No otherwise qualified individual with a disability ... shall solely by reason of her or his disability be excluded from the participation in, be denied the benefits of, or be subjected to discrimination under any program or activity receiving Federal financial assistance" (29 U.S.C.A. § 794).
- Learning disabilities, which "is a general term that refers to a heterogeneous group of disorders manifested by significant difficulties in the acquisition and use of listening, speaking, reading, writing, reasoning, or mathematical skills. These disorders are intrinsic to the individual, presumed to be due to central nervous system dysfunction, and may occur across the life span...."
  - º "Learning Disabilities can be divided up into three broad categories. These types of learning disabilities include: developmental speech and language disorders, academic skills disorders, [and] 'other', a catch-all that includes certain coordination disorders and learning handicaps not covered by the other terms. Each one of these categories includes a number of more specific disorders."

º Dyslexia, which is a severe difficulty in understanding or using one or more areas
   of language (including listening, speaking, reading, writing, and spelling), is the
   most common learning disability.[10]

The World Health Organization's (WHO) *International Classification of
Functioning, Disability and Health,* commonly known as ICF, regards all
human beings as having some decrement in health and therefore some disability.[11] What the ICF endeavors to do is to classify in a specific way all of the
body's functions and structure, what a person can do in a standard environment, and what that person actually does in his or her usual environment
(performance). Disability thus becomes an umbrella term for impairments,
activity limitations, and participation restrictions.[12] In the ICF view, it is not
a matter of the body having a problem with a particular function, a disability
only becomes apparent when the person is confronted with an environment
that constrains his or her performance.

Interestingly, disability, in effect, might be viewed as beginning when good
health has ended or the person has no fundamental physical impairment.
In such instances, once an individual is disabled, he or she enters a special
category. The WHO, through its ICF, wants to shift the focus from cause to
impact. It is not a disability that affects an individual; it is that person's interaction with the environment that causes the problem. As a result, in this *social
model* the problem of disability is a creation of society and not an attribute of
the individual. This is why some people say that they are not disabled, but
they have an *impairment.* They only have a disability when they try to do
something that the standard-built environment makes difficult for them; this
applies in a library as much as anywhere else. According to the WHO,

- A man with two fingers on one hand has an impairment, but this becomes a disability
  when he is expected to use a swipe card to enter a locked room in the library;
- A blind woman experiences a disability if important study materials are only available in print form and the library cannot or will not provide her with the necessary
  texts in Braille or audio formats;
- A man in a wheelchair does not experience a problem until he arrives at steps
  leading up to the library's front door; and
- A female student with poor hearing but the ability to lip read receives poor service
  if a library staff member turns away while speaking to her so that she cannot see the
  staff member's lips.

The ICF is intended to be a tool that assists planning and policy development. By itself, it is not an assessment or measurement tool, but rather it
represents a framework and set of classifications on which assessment and
measurement tools may be based and to which they can be mapped.[13] Internationally, the ICF has had only a slight impact on library thinking,[14] and,
as yet, no impact on library policies.

THE PICTURE IN OTHER COUNTRIES

Although the literature tends to focus on the situation in individual countries, there are some cross-country analyses and comparisons. One example, *Disability in Higher Education*, provides case studies of the practices in Canada (Ontario), France, and the United Kingdom.[15] It also describes the situation in Germany and Switzerland. Although the statistics do not allow for a detailed comparison across the countries, they reflect conditions in each of the five countries. The universities in each of the countries have a long way to go before they respond fully to the needs of disabled students. Achieving full service to these students requires the development of open attitudes toward students with disabilities, close review of the funding mechanisms, improvements in data collection, better identification and assessment procedures, and improved links with secondary schools and other groups in the community. This section of the chapter portrays another country—New Zealand.

New Zealand

As reported in the 2001 Census, "743,800 New Zealanders or 20 percent of the total population (excluding people living in some special types of residential facilities) are limited in their daily activities because of the long-term effects of a disability." This number represents "an increase of 41,800 since 1996–1997. However, the overall disability rate of 1 in 5 has not changed." Additionally,

- One in five New Zealanders has a disability.
- Disability increases with age.
- The majority of disabled people have more than one disability.
- Physical disabilities are the most common type of disability; two-thirds of disabled people reported a physical disability.
- The number of people with mild disabilities has decreased whereas the number with moderate disabilities has increased.
- The disability rate for Maori children is 15 percent, which is also higher than the national rate for children (11 percent).
- More females reported disabilities (384,900) than did males (358,900).[16]

Nonetheless, the overall disability rate for males and females is the same.

In the second in a series of annual reports that identify trends in participation in tertiary education, the Ministry of Education observed that "although the number of students with disabilities has been increasing strongly in recent years, the rate of participation by this group is less than a quarter of that of people with disability." Students with disabilities "are more likely to be older than the general student body." Furthermore, for the year 2002, students with disabilities were more likely to study part-time and at a certificate or diploma level, and to be enrolled in mixed field programs (e.g., employment-related programs and social and life skills–related training).[17] Viewed from another perspective, of the 743,800 people previously mentioned who have disabilities, approximately 7 percent comprised students enrolled in tertiary education. (Thus, in 2001, there were 15,160 students with disabilities of at least fifteen years of age.) These statistics become even more dramatic when race and ethnicity are considered; however, "Asian students were far less likely to report having a disability."[18]

Given the growth in the population with disabilities and the aging of this population, in April 2001, Prime Minister Helen Clark launched the New Zealand Disability Strategy, "Making a World of Difference—Whakanui Oranga," whose purpose "is to remove the barriers which prevent disabled people from participating fully in society." She said,

Our society is built in ways which assume we can all move quickly from one side of the road to the other, that we can all see signs, read directions, hear announcements, reach buttons, climb stairs, open heavy doors, interpret complex information and that we all have stable moods and perceptions. For one in five New Zealanders with a long-term disability, that is not necessarily the case. Many can't reach their potential, or participate fully in our communities because of the barriers they face doing everyday things.[19]

As part of the national strategy, each government department has been instructed to develop an annual implementation work plan with goals and actions. At the end of each year, the departments are required to prepare a progress report for the Office for Disability Issues. The Minister for Disability Issues then reports annually to Parliament on progress in implementing the strategy.[20] The New Zealand Disability Strategy accepts the ICF approach when it says "Disability is not something individuals have. What individuals have are impairments." It then goes on to state, "Disability is the process which happens when one group of people creates barriers by designing a world only for their way of living, taking no account of the impairments other people have."[21]

It is instructive, therefore, to compare the New Zealand Disability Strategy with the draft New Zealand Digital Strategy, for this document, issued by the Ministry of Economic Development, applies the typical definition of disability, not the ICF version. While apparently recognizing the potential benefits of giving each person the opportunity to acquire the skills needed for an information-powered society (e.g., "the use of ICT [information and communications technologies] should be promoted at all stages of education and in all forms of training, taking into account the special needs of persons with disabilities and disadvantaged groups"),[22] it fails to provide any specific reference to how ICT could improve the educational opportunities of these people. There are reminders of the need to promote the use of ICT in health and disability services,[23] but almost nothing is said on behalf of the people with the disabilities. The draft Digital Strategy often refers to the importance of the government providing leadership, but this does not seem to be translated into specific references to improving the life of people with disabilities.

The New Zealand Human Rights Act of 1993 was designed as antidiscrimination legislation with the aim of guaranteeing equal access to facilities, such as library buildings.[24] Although, as Mary A. Schnakenberg explained, this law allows disabled persons to have access to public buildings,[25] no legislation makes it mandatory that information be made available in a format that visually impaired people find easy to access.[26] Librarians who meet the letter of the law are not necessarily providing equal service to the entire community served so that everyone will be able to achieve his or her potential.

ISSUES

Numerous studies have been conducted in the area of higher education and disabilities, and these works have identified various issues. As a consequence, this section is very selective in its coverage. It is important to note that the literature tends not to connect the library with the rest of the institution; therefore, the library becomes irrelevant to the issues as presented in the overwhelming body of reported studies. Some of the pressing issues discussed include the removal of architecture barriers, the need to make technology accessible to all distance education programs, ensuring that students with disabilities are not disadvantaged in distance education courses delivered electronically, helping faculty who have disabilities, providing sufficient financial aid, determining who is protected by law and what reasonable accommodations are required,[27] and supporting efforts to make faculty effective teachers and to meet the educational needs of all students, whether or not they have disabilities. Faculty need to realize that, in general, students with disabilities can do the same academic work as their peers without disabilities, but they cannot do it as rapidly.

Wolanin and Steele, as well as Henderson, discuss a number of key issues.[28] Among the issues that Wolanin and Steele present is the fact that "students with disabilities do not receive the same level of academic preparation in K-12 education as their peers without disabilities and consequently do not go on to higher education in large numbers."[29] Thus, they may require some remedial education and/or auxiliary services to assist them in completing their coursework. Furthermore, "faculty attitudes and the academic culture are the major barriers to the successful implementation of accommodations for students with disabilities. Faculty are often ignorant about their responsibilities and about how to relate to students with disabilities."[30] Wolanin and Steele also present two models of disability: the *medical* and *social* models. The former, which views students with disabilities as being different from other students, focuses on physical or mental impairments. The latter model considers students and others with disabilities as productive members of society; they make positive contributions. The social model asks that students be viewed as students—whether or not they have disabilities.

Shaila Rao provides a literature review that is international in scope and that examines attitudinal barriers, which "happens to be the least researched variable in studies done with faculty and students with disabilities in higher education." One of the conclusions reached from reviewing various studies is that "faculty at institutions of higher education need to be better informed about disabilities and students with disabilities to improve their attitudes."[31] D. Roer-Strier echoes Rao's theme that faculty awareness and involvement must be increased.[32] Stanley Paul argues that "respect and cooperation from faculty, students, and administration can lead to a more effective educational experience for students with disabilities."[33] At the same time, those without disabilities gain opportunities to interact with a diverse community, some of whose members have disabilities. Margaret Taylor suggests that the behavior of faculty and the administration towards students with disabilities is similar to a "lottery" and that "tutors' understanding of students' needs is inconsistent and that some are unsure of how to interact with disabled people."[34]

In *The Condition of Education 2003: Services and Accommodations for Students with* Disabilities, the National Center for Education Statistics noted that, for whatever reason, more than 20 percent of the students with disabilities reported that they did not receive the services or accommodations they needed.[35] However, the report did not fully delve into the question of why not. Briley S. Proctor points out that institutions of higher education do not have to offer all of the services that students received in their secondary education. Consequently, some college students may find that they receive fewer accommodations than they were accustomed to in high school.[36]

A final issue relates to college attainment. According to the National Organization on Disability,

There seems to have been a decline since 1998 from 30% to 26% among people with disabilities who have completed some college, and an even sharper decline from 19% to 12% for people with disabilities who have graduated from college. Given the importance of educational attainment in obtaining employment, it is important to explore more fully the cause of this decline.[37]

Salome Heyward provides an excellent discussion of (and introduction to) the legal responsibilities of higher education to students with disabilities. She notes that today's students who identify themselves as disabled and requesting accommodation "have greater sophistication and awareness regarding their legal rights"[38] and

Assuming an individual can establish that he or she has an impairment that satisfies the legal definition of disability, there is an additional hurdle that must be cleared. The individual must also be "otherwise qualified." "[T]he definition of '[disabled] individual' [in Section 504] is broad, but only those individuals who are both [disabled] and otherwise qualified are eligible for relief."[39]

What does "otherwise qualified" mean? Assuming that someone applied for admissions into a program of study (or was already enrolled and in the process of completing the program) and did not meet one criterion (e.g., had not taken the SAT examination or had a grade point average less than the program requires for graduation) but was "otherwise qualified," what is to be done? Clearly, the question illustrates that colleges and universities would turn to their legal counsels to answer the question; actually the counsels would expect programs already to have in place procedures that address the question and to maintain an extensive documentation trail.

The faculty might perceive a clash between ADA compliance and their academic freedom. An example that Heyward does not present involves course syllabi stating that unless students attend a certain number of classes, their final grade will be penalized. To what extent would the Department of Education's Office of Civil Rights (see the next chapter) accept academic freedom as a sufficient justification if a student has a disability prohibiting regular attendance or the completion of a particular lab experiment? The faculty member might be expected to demonstrate that class attendance did indeed add to the understanding of course content and that the content could not be presented through other means (e.g., PowerPoint slides distributed to the class).

Should policies covering equal opportunities for students in higher education be based on a liberal as opposed to a rights-based approach? Sheila Riddell maintains that a rights-based approach focuses on equality of access rather than on outcomes and that it favors individual over structural explanations.[40] Taylor expresses some reservation about a rights-based approach, which she says "places the onus on the individual to effect change for him/herself [and] which can potentially lead to victim blaming." Her preference for a liberal approach is that it "is not automatically assumed that individuals are inevitably subject to the crushing power of patriarchy, capitalism, racism or disablism."[41] She makes it clear that there can nevertheless be a lack of resources and that physical and attitudinal barriers stand between the students with disabilities and academic success.

Faculty and staff already working at the institution might have a chronic illness or disease. In such an instance, employment law applies. One final issue to mention here is that academic institutions might acquire high-speed scanners that convert written text into the spoken word. When copyrighted material is scanned, how well do the policies and procedures conform to intellectual property rights? Clearly, the issues raised do not apply solely to the provision of adaptive technology. The United Kingdom, for instance, has the Copyright (Visually Impaired Persons) Act of 2002, which sets out two situations in which visually impaired people (or those gathering information for them) do not have to seek prior permission from the rights holder before making copies.[42] First, single copies can be made as long as the original work has been lawfully obtained and an alternative accessible copy is not available. Second, multiple copies can be provided by educational establishments as long as the author's moral rights are protected.

TRENDS

As already noted, approximately 10 percent of the U.S. student population (undergraduate and graduate) has a disability. As the population ages, more people (administrators, faculty, staff, and student) face the likelihood of becoming physically disabled. More people may also experience psychological disabilities. The percentage of students with documented learning disabilities will remain high, especially if there is diagnosis (even over-diagnosis) at an early age. The category of student disabilities that is likely to increase the most over time relates to psychological disabilities. More instances are being diagnosed and those individuals might receive medication.

Some key questions meriting consideration are:

- How well do libraries serve the student body that has disabilities?
- With libraries embarking on the provision of service 24/7/365, how well are they meeting or exceeding the service expectations of the different communities served?
- With libraries placing increasing emphasis on information literacy and trying to produce evidence that such instruction makes a difference (students, for example, demonstrate critical thinking, problem solving, and good communication skills; and become lifelong learners who can evaluate the information they find), what impact do such programs have on students with disabilities?
- When libraries hire instructional and reference librarians, to what extent are these individuals able to interact effectively with all of the communities covered in the library's (and broader organizational) mission statements?
- To what extent can librarians create twenty-first-century library services "without bringing along patrons with disabilities?"[43]

CONCLUSION

Academic institutions have developed policies and procedures to respond to and accommodate students with disabilities and to deal with the employment of faculty and staff who become ill or suffer from a disability.[44] Student rights and institutional responsibilities extend beyond the classroom to the support services, including the library. Librarians likely provide service to students with disabilities—hidden (not readily apparent) and otherwise—when they visit the library. As well, students with disabilities use the library's Web site and online databases, and they participate in instructional sessions that librarians provide, perhaps in conjunction with the teaching faculty. These sessions might involve the completion of assignments or testing about the extent to which the sessions were successful—learning occurred.

As administrators, teaching faculty, and librarians compile data regarding student learning over the duration of a program of study and use those data to improve the educational experience, students with physical, medical, learning, and psychological disabilities become part of the outcomes assessment that accrediting organizations expect of academic institutions and some programs (e.g., accounting and library and information science). Of course, there is a definite need for the librarians to be aware of the legal requirements as well as how to serve any population of library users better— better includes recognition that service quality and satisfaction, multifaceted concepts, apply to *everyone* identified in the institutional and library mission and vision statements. Knowledge of the service expectations and information needs for all segments of the academic community is essential for the continuous quality improvement of library services and programs. Reinforcing the importance of this is the fact that academic libraries are both service and learning organizations.

> [The] human potential [of students with disabilities] still needs to be fully recognized, nurtured, and developed.[45]

NOTES

1. Delar K. Singh, "Students with Disabilities and Higher Education," *College Student Journal* 37 (September 2003), 367. See also U.S. Bureau of the Census, "Facts for Features" (Washington, D.C.: Bureau of the Census, 2002). Available at http://www.census.gov/Press-Release/www/2002/cb02ff11.html (accessed September 7, 2004).

2. U.S. Bureau of the Census, *Census Brief,* CNBR-97-5 (Washington, D.C.: Bureau of the Census, 1997), 1.

3. U.S. Bureau of the Census, "Disability Status: 2000—Census 2000: Table 1. Characteristics of the Civilian Noninstitutionalized Population by Age, Disability Status, and Type of Disability: 2000" (Washington, D.C.: Bureau of the Census, 1997). Available at http://www.census.gov/hhes/www/disable/disabstat2k/table1.html (accessed September 5, 2004).

4. Thomas R. Wolanin and Patricia E. Steele, *Higher Education Opportunities for Students with Disabilities: A Primer for Policymakers* (Washington, D.C.: The Institute for Higher Education Policy, June 2004), vii. Available at http://www.ihep.com/Pubs/PDF/DisabilitiesReport2004.pdf (accessed September 4, 2004).

5. Ibid., ix.

6. Ibid., 20.

7. U.S. Department of Education, National Center for Education Statistics, *The Condition of Education 2003: Services and Accommodations for Students with Disabilities: Services and Accommodations for Students with Disabilities* (Washington, D.C.: National Center for Education Statistics, 2003). Available at http://nces.

ed.gov/programs/coe/2003/section5/indicator34.asp (accessed September 4, 2004). Note: the percentages do not total 100 due to rounding.

8. Ibid.

9. Cathy Henderson, *2001 College Freshmen with Disabilities: A Biennial Statistical Profile* (Washington, D.C.: The George Washington University HEATH Resource Center, 2001). Available at http://www.heath.gwu.edu/PDFs/collegefreshmen.pdf (accessed November 22, 2004). The Graduate School of Education and Human Development, The George Washington University maintains the HEATH Resource Center, from which the report was produced.

10. See National Joint Committee on Learning Disabilities, "The ABCs of LD and ADHD" (Rockville, MD: National Joint Committee on Learning Disabilities, 2004). Available at http://www.ldonline.org/abcs_info/articles-info.html (accessed September 8, 2004).

11. World Health Organization, *Towards a Common Language for Functioning, Disability and Health: ICF* (Geneva: World Health Organization, 2002). Available at http://www3.who.int/icf/beginners/bg.pdf (accessed October 2, 2004).

12. Ibid., 2.

13. *ICF Australian User Guide V1.0* (Canberra: Australian Institute of Health and Welfare, 2003). Available at http://www.aihw.gov.au/publications/dis/icfaugv1/icfugv1.pdf (accessed October 3, 2004).

14. Katherine J. Miller-Gatenby and Michele Chittenden, "Reference Services for All: How to Support Reference Service to Clients with Disabilities," *The Reference Librarian* 69/70 (2000): 313–326.

15. See Organisation for Economic Co-operation and Development, *Disability in Higher Education* (Paris: Organisation for Economic Co-operation and Development, 2003).

16. New Zealand, Statistics New Zealand, *Disability* (Wellington: Statistics New Zealand, 2002). Available at http://www.stats.govt.nz/domino/external/web/Prod_Serv.nsf/htmldocs/Disability (accessed September 5, 2004); New Zealand, Statistics New Zealand, *New Zealand Disability Survey Snapshot 1: Key Facts* (Wellington: Statistics New Zealand, 2002). Available at http://www.stats.govt.nz/domino/external/pasfull/pasfull.nsf/web/Media+Release+2001+Disability+Survey+Snapshot+1+Key+Facts?open (accessed September 5, 2004).

17. New Zealand, Ministry of Education, *Participation in Tertiary Education 2003* (Wellington, NZ: Ministry of Education, 2003), 33–35. Available at http://www.minedu.govt.nz/index.cfm?layout = document&documentid = 8811&indexid = 8655&indexparentid = 8654 (accessed September 5, 2004).

18. Ibid., 33–34.

19. New Zealand, Ministry of Education, *New Zealand Disability Strategy—Education's Implementation Work Plan* (Wellington, NZ: Ministry of Education, 2004). Available at http://www.minedu.govt.nz/index.cfm?layout = document&documentid = 7356&data = 1 (accessed September 4, 2004).

20. For information about the strategy, see New Zealand, Office for Disability Issues, *Publications: NZ Disability Strategy Publications* (Wellington: Ministry of Social Development, Office for Disability Issues, 2004). Available at http://www.odi.govt.nz/publications/publications.html (accessed September 5, 2004).

21. Ministry of Education, *New Zealand Disability Strategy*, 3.
22. Ministry of Economic Development, *Digital Strategy: A Draft New Zealand Digital Strategy for Consultation* (Wellington, NZ: The Ministry, 2004). Available at http://www.med.govt.nz/pbt/infotech/digital-strategy/draft/draft.pdf (accessed September 15, 2004), 21
23. Ibid., 7, 52, 98.
24. New Zealand. Public Access to Legislation Project (Wellington, New Zealand: Parliamentary Counsel Office, 2005). Available at http://www.legislation.govt.nz/ (accessed January 24, 2005).
25. Mary A. Schnakenberg, "Access to Information for the Visually Impaired in New Zealand," *New Zealand Libraries* 46 (1990): 18.
26. Catherine Bardwell, "Users with Disabilities: Barriers in the Electronic Age: Challenges Faced by New Zealand University Libraries," *New Zealand Libraries* 48 (1997): 184.
27. See Laura Rothstein, "Disabilities and Higher Education: A Crystal Ball?," *Change* 35 (May–June 2003): 39–40.
28. Wolanin and Steele, *Higher Education Opportunities for Students with Disabilities;* Henderson, *2001 College Freshmen with Disabilities.*
29. Wolanin and Steele, *Higher Education Opportunities for Students with Disabilities,* vii.
30. Ibid., ix.
31. Shaila Rao, "Faculty Attitudes and Students with Disabilities in Higher Education: A Literature Review," *College Student Journal* 38 (June 2004): 191–197. [Electronic Version available through Infotrac.]
32. D. Roer-Strier, "University Students with Learning Disabilities Advocating for Change," *Disability and Rehabilitation* 24 (2002): 914–924.
33. Stanley Paul, "Students with Disabilities in Higher Education: A Review of the Literature," *College Student Journal* 34 (June 2000). [Electronic Version from Infotrac.]
34. Margaret Taylor, "Widening Participation into Higher Education for Disabled Students," *Education + Training* 46 (2004): 44.
35. U.S. Department of Education, National Center for Education Statistics, *The Condition of Education 2003.*
36. Briley S. Proctor, "Social Policy and Its Application to Students with Learning Disabilities in U.S. Institutes of Higher Education," *International Journal of Sociology and Social Policy* 21 (2001): 49–50.
37. National Organization on Disability, "Education Levels of People with Disabilities" (Washington, D.C.: National Organization on Disability, 2001). Available at http://www.nod.org/content.cfm?id = 130 (accessed September 8, 2004).
38. Salome Heyward, *Disability and Higher Education: Guidance for Section 504 and ADA Compliance* (Horsham, PA: LRP Publications, 1998), 1: 9.
39. Ibid., 4: 1.
40. Sheila Riddell, "Chipping away at the Mountain: Disabled Students' Experiences of Higher Education," *International Studies in the Sociology of Education* 8 (1998): 203–222.
41. Taylor, "Widening Participation into Higher Education for Disabled Students," 44.

42. United Kingdom. Her Majesty's Stationery Office, *Copyright (Visually Impaired Persons) Act 2002* (London: Her Majesty's Stationery Office, 2002). Available at http://www.legislation.hmso.gov.uk/acts/acts2002/20020033.htm (accessed January 24, 2005).

43. Heyward, *Disability and Higher Education*, 8: 7.

44. For background information, see Ted Wattenberg, "Beyond Legal Compliance: Communities of Advocacy That Support Accessible Online Learning," *The Internet and Higher Education* 7 (2004): 123–139.

45. Singh, "Students with Disabilities and Higher Education," 367.

2

————◆◆◆◆————

CONTEXT

Peter Hernon

[T]he history of library services to people with disabilities is recent and comparatively short.[1]

Higher education is a complex enterprise that goes beyond the realm of individual faculty members and programs of study (both undergraduate and graduate) to include various stakeholders and oversight bodies. The result is that institutions of higher education face numerous pressures and challenges. Faculty pursue their scholarship, funded research, consulting, and teaching, while other actors (including accrediting organizations and oversight bodies) expect educational programs and institutions to meet their stated mission and to maintain quality assurance and to foster student learning. These stakeholders therefore insist that higher education be affordable, widely available, and of high quality. They also insist that institutions be in full compliance with existing laws and that they can influence institutional policies and change organizational and institutional cultures.

Congress passed the Rehabilitation Act of 1973, which contains Section 504 prohibiting discrimination on the basis of physical or mental disability, and the Americans with Disabilities Act of 1990 (ADA), Title II of which prohibits state and local government from discriminating on the basis of disability. To be in compliance with these statutory laws, institutions of higher education have expressed a commitment to providing reasonable workplace accommodations for employees and applicants for positions who have disabilities. Typical of such a commitment, Curry College in Milton, Massachusetts

recognizes that people with disabilities can need assistance in order to enable them to engage in life equitably. The College aims to provide services to persons with disabilities which will result in the attainment of a quality experience while participating in all institutional events, and to ensure the services are delivered in a manner which incurs the least restriction of their human rights and dignities.[2]

To achieve such a goal, colleges and universities might assign responsibilities for various aspects of disability services to the directors of three different offices: human resources, student disabilities, and buildings and grounds. Faculty members mostly work with the student disabilities officer and those students declaring their disabilities who have communicated with that officer. Service organizations such as libraries work with all three offices: human resources for library employees, student disabilities for student support in using library collections and services, and buildings and grounds on physical access issues. As Curry College declares, the goal is to ensure "the provision of services necessary to enable students with disabilities to achieve their maximum potential as members of the College Community," to facilitate "the integration of students with disabilities within our community," and to promote "a positive image of persons with disabilities."[3]

EXAMPLES

A number of academic institutions have accessibility and service statements that identify relevant services or confirm a commitment to serving students (and often others) with disabilities. These statements might reflect core values and principles and they frequently identify the staff who have responsibilities in accordance with those policies. Examples of such statements for entire institutions and/or for their libraries can be found at the Web sites of Amherst College (Amherst, MA), Boston College (Newton, MA), Bridgewater State College (Bridgewater, MA), Earlham College (Richmond, IN), Griffith University (Queensland, Australia), Montgomery College (Montgomery County, MD), North Lindsey College (Scunthorpe, United Kingdom), Roanoke College (Salem, VA), Rutgers University (New Brunswick, NJ), the University of Canterbury (Christchurch, New Zealand), the University of Manitoba (Winnipeg, Canada), the University of Notre Dame (Notre Dame, IN), and Washington State University (Pullman, WA).[4] Chapter 6 offers other examples. To be most effective, statements of values and principles should be linked to the mission statement, and all staff should be familiar with them and committed to their accomplishment.

The students at Beacon College (Leesburg, FL) and Landmark College (Putney, VT) have learning disabilities. Beacon College offers the arts associate and baccalaureate degrees and Landmark College provides the arts associate degree. Landmark's National Institute "develops and disseminates educational research and theory-based teaching practices."[5] Gallaudet University (Washington, D.C.) "is the only liberal arts university in the world designated exclusively for deaf and hard of hearing students." It has a mission and visual statement, and a statement on sign communication that reflects its commitment to a visual communication environment.[6]

In 2001, Dean College in Franklin, Massachusetts, established an Institute for Students with Disabilities for the expressed purpose of improving instructional and support services for students with disabilities. The institute's programs revolve around four goals:

1. Increase awareness, knowledge, and understanding of disabilities. Activities to achieve this goal include faculty and staff training and development, including pedagogical coaching; integration of learning services into one organizational unit—The Center for Learning; dissemination of resource information; and acquisition of training in, and use of, assistive technology and adaptive equipment.

2. Improve the methodologies, pedagogy, and curriculum used by faculty. Activities to achieve this goal include faculty and staff training and development, including pedagogical coaching; providing laptops and technology training to all full-time faculty to enable them to integrate technology into their classroom for students with disabilities; establishing a library of resource materials; developing and implanting the Arch Program, a college preparatory program designed for students with learning disabilities who need or want some intensive academic skill development prior to entering the associate degree program;[7] and more.

3. Provide a unified, integrated, and comprehensive approach. The college has integrated learning services under the umbrella of the Center for Learning, and the Arch Program is one of the programs offered.

4. Improve the academic success of students with disabilities. To determine the impact of this overarching goal, the college uses student outcomes, which are aggregate statistics on groups of students that are often compiled and reported at the institutional level. Examples of these outcomes include retention rates, percent of students placed on academic probation or academic suspension, and dean's list statistics. The college tracks and compares statistics about student outcomes for three groups: those who have submitted documentation of a disability, students classified as at-risk upon admission, and all other students.[8]

Another example is Texas Tech University Libraries, whose mission is to "connect users with resources that advance intellectual inquiry and discovery." Under the goal of "access and diversity: serve a larger, more academically prepared, and diverse student body," the first objective specifies "provide access and services to meet the needs of students, faculty, and staff." One of the so-called methods for assessment is really an output metric that indicates the amount of business handled. It centers on a determination of the "number of requests for Americans with Disabilities Act services."[9]

Finally, it merits mention that Valle Verde Library, part of El Paso Community College (El Paso, TX) has a useful page entitled "Designing Web Pages for People with Disabilities" that complements the information provided in the chapter appendix. The sites listed on that Web page illustrate how to apply appropriate design architecture to Web sites.[10]

ENFORCEMENT

The Office for Civil Rights (OCR), U.S. Department of Education, enforces regulations that implement Section 504 and Title II. According to those requirements, institutions of higher education must provide students with disabilities with "auxiliary aids" (e.g., assistive listening devices and telecommunications devices for deaf persons); however, "colleges are not required to provide the most sophisticated auxiliary aids available." Still,

the aids provided must effectively meet the needs of a student with a disability. An institution has flexibility in choosing the specific aid or service it provides to the student, as long as the aid or service selected is effective. These aids should be selected after consultation with the student who will use them.[11]

According to OCR,

Libraries and some of their significant and basic materials must be made accessible ... to students with disabilities. Students with disabilities must have the appropriate auxiliary aids needed to locate and obtain library resources. The college library's basic index of holdings (whether formatted on-line or on index cards) must be accessible. For example, a screen and keyboard (or card file) must be placed within reach of a student using a wheelchair. If a Braille index of holdings is not available for blind students, readers must be provided for necessary assistance.

Articles and materials that are [among] library holdings and are required for course work must be accessible to all students enrolled in that course. This means that if material is required for the class, then its text must be read for a blind student or provided in Braille or on tape. A student's actual study time and use of these articles are considered personal study time and the institution has no further obligation to provide additional auxiliary aids.[12]

Given these requirements, academic libraries have tended to focus on issues of accessibility and the nondiscrimination of their customers and employees. They might view assistance to students with disabilities largely as the responsibility of the student disabilities officer, who provides students with auxiliary aids and services (see chapter 6).

Complicating matters for public services (e.g., interaction at a public service desk), students may have hidden disabilities, which

are physical or mental impairments that are not readily apparent to others. They include such conditions and diseases as specific learning disabilities, diabetics, epilepsy, and allergy. A disability such as a limp, paralysis, total blindness or deafness is usually obvious to others. But hidden disabilities such as low vision, poor hearing, heart disease, or chronic illness may not be obvious. A chronic illness involves a recurring and long-term disability such as diabetes, heart disease, kidney and liver disease, high blood pressure, or ulcers.[13]

As a result, it is possible to document the number of students who do not have hidden disabilities, that is, if they inform the institution of their disability.[14] At the same time, the possibility of students having hidden disabilities increases the need for reference and other public service staff to receive proper training in how to deal with anyone who requests assistance. Linda L. Walling suggests that the preparation should also extend to students in schools of library and information studies.[15] However, that training needs to go beyond exposing students to information about adaptive technologies.

With the passage of revisions to Section 508 in 2001, equal access applies to Web pages in a wide assortment of institutions and agencies, such as those associated with higher education. Equal access refers, in general, to accessible Web design and appropriate adaptive technologies.

Of particular interest is OCR's *Annual Report*, which lists the types of complaints that the office has received. A number of these relate to the failure of an institution to provide auxiliary aids and services. Although not specified in the report, OCR could interact with libraries over accessibility issues (discrimination) related to the online public access catalog, the Web site, or individual databases. OCR involvement could also arise over distance learning courses offered through the Internet and the provision of library resources to students enrolled in those courses.

In Section V, "Educational Support Services," of its self-study, the University of Kentucky sounded a warning: "in the area of distance learning, many colleges seem to be handling students with disabilities differently and seem confused about where students should be sent to seek special accommodations required by law."[16] *Disabilities Compliance for Higher Education* clarifies the matter. LRP Publications (Horsham, PA) publishes this most informative newsletter, which focuses on OCR rulings related to accommodations and coverage of issues, as well as recent developments. In one issue, a doctoral student reporting on her dissertation research commented, "Students … see DS [Disability Service] officers, to a great extent, as places of last resort. They would like to get their needs met through other channels first, ones that do not single them out as being different from other students."[17] Another issue (April 2004, p. 4) identifies key Web sites that provide information on assisting students with disabilities.

As highlighted in the newsletter, OCR ruling might apply to libraries and their administration. For example, a university might agree to build sanitary services in libraries and other buildings that are accessible to individuals with disabilities (July 2004, p. 10). In another instance, a librarian sued the university, charging it violated state "discrimination laws by terminating her based on her disability and refusing to accommodate her disability" (May 2004, p. 13). The issue revolved around the extent to which retrieving and shelving material constitute essential duties for a librarian. Another ruling related to a student's sensitivity to fluorescent lighting in the library and classroom (September 2001, p. 11).

SOME RELEVANT ASSOCIATIONS, ORGANIZATIONS, AND GOVERNMENT AGENCIES

The chapter appendix offers twenty-five examples of relevant bodies in selected countries that provide information and guidance for any institution or organization dealing with accessibility issues. In the United States, perhaps the overall leading organization is the Association on Higher Education and Disability (AHEAD), which offers pertinent guidelines. CLAUD, which was formed in 1998, involves "librarians in higher education networking to improve library access for disabled users in the South and South-West of England." Its aims are to disseminate information on disability and to establish good practice. Among the useful material that CLAUD offers is a paper by Sandra Jones called "Recommendations to Improve Accessibility for Disabled Users in Academic Libraries" (2002). The recommendations are based on a survey that she conducted for CLAUD. Those recommendations, in essence, form a set of standards (see this chapter's appendix for more information on CLAUD).

The Quality Assurance Agency for Higher Education (QAA) in the United Kingdom has implemented a detailed code of practice for the assurance of academic quality and standards in higher education. In October 1999, QAA adopted Section 3, which applies to students with disabilities; "the object of the code is to assist institutions in ensuring that students with disabilities have access to a learning experience comparable to that of their peers." The code assumes that each institution takes nationally agreed-upon principles and practices into account and "has its own systems for independent verification both of its quality and standards and of the effectiveness of its quality assurance systems."[18]

In 1998, the Australian Library and Information Association (ALIA) implemented detailed "Guidelines on Library Standards for People with Disabilities,"[19] and there are also guidelines on information access for students with print disabilities. These guidelines date from the 2002 Forum on Library Services for People with Disabilities, at which the Australian Vice-Chancellors™ Committee agreed to chair an Accessible Curricular Materials Steering Committee to implement recommendations from the forum.[20] The guidelines are not prescriptive but offer advice on good practice. They cover the provision of student assistance, teaching materials, Internet access, the encouragement of inclusion, equipment and technology, practical classes and practicum placements, and policy implementation. They adhere to the general principle that students with print disabilities should be able to realize their full potential in university life, and that the universities need to act to help them do this. It cannot be assumed that because something is hard, it is therefore unreasonable. Although the guidelines address such matters as adaptive technology, the ultimate aim is to develop the student's capacity to undertake independent research. The library is expected to consider the needs of students with print disabilities when purchasing new equipment and software. It is worth noting that not all the responsibility is left with the university. All print disabled students are expected to notify the university of their intention to enroll in specific courses, and of their needs for texts/course materials as early as possible. They should also look to acquiring appropriate adaptive technology skills prior to commencing their courses.

Finally, it merits mention that various universities have centers and other organizations that assist students with disabilities and those working with them. For example, Disabilities, Opportunities, Internetworking, and Technology (DO-IT) of the University of Washington hosts Web sites for postsecondary faculty and administrators and also student services staff; sponsors AccessDL for the National Center on Accessible Distance Learning; and more.[21] The National Center on Accessible Information Technology at the university operates AccessIT, which "promotes the use of electronic and information technology (E&IT) for students and employees with disabilities in educational institutions at all academic levels. This Web site features the AccessIT Knowledge Base, a searchable, growing database of questions and answers regarding accessible E&IT."[22]

Founded at Stanford University in 1990, the Archimedes Project "studies barriers to accessing and using information, computers, and information appliances and identifies and designs innovative solutions...."[23] Founded in 1971, the Trace Research and Development Center, which is affiliated with the College of Engineering at the University of Wisconsin–Madison, is "working on ways to make standard information technologies and telecommunications systems more accessible and usable by people with disabilities."[24]

CONCLUSION

Numerous organizations and other bodies assist those with disabilities as well as groups that try to work with students in higher education who have physical and other disabilities. Librarians and teaching faculty might learn much from a perusal of the types of Web sites listed in the chapter appendix. Gary Greene of California State University, Long Beach, for instance, reminds us, "spelling problems in students with LD [learning disabilities] may be more severe than reading disabilities and have proved more difficult to remediate."[25] Thus, to what extent should such students be penalized for spelling mistakes in their papers and PowerPoint presentations? Should we expect them to use spelling check software, and, if they do, should the paper or slide set be error free? Error free includes catching all word similarities (e.g., "to" for "too").

Both librarians and teaching faculty have a role to play in advancing learning and ensuring that the student population becomes better educated and able to function effectively in a global society that continues to change. As educators, both librarians and teaching faculty need to recognize differences among students and to implement strategies to advance learning for students with assorted disabilities, generational orientations (e.g., the millennia generation, which dislikes reading), and so on.[26]

> When a person appears to be different, we attach a stigma to him or her.... "Stigma is about disrespect. Stigma is the use of negative labels to identify a person.... Stigma is a barrier."[27]

APPENDIX: EXAMPLES OF RELEVANT ASSOCIATIONS, ORGANIZATIONS, AND GOVERNMENT AGENCIES

Name	Country	Activities
The Access Board, http://www.access-board.gov/	U.S.	This government agency offers building and facility design guidelines and standards.
American Foundation for the Blind, http://www.afb.org/Section.asp?SectionID=42	U.S.	The Foundation "promotes wide-ranging, systemic change by addressing the most critical issues facing the growing blind and visually impaired population—employment, independent living, literacy, and technology." The homepage offers a press office, bookstore, links to related sites, an annual report, and more.
American Library Association, Association of Specialized and Cooperative Library Agencies, http://www.ala.org/ASCLAMAINTemplate.cfm?Section=ascla	U.S.	Among the issues that this site covers are the ADA, "blind and physically handicapped," "assistive technology," "equity of access," "Web accessibility tools," "impaired elderly library patrons," and "learning disabilities."
Assistive Devices Industry Office (Industry Canada), http://www.at-links.gc.ca/IndexE.asp	Canada	One option here is "Welcome to Persons With Disabilities Online, a site where persons with disabilities, their family members, caregivers and service providers can access a full range of information on disability-related programs and services in Canada."

Name	Country	Activities
Association for Higher Education Access and Disability (AHEAD), http://www.ahead.ie	Ireland	This independent non-profit organization promotes full access to, and participation, in third-level education for students with disabilities. It undertakes research in areas relating to disability and third level education and acts in a consultative capacity to the Higher Education Authority, educational institutions and other bodies in the education sector. AHEAD lobbies to improve access to and increase the participation of students with disabilities in higher and further education in Ireland. It also strives to inform and change national policy in the areas of education and the employment of graduates with disabilities.
Association on Higher Education and Disability http://www.ahead.org	U.S.	"AHEAD is an international, multicultural organization of professionals committed to full participation in higher education for persons with disabilities." The site offers "information such as DSS Links, articles and papers, the Alert Newsletter, JPED, legal resources, and Association business;" AHEAD's "Code of Ethics, Professional and Program Standards, and publications;" and more.
Australian Human Rights & Equal Rights Commission, http://www.hreoc.gov.au/disability_rights/webaccess/	Australia	This site covers disability rights, including standards, guidelines, tools and techniques, workshops and training, legal issues, and more.
CLAUD (Consortium for Libraries in Higher Education Networking to Improve Library Access for Disabled Users in South and Southwest England), http://www.bris.ac.uk/claud/welcome.html	United Kingdom	This Web site is aimed at "librarians in higher education working to improve library access for disabled users in the south and south-west of England."
Department of Justice, Americans with Disabilities Act, ADA HOME PAGE, http://www.usdoj.gov/crt/ada/adahom1.htm	U.S.	This page provides resources on the ADA, links to pages of other government departments and agencies, ADA standards for accessible design, and more.

Name	Country	Activities
Disabled People's Association http://www.dpa.org.sg/	Singapore	The site of this cross-disciplinary organization has many links to related organizations in Singapore and the rest of South East Asia. It will run with Speech First software.
EASI: Equal Access to Software and Information, http://www.rit.edu/~easi	U.S.	Its "mission is to serve as a resource by providing information and guidance in the area of access-to-information technologies by individuals with disabilities. We stay informed about developments and advancements within the adaptive computer technology field and spread that information to colleges, universities, K-12 schools, libraries and into the workplace."
Enable New Zealand, http://www.enable.co.nz	New Zealand	This multi-service organization assists disabled people and their families, employers, health professionals, and disability support organizations. It has a contracted responsibility for administering funding designated to improve the quality of life for disabled people, which it achieves by providing access to information, research, and other direct assistance. Enable Information is a national disability information and referral service. There is a Web site for accessing disability information at http://www.weka.net.nz.
Learning Disabilities Worldwide, http://www.ldam.org/	U.S.	LDW "serves the educational needs of individuals with learning disabilities in this country, and to a significant extent, in other parts of the world." It publishes a wide range of journals, books and videos designed to guide parents, educators, practitioners, and individuals with learning disabilities.
Library of Congress, http://www.loc.gov/	U.S.	Among its many offerings is a Web page entitled "Especially for People with Disabilities," which provides technical and program accommodations for the public" (see http://www.loc.gov/access).
National Center for Education Statistics, http://nces.ed.gov/	U.S.	NCES provides data on education from elementary school through postsecondary education. There is information specifically on students with disabilities.

Name	Country	Activities
National Center for the Dissemination of Disability Research, http://www.ncddr.org/	U.S.	Established in 1995, the Center funds research studies, with its "priorities being in the areas of Employment Outcomes Research, Health and Function Research, Technology for Access and Function Research, Independent Living and Community Integration Research, Associated Disability Research, Knowledge Dissemination and Utilization Activities, Capacity Building for Rehabilitation Research Training Activities, and state Technology Assistance Projects."
National Council on Disability, http://www.ncd.gov/	U.S.	This independent federal agency "promotes policies, programs, practices, and procedures that guarantee equal opportunity for all individuals with disabilities."
National Information Library Service, http://www.nils,org.au	Australia	Joint venture of RVIB, Royal Blind Society, and Vision Australia Foundation. Offers guidance and various resources related to audio publishing and accessibility.
National Organization on Disability, http://www.nod.org/	U.S.	Its mission "is to expand the participation and contribution of America's 54 million men, women and children with disabilities in all aspects of life." It seeks to raise disability awareness through programs and information.
Office for Disability Issues, http://odi.govt.nz	New Zealand	The Office promotes "the participation and inclusion of disabled people in our society." The Web site offers "information about the Office, disability in New Zealand, and what the government is doing to promote the well-being and inclusion of disabled people." There are links to key government and non-government organizations and associations.
The Open Road, http://www.openroad.net.au/	Australia	"The Open Road project, an initiative to assist public libraries and community organizations to explore the potential of using the internet to provide services to their diverse communities. The Open Road will explore issues relating to the both the provision of accessible and multilingual internet access, and the provision of accessible and multilingual community information (e-diversity)."

Name	Country	Activities
		The Open Road offers a Disability Awareness Kit, a home page covering different types of disabilities and trying to increase awareness of disability issues (see http://www.openroad.net.au/access/dakit/).
Section508.gov, http://www.section508.gov/	U.S.	This Web site of the General Services Administration provides resources to enable government employees and the public understand and implement the requirements of Section 508 of the Workforce Investment Act of 1998.
WebAIM (Web Accessibility in Mind, http://www.webaim.org/	U.S.	Its goal "is to improve accessibility to online learning opportunities for all people; in particular to improve accessibility for individuals with disabilities who currently may have a difficult time getting access to online learning opportunities." The site offers tutorials, materials, and more.
WorkAble Electronic Network, http://www.workable.org.au	Australia	Funded by the Department of Family and Community Services, WorkAble is aimed "vocational training and employment for people with a disability." The "site has a range of features for people with a disability and their families, and staff of service provider agencies."
World Wide Web Consortium (W3C), http://www.w3.org/WAI/	U.S.	The Web Accessibility Initiative includes coverage of disabilities (e.g., Web accessibility guidelines).

NOTES

1. Rosemary Griebel, "If Helen Keller Lived North of the 49th: Canadian Library Services for People with Disabilities," *Feliciter* 49, no. 3 (2003): 155.

2. Curry College, *Curry College Disability Services*, 1. Available at http://www.curry.edu/hr/files/disability_serv.html (accessed July 7, 2004).

3. Ibid., 2.

4. Amherst College Library, "ADA Accessibility" (Amherst, MA: Amherst College Library, 2004). Available at http://www.amherst.edu/library/info/ada.html (accessed September 3, 2004); Boston College Library, "Services for Persons with Disabilities" (Newton, MA: Boston College, O'Neill Library, 2004). Available at http://www.bx.edu/libraries/centers/oneill/about/s-disabilities/ (accessed September 4, 2004); Bridgewater State College Library, "Services for

Users with Disabilities" (Bridgewater, MA: Bridgewater State College, Maxwell Library, 2004). Available at http://www.bridgew.edu.edu/Library/disability. cfm (accessed September 3, 2004); Earlham College Libraries, "Library Services for Persons with Disabilities" (Richmond, IN: Earlham College Libraries, 2004). Available at http://www.earlham,edu/~libr/library/access.htm); Griffith University, "Students with Disabilities Policy" (Queensland, Australia: Griffith University, n.d.). Available at http://www.62.gu.edu/au/policylibrary. nsf/mainsearch/c5572a3154e0fefd4a256bba0063129f (accessed September 4, 2004); Montgomery College Libraries, "Library Services for Patrons with Disabilities" (Montgomery County, MD: Montgomery College Libraries, 2004). Available at http://www.montgomerycollege.edu/library/library_ services-for_disabilities.htm (accessed September 3, 2004); North Lindsey College, "Disability Statement" (Scunthorpe, UK: North Lindsey College). Available at http://www.northlindsey.ac.uk/nlcds.htm (accessed September 3, 2004); Roanoke College, "Services for Students with Disabilities" (Salem, VA: Roanoke College Library, 2004). Available http://www.roanoke.edu/library/ disability.htm (accessed September 3, 2004); Rutgers University Libraries, "Library Services for Persons with Disabilities"(New Brunswick, NJ: Rutgers University Libraries, 2004). Available http://www.libraries.rutgers.edu/rul/ lib_servs/disabil.shmtl); University of Canterbury, "Facilities for Users with Disabilities" (Christchurch, New Zealand: University of Canterbury, 2004). Available at http://library.canterbury.ac.nz/services/disabled.shtml (accessed October 5, 2004); University of Manitoba, "Information for Library Users with Disabilities" (Winnipeg, CA: University of Manitoba Libraries, 2004). Available at http://www.umanitoba.ca/libraries/get_it/disability_services. shmtl (accessed September 3, 2004); University of Notre Dame, "University Libraries: Services for Students with Disabilities" (Notre Dame, IN: University of Notre Dame Libraries, 2004). Available at http://www.library.nd.edu/ services/disabilities/index.shtml); Washington State University Libraries, "WSU Library Services for Users with Disabilities" (Pullman, WA: University of Washington Libraries, 2004). Available at http://www.wsulibs.wsu.edu/ govdoc/disabilities.htm (accessed September 3, 2004).

5. Landmark College, "National Institute at Landmark College" (Putney, VT: Landmark College, 2003). Available at http://www.landmarkcollege.org/ institute/index.html (accessed September 7, 2004).

6. Gallaudet University, "The Gallaudet Mission, Vision and Communication Statements" (Washington, D.C.: Gallaudet University, n.d.). Available at http://www.gallaudet.edu/mission.htm (accessed September 14, 2004).

7. "The program combines coursework in the liberal arts with skill development coursework in study strategies, personal development and learning, reading and writing, mathematics, and technology. The program also provides comprehensive advising and academic support, including individual tutoring." See Dean College, "The Institute for Students with Disabilities at Dean College: Summary of Results and Findings, 2001–2003" (Franklin, MA: Dean College, 2004), 2.

8. Ibid., 4–5.

9. Texas Tech University Libraries, "University Libraries Strategic Plan" (Lubbock, TX: Texas Tech University Libraries, 2004). Available at http:// library.ttu.edu/sp/ulsp_text.php (accessed September 26, 2005).

10. Valle Verde Library, "Designing Web Pages for People with Disabilities" (El Paso, TX: El Paso Community College, Valle Verde Library, 2004). Available at http://www.epcc.edu/vvlib/webada.html (accessed September 4, 2004).

11. U.S. Department of Education, Office for Civil Rights, "Auxiliary Aids and Services for Postsecondary Students with Disabilities," 3 (Washington, D.C.: Office for Civil Rights, 1998). Available at http://www.ed.gov/about/offices/list/ocr/docs/auxaids.html (accessed July 7, 2004).

12. Ibid., 4–5.

13. U.S. Department of Education, Office for Civil Rights, "The Civil Rights of Students with Hidden Disabilities under Section 504 of the Rehabilitation Act of 1973," 2 (Washington, D.C.: Office for Civil Rights, n.d.). Available at http://www.ed.gov/about/offices/list/ocr/docs/hq5269.html (accessed July 7, 2004).

14. "At the postsecondary level it is the student's responsibility to make his or her handicapping condition known and to request academic adjustments." Ibid., 4.

15. Linda Lucas Walling, "Educating Students to Serve Information Seekers with Disabilities," *Journal of Education for Library and Information Science* 45 (Spring 2004): 137–148.

16. University of Kentucky, "Self-study: Section V, Educational Support Services" (Lexington, KY: University of Kentucky, n.d.). Available at http://www.uky.edu/SelfStudy/VCOMMREPORT/SectionV.pdf (accessed August 31, 2004).

17. Rebecca Cory, "Students, DS Providers Often Can View Issues Differently," *Disability Compliance for Higher Education* 9, no. 11 (June 2004): 2.

18. Quality Assurance Agency for Higher Education, *Code of Practice for the Assurance of Academic Quality and Standards in Higher Education. Section 3: Students with Disabilities* (Gloucester, UK: Quality Assurance Agency for Higher Education, October 1999). Available at http://www.qaa.ac.uk/public/COP/COPswd/contents.htm (accessed November 24, 2004).

19. Australian Library and Information Association, "Guidelines on Library Standards for People with Disabilities" (Kingston, Australia: Australian Library and Information Association, 1998). Available at http://alia.org.au/policies/disability.standards.html (accessed January 24, 2005).

20. National Library of Australia. Forum on Library Services for People with Disabilities, Homepage (Canberra, Australia: National Library of Australia, 2002). Available at http://www.nla.gov.au/initiatives/meetings/disabilities/index2002.html (accessed January 24, 2005). For papers that the Forum produced, see http://www.nla.gov.au/initiatives/meetings/disabilities/papers.html (accessed January 24, 2005).

21. University of Washington, Disabilities, Opportunities, Internetworking, and Technology (DO-IT) (Seattle,WA: University of Washington). Available at http://www.washington.edu/doit/ (accessed November 5, 2004).

22. University of Washington. National Center on Accessible Information Technology at the University, AccessIT (Seattle,WA: University of Washington). Available at http://www.washington.edu/accessit/index.php (accessed November 5, 2004).

23. Stanford University, Archimedes Project (Palo Alto, CA: Stanford University). Available at http://archimedes.stanford.edu/ (accessed November 5, 2004).

24. University of Wisconsin–Madison, College of Engineering, Trace Research & Development Center, Homepage (Madison, WI: University of Wisconsin). Available at http://trace.wisc.edu/ (accessed November 5, 2004).

25. Gary Greene, "A Spelling Test for Teachers of Students with Learning Disabilities," *LD Forum* 20, no. 3 (1995). Available at http://www.ldonline. org/ld_indepth/teaching_techniques/spelling_test.html (accessed November 8, 2004).

26. See David Pollak, *Dyslexia, the Self and Higher Education* (Sterling, VA: Stylus Publishing, 2005). Although more dyslexic students enter academic institutions, little has been done to identify their needs. Pollak discusses what institutions can do as they try to work effectively with these students.

27. Kathy Wollam and Barbara Wessel, "Recognizing and Effectively Managing Mental Illness in the Library," *Colorado Libraries* 29, no. 4 (Winter 2003): 17.

3

LEGAL CONTEXT WITHIN THE UNITED STATES

Kathleen Rogers

> Education is a key determinant of future success, and every American deserves equal access to education.[1]

A few years ago, I received a call from a senior administrator of a nursing program seeking reassurance that "common sense was not outlawed when the Americans with Disabilities Act was enacted." The administrator had recently learned that a high school student who was "legally blind" was considering applying to the college's nursing program and she wanted confirmation that she could deny admission to a student who could not see without running afoul of the Americans with Disabilities Act (ADA).

Although the notion of matriculating a sightless student into a nursing program may be inconceivable to many inside and outside of the profession, I knew it was not beyond the realm of possibility. Moreover, I knew that neither the ADA nor the law commonly referred to on U.S. campuses as "Section 504" would permit the administrator from doing what she wanted to do: make a certain educational program off-limits to students with a particular disability or diagnosis or to exclude students from enrolling in a program because of their disability.

That evening, I searched the Internet for stories of individuals who worked as nursing professionals although they could not see. It did not take long to find two stories about two different women who worked as registered nurses despite being blind. Both women worked for large health care organizations in different parts of the country as phone intake nurses. They took calls from sick patients and children's parents and both used their considerable knowledge and skills to listen to callers' questions, to probe them about symptoms, and to relay medical advice.

The callers were unaware that the nurse on the other end of the phone could not see, and the nurses' lack of vision did not compromise their ability to administer to the patients. These were remarkable women who worked in the nursing profession despite their disabilities. Their life stories gave me the "ammunition" I needed to coax the administrator into opening her mind to the possibility of enrolling a student who could not see into the nursing program.

When I went to speak with the administrator, I brought these articles with me. She wasted no time pointing out that the articles made clear that both women had received their nursing degrees while they still had some or mostly all of their sight. Nevertheless, these stories moved the discussion from the certainty of exclusion to the possibility of inclusion.

Together, we made a list of questions that we thought might shape our discussion:

- Was the student "otherwise qualified" to enter the program?
- Was the student blind or did she have low vision?
- Was the disability recent or since birth?
- How serious was she about nursing; how well had she thought through her career goals?
- Was her family supportive of her career goal? Or, were they waiting for someone else to raise concerns and discuss obstacles?
- Will she be able to get the necessary clinical placements?
- What do state nursing licensing requirements say?
- What kind of auxiliary aids are available to assist the student?
- Are there no professional possibilities for this student or just remote ones? Could this student be the exception?

The high school student never did apply, and the issue became moot. However, the administrator's question offered a valuable teaching and learning opportunity to everyone, including me. It forced us to test our prejudices and fears and to consider the possibility that a high school student with little or no vision may someday seek to purse a dream of being a registered nurse. (I sometimes wonder whether we would have had this same discussion if Section 504 and the ADA were not enacted.)

Today, in elementary schools across the United States, children with disabilities are growing up believing that no degree or profession is beyond their reach solely because they have a physical, learning, or psychological disability. These children will finish high school and many will pursue undergraduate and graduate degrees. When they arrive on campus, they will need informed, creative, and supportive faculty, staff, and administrators who are committed to helping them navigate the many challenges of higher education.

Within this context, the purpose of this chapter is to provide a primer on what I believe every college and university faculty and administrator needs to know about disability rights and responsibilities in the university setting.

WHAT IS THE ADA AND SECTION 504?

In 1973, Congress passed Section 504 of the Rehabilitation Act of 1973, which the president signed into public law. This act, which was the first federal statute containing civil rights protection for persons with disabilities, prohibits discrimination on the basis of physical or mental disability (see 29 U.S.C. 794). It provided that:

No otherwise qualified individual with a disability in the United States ... shall, solely by reason of his or her disability, be excluded from the participation in, be denied the benefits of, or be subjected to discrimination under any program or activity receiving federal financial assistance. . . .

In the United States, virtually all public schools, including public colleges and universities, are covered by Section 504 because they receive some federal financial assistance. Most private U.S. colleges and universities are subject to Section 504 because they, too, receive federal financial assistance in the form of financial aid for their enrolled students, federal loans for programs, and research grants from various governmental agencies.

In 1990, Congress sought to expand legal protections to persons with disabilities and the result was the Americans with Disabilities Act (the ADA). Title II of the act requires public entities to furnish "appropriate auxiliary aids and services where necessary to afford an individual with a disability an equal opportunity to participate in and enjoy the benefits of a service or program or activity conducted by a public entity." Title III of the ADA expanded the protection to all private entities which operate places of "public accommodation." A private college or university is a place of public accommodation just like a shopping mall, restaurant, cinema, hotel, or sports arena.

Both Section 504 and the ADA prohibit discrimination against individuals with disabilities, albeit in slightly different terms. Three broad principles underlie the nondiscrimination requirements of both these laws:

1. Students with disabilities must be given equal opportunities to participate;
2. Students with disabilities must be given an equal opportunity to benefit; and[2]
3. Schools must permit students with disabilities to participate in programs and activities in an integrated setting "to the maximum extent appropriate."

So, what actions by a university would violate federal disability laws? Under Section 504 and the ADA, a college or university may not:

- Limit the number of students with disabilities admitted;
- Make preadmission inquiries into whether an applicant has a disability or a history of a disability;

- Exclude a student with a disability from a program or course of study solely on the basis that the student has a particular disability or diagnosis;
- Counsel students with disabilities towards particular programs or career paths different from those suggested for students without disabilities; or
- Restrict students with disabilities from living in particular dormitories or from participating in college activities (such as study abroad programs) solely because of their disability.

Put another way, to meet its obligations under Section 504 and the ADA, colleges and universities must:

- Admit qualified students who have disabilities;
- Eliminate criteria that screen out persons with disabilities;
- Eliminate testing methods that measure a person's disability, rather than his or her ability;
- Refrain from creating a hostile environment for students with disabilities in any program or activity provided by the school;
- Provide reasonable accommodations to students who qualify for them;
- Remove architectural barriers in existing facilities if the removal is "readily achievable"[3] without much difficulty or expense; and
- Provide assistive technology to students who qualify for such technology.

Although the mandates of these two laws appear broad, they are not limitless. Nothing in either Section 504 or the ADA requires colleges and universities to:

- Admit students who are not otherwise qualified for admission;
- Lower academic standards to accommodate students with disabilities;
- Alter or compromise essential academic or programmatic requirements for students with disabilities;
- Alter fundamental performance standards or standards of behavior for students with documented disabilities; or
- Produce identical results or levels of achievement for student with disabilities.

Obviously, this list of do's and don'ts is not exhaustive and the responsibilities of colleges and universities are ever-changing as courts continue to interpret Congress's intent when it enacted both Section 504 and ADA many years ago.

WHO IS PROTECTED UNDER SECTION 504 AND THE ADA?

Section 504 prohibits discrimination against an "otherwise qualified individual with a disability," while the ADA protects "individuals with disabilities." With the exception of the phrase "otherwise qualified" contained in Section 504, the two laws contain nearly identical definitions of an individual with a disability, namely

An individual with a disability is someone who (i) has a physical or mental impairment which substantially limits them in one or more major life activities, such as caring for one's self, performing manual tasks, learning, walking, seeing, hearing, breathing and working; (ii) has a record of such impairment; or (iii) is regarded as having such an impairment.

The definition includes learning disabilities (such as dyslexia) that are reading disorders, including some processing disorders; dysgraphia, which is comprehensive of all written disorders, including grammar and spelling difficulties as well as processing problems; dyscalculia, which is a mathematic disorder, including numeric ordering, numeral recognition, and so on; dyspraxia, which are learning disorders of motor skills; auditory processing disorder, which is difficulty with understanding/comprehending/decoding auditory information; and visual processing disorder, which is difficulty with understanding/comprehending/decoding visual information.

Certain phrases are central to this definition, in particular:

A physical impairment: A physical impairment includes physiological disorders or conditions, cosmetic disfigurement, or anatomical loss affecting one or more major body systems.[4] Hearing and speech impairments, visual impairments, cerebral palsy, multiple sclerosis, diabetes, epilepsy, migraines, and HIV are all examples of physical impairments.

A mental impairment includes psychological conditions such as major depression, bipolar disorder, schizophrenia, and multiple personality disorder.

Substantially limiting: Not everyone who has a mental impairment is covered by Section 504 and the ADA, however. To constitute a "disability" under federal law, the condition must "substantially limit" a major life activity. The phrase "substantially limit" has been hotly debated among lawyers and practitioners. Federal legislation gives only limited guidance as to what is meant by "substantially limiting" and the phrase has spawned litigation across the country even up to the U.S. Supreme Court.

Impairments are considered "substantial" when they restrict important life activities or affect the manner in which the critical life activities can be performed in comparison to most people. There must be a direct connection between the limitation and the disability, and the conditions, manner, and duration of the impairment must be considered. Mild, temporary, or even "moderately severe" conditions may not be considered "substantial."[5]

Where a student had, at times, excelled in the classroom even without accommodations, a court has found that he was not "substantially limited" for purpose of the ADA.[6] The student had a documented learning disability that interfered primarily with his ability to read quickly. When given additional time to read, however, his comprehension was, in fact, very high. In

addition, throughout his educational career, the student sometimes performed very well in his studies without receiving any accommodations.
When the university denied the student an accommodation he was seeking
in conjunction with a clinical program, he sued his school. Although the
court found that there was no question that the student had a medical condition, it also ruled that the student was not "substantially limited" in a
major life activity, at least in part because he had, at times, excelled even
without accommodations.

In another case,[7] a court was faced the question of whether a student diagnosed with multiple personality disorder was substantially limited for purposes of the ADA. The court decided that, even assuming that learning or
"attending college" was a major life function, the plaintiff's medical condition only limited her from a narrow range of educational opportunities, which
it held to be insufficient to establish a disability claim.

Courts have held that a student alleging a violation of the ADA could not
simply rely upon a diagnosis of a disability but had to demonstrate that the
disability substantially (and specifically) limited his or her ability to learn,
particularly in the classroom setting. Put another way, courts have ruled that
the limitation could not simply affect the student's ability to learn a specific
subject or field of study, but had to more generally limit the student's overall
ability to learn.[8]

In yet another case, a student alleged his significant vision problems constituted a disability, but the court found that, with glasses and/or contact
lenses, he was able to significantly improve his vision to the point where he
could read everything but very small print. The court held that, once amelio-
rating measures were considered, the plaintiff's medical condition no longer
constituted a serious limitation on a major life function.[9]

Moreover, students are not substantially limited for purposes of the ADA
if their medical condition simply brought them down to the level of an
average person. The question was not whether a student was limited from
performing up to his or her potential, but rather it needed to focus on
whether the plaintiff was impaired in comparison to the average population.[10]
Consequently, students who had requested additional time and a separate
room to take the medical boards were not discriminated against when the
university denied their request because "an individual is not substantially
limited in a major life activity if the limitation does not amount to a significant restriction when compared with the abilities of the average person."

Major life activity: Congress did not provide a list of "major life activities"
when it passed the ADA. Perhaps members thought such guidance was
unnecessary, or such a list superfluous to those with responsibility for implementing this law. In the years since passage of the ADA, there has been broad
consensus on what likely constitutes a "major life activity" and litigation
where reasonable minds have disagreed. Most experts and observers agree
that Congress was thinking about these activities when it crafted the phrase

"major life activities:" seeing, hearing, speaking, performing manual tasks, breathing, sleeping, walking, concentrating, caring for oneself, and learning.

Record of impairment: The ADA protects not only those persons who currently have a physical or mental impairment or learning disability, but also those who may have *record* of a disability that substantially limited them in a major life activity sometime in their past. The ADA protects those who have recovered from their impairment, as well as those who may have been misdiagnosed or misclassified as having an impairment or disability. So, an otherwise qualified[11] student who has been treated successfully for an eating disorder, cancer, alcoholism, drug addiction, or other impairment or disease cannot be denied admission to an educational program solely on the basis that the student has a history of disability.

Regarded as having an impairment: The ADA also protects persons who are regarded as having a physical or mental impairment that substantially limits them, whether or not that person actually has an impairment. The *ADA Title III Technical Assistance Manual,* a manual written and issued by the U.S. Department of Justice (see http://www.usdoj.gov/crt/ada/taman3.html), sets forth three "typical" situations covered by this category. Here, quoting in pertinent part from that manual, are three "illustrations" to explain this category of protection.

- Illustration A: An individual with mild diabetes, controlled by medication, is barred by the staff of a private summer camp from participation in certain sports because of her diabetes. Even though A does not actually have an impairment that substantially limits a major life activity, she is protected under the ADA because she is treated as though she does.

- Illustration B: A three-year-old child born with a prominent facial disfigurement has been refused admittance to a private day care program on the grounds that her presence in the program might upset other children. B is an individual with a physical impairment that substantially limits her major life activities only as a result of the attitudes of others towards her impairment.

- Illustration C: C is excluded from a private elementary school because the principal believes rumors that C is infected with HIV. Even though these rumors are untrue, C is protected under the ADA because he is being subjected to discrimination by the school based on the belief that he has an impairment that substantially limits major life activities.

Simply put, the ADA protects not only those with a disability but also persons who do not have a disability (but who are perceived as having one).

WHAT IS A "REASONABLE ACCOMMODATION?"

Reasonableness, like beauty, often lies in the eye of the beholder. What you may consider reasonable, I may not. What a faculty member may consider reasonable, a student may not. What a judge or jury may consider a reasonable accommodation, a university may not. Moreover, a reasonable accommodation for one student might not be a reasonable accommodation for another at the same school, in the same program, or in the same class. Reasonableness depends on the facts and circumstances of each case and each case is different.

When the U.S. Congress passed Section 504 and the ADA, it did not provide colleges and universities (or any entity) with a list of accommodations that it considered reasonable, specifically or generally so. Congress provided no tools by which university administrators could evaluate or calibrate the reasonableness of a student's request for an accommodation. Here is what we do know, however:

- Educational institutions must remove architectural barriers in existing facilities if the remove is "readily achievable" or can be accomplished without much difficulty or expense. If the removal is not "readily achievable," the university must find an alternative way to provide the services (such as moving a class in a building without an elevator from the second floor to the ground level to accommodate a student in that class who uses a wheelchair).

- Educational institutions must provide auxiliary communication aids to students with impaired sensory, manual, or speaking skills.

- Educational institutions must make reasonable modifications in their policies and practices unless to do so would fundamentally alter the nature of the educational program or service being provided.

- An accommodation is not reasonable if it fundamentally alters the nature of the education program or a requirement essential to that educational program.

- An accommodation is not reasonable if it results in an "undue burden" to the institution. Undue burden is very high standard to meet under U.S. law. Indeed, it is hard to find a legal case in which a court has upheld the denial of a requested accommodation on the grounds that granting the accommodation would have posed an "undue burden" on the institution. An "undue burden" means an undue *financial* burden (not an administrative burden) and the institution must take into account the resources of the *whole* institution when it determines whether or not a request is truly an undue burden.

- Colleges and universities are not required by law to provide personal aide or personal care attendants, individually prescribed devices, readers for personal use or study, or other devices or aides of a personal nature.[12]

ACCOMMODATING PSYCHOLOGICAL DISABILITIES

The interplay of psychological disabilities and civil rights protection is perhaps the most challenging and interesting for experts and observers in this area. It is unlikely that the representatives and senators who passed Section 504 and the ADA could have predicted how their legislation for more ramps and wider doors has created broad protections (and challenging questions) about accommodating citizens of all ages who live with a wide variety of psychological disabilities. The topic of psychological disabilities is so complex that it is deserving of its own section.

Accommodations for psychological disabilities may be as varied as the conditions that necessitate them. Here are some examples of accommodations that schools have made for students with documented psychological disabilities:

- Permit a tape recorder in class;
- Permit extended time for examinations;
- Allow students to take a break and leave the classroom during the lecture;
- Assign a "buddy" in class to answer questions about assignments and so forth;
- Permit beverages or food in class;
- Provide preferential seating (near a door or window; away from others; on an aisle);
- Provide preferential assignment to course sections (morning-only section meetings; no morning section meetings);
- Permit make-up tests and quizzes missed as a result of a psychological episode;
- Permit reduced course loads; and
- Permit examinations to be held in hospitals.

Psychological Disabilities and Policy Exemptions

Students sometimes seek exemptions or exceptions from university policies because of their psychological disabilities. Although a student with a particular kind of disability may be entitled to a course exemption (from a foreign language or math requirement), the ADA/Section 504 does not require schools to give exemptions from or make exceptions to university policies for students with psychological disabilities. Schools are not required to:

- Extend a drop/add deadline;
- Offer tuition reimbursement past deadlines;
- Excuse poor performance;
- Change a failing grade to pass/fail;
- Remove a grade from a transcript;
- Waive infractions of a code of conduct;
- Waive all course attendance requirements;
- Alter or eliminate testing requirements; or
- Excuse students from internal judicial proceedings.

Schools are also not required to grant an accommodation if that request compromises the essential requirements of an academic course or program, poses a threat to personal or public safety, or is of a personal nature.

Dismissal from the University

Nothing contained in Section 504 or the ADA prohibits a university from dismissing a student even if the student has a psychological disability that may impede his or her success inside or outside of the classroom.

Poor Academic Performance

Students with psychological disabilities may be dismissed[13] for poor academic performance. Neither the ADA nor Section 504 requires a school to lower its academic standards in order to accommodate a student with a psychological disability. Students who cannot maintain the requisite grade point average may be dismissed even if the student's poor academic performance can be traced, in whole or in part, to a psychological disability. Schools are not required to fundamentally alter their performance standards or programs of study.

Unacceptable Behavior

A student who cannot participate effectively[14] in the university's program of study may be required to withdraw, regardless of whether he or she has a disability and regardless of whether that disability is documented. Students with documented psychological disabilities may be dismissed if their behavior disrupts university activities or disturbs or threatens students, faculty, and staff. Students may be held accountable for their actions even if they cannot control their behavior because of their disability.

The decision to dismiss a student with a documented disability must be based on a fair, stereotype-free assessment, by objective sources, such as knowledgeable medical professionals. In other words, the decision to dismiss a student should be based on the documented, professional opinion of those clearly qualified to make judgments about a student's mental health.[15]

STUDENTS WHO MAY POSE A DIRECT THREAT

What if a university believes that a student's disability poses a threat to the health and safety of the student or to that of others? Does Section 504 or the ADA tie the hands of university administrators who are concerned that a student with a contagious disease (tuberculosis) or a student with a serious mental or emotional diagnosis (schizophrenia) may put himself or herself or others at risk by attending classes, living in the residence halls, or participating in the life of the college?

Concern that the student will harm himself or herself is not, by itself, a sufficient basis for excluding the student from school. However, both Section 504 and the ADA permit the exclusion of an individual with a disability from participation in an activity if that individual's participation poses a "significant" risk to others that "cannot be eliminated or reduced to an acceptable level by reasonable modifications . . . or by the provision of appropriate modifications or services."

Both the ADA and Section 504 set a high threshold for excluding students. The decision to bar or terminate a student's participation cannot be made lightly. The direct threat to others must be real, substantial, and articulable. The risk cannot be based on general knowledge about a certain diagnosis; and prejudice, stereotypes, and fear cannot play a role.

Just as the ADA and Section 504 require a thoughtful, individual assessment in determining the reasonable accommodation(s) for a disability, these same laws mandate an "individual assessment" based on "reasonable judgment" that relies on "current medical evidence" or on the "best available objective evidence" in determining:

- The nature, duration, and severity of the risk, and
- The probability that the potential injury will occur.

Even if university administrators conclude that the risk is severe and the potential for injury to others is great, exclusion may still be unlawful. The institution must take the additional step of determining whether the risk can be mitigated or eliminated by a "reasonable modification of policies, practices or procedures." If some other course less than full and permanent exclusion from the program may mitigate the direct threat, that avenue must be reasonably explored.

The proper legal analysis is not what the university believes may be best for the student with that diagnosis or what may be the easiest course for the university to follow. Rather, the correct approach is for schools to make the needed individual assessment and to balance their responsibilities to protect others against the rights of the student with a disability. For example, a student has a diagnosis of bipolar disorder and is experiencing frequent manic episodes followed by bouts of depression. His behavior is disruptive to his roommates and other members of his residence hall and his resident director is spending a disproportionate amount of time managing the student and his behavior. The student is not failing his courses. Some university administrators are calling for him to be involuntarily withdrawn from school and sent home to his parents. In this case, the proper course may be to have the student live off campus for the remainder of the semester (or until his medication condition permits him to return to the dorm) but allow him to remain in his classes, particularly in the short term.

CONCLUSION

The ADA is a complicated, dynamic, and frequently misunderstood U.S. federal law. I encourage every faculty member I encounter to learn about the

ADA and Section 504 and the rights they give and responsibilities they impose on universities, their employees (especially faculty), and their students.

It is not easy to summarize the directives and implications of the ADA, particularly in the form of a short list. But, if I had to do so, my list might look like this:

- The ADA covers three broad types of disability: physical, learning, and psychological. Do not treat students with learning and psychological disabilities differently than those with physical disabilities.
- To fulfill your legal obligations under the ADA, you must:
  - Admit qualified students who have disabilities into your school and programs;
  - Eliminate criteria that screen out persons with disabilities or testing methods that measure a person's disability, rather than her/his ability;
  - Refrain from creating a hostile environment in your classroom or program for persons with disabilities; and
  - Make reasonable modifications to policies, practices, and procedures to enable students with disabilities to satisfy fundamental requirements and standards of performance.
- Academic freedom is important, but it is not absolute in the United States. A student's ADA rights can trump a faculty's right of academic freedom on U.S. soil. Attendance requirements, testing formats, coursework deadlines, and curriculum requirements are just a few of the areas where a faculty's preferences may be outweighed by ADA requirements.
- Give accommodations to students who have gone through the appropriate process for documenting and requesting reasonable accommodations. Do not permit students to circumvent the process. Faculty should not honor requests for modifications unless the student has followed the appropriate process.
- In the United States, the university (not individual faculty members) determines who shall receive accommodations and the accommodations that shall be granted to individual students. Faculty should not deviate and give students more, fewer, or different accommodations than the student has been authorized to receive.
- A documented disability does not excuse bad behavior, poor academic performance, or irresponsibility. Do not confuse a request for a reasonable accommodation with a request for an exemption from a university policy. The ADA requires the former, but not the latter.
- Respect and uphold a student's broad right of confidentiality. Faculty should not disclose to others whether a student has a disability, the nature of that disability, or the accommodation being requested or granted to the student. Faculty should be particularly vigilant not to disclose a student's disability and accommodation needs to other students.
- Act fairly and prudently. Respect and understanding can go a long way in creating an atmosphere in which students with disabilities can learn and thrive.

- Do not go it alone. Get advice and assistance from those with expertise in this disability area. Do not be embarrassed if you do not know how to respond to a request for an accommodation. Seek advice early and as often as you need to.

- Recognize that there are no easy answers. Issues regarding disabilities are constantly evolving. Last week's approach may not be the best approach for this week's situation or for this student at this time.

> The opportunity for a quality education should not be denied on the basis of physical, mental, or cognitive disability.[16]

NOTES

1. Disabilityinfo.gov. "Education: Knowledge and Skills That Support Future Success" (Washington, D.C.: Disabilityinfo.gov, n.d.). Available at http://www.disability.gov/digov-public/public/DisplayPage.do?parentFolderId=61, (accessed June 10, 2005).

2. The requirement to provide equality in participation and benefit "does not guarantee that an individual with a disability must achieve an identical result or level of achievement as persons without disabilities" (Title III [ADA] 3.3000).

3. "Readily achievable" for the purpose of these laws means that if the removal or alteration is not readily achievable, the institution must use other "readily achievable" means to accommodate the individual. A common example of this is to relocate a class to a handicapped-accessible classroom if a student with a mobility impairment cannot access the assigned classroom and the university cannot make the assigned classroom accessible for the student "readily."

4. Major body systems would include neurological, musculoskeletal, special sense organs (which would include speech organs that are not respiratory associated such as vocal cords, soft palate, and tongue); respiratory, cardiovascular, reproductive, digestive, genitourinary, hemic and lymphatic, and skin and endocrine.

5. Whether a temporary condition is substantially limiting is a question to be resolved on a case-by-case basis, taking into consideration both the duration (or expected duration) of the impairment and the extent to which it actually limits a major life activity of the affected individual.

6. See *Wong v. Regents of the University of California,* 379 F.3d 1097 (9th Cir. 2004) and *Betts v. Rector & Visitors,* 18 Fed Appx. 114 (4th Cir. 2001). The courts examined the question of whether a student who had demonstrated significant academic achievement without accommodation could be considered to have a medical condition that substantially limited a major life activity and ruled that the student could not show a substantial limitation.

7. See *Davis v. University of North Carolina,* 263 F.3d 95 (4th Cir. 2001).

8. See *Marlon v. Western New England College,* 2003 U.S. Dist. LEXIS 22095 (D. Mass. 2003), *aff'd* 2005 U.S. App. LEXIS 407 (1st Cir. 2005).

9. See *Pacella v. Tufts University School of Dental Medicine,* 66 F. Supp. 2d 234 (D. Mass. 1999).

10. See *Price v. National Board of Medical Examiners,* 966 F. Supp. 419 (S.D.W.V., 1997).
11. "Otherwise qualified" is another term frequently used when discussing students with disability and the laws that govern disability status.
12. For a list of common auxiliary aids and an excellent summary regarding the provision of aids and services for postsecondary students with disabilities, see U.S. Department of Education. Office for Civil Rights, *Auxiliary Aids and Services for Postsecondary Students with Disabilities* (Washington, D.C.: Department of Education, 1998). Available at http://ed.gov/print/about/offices/list/ocr/docs/auxaids.html, (accessed June 8, 2005).
13. Withdrawal and dismissal are, of course, extreme outcomes. Lesser responses may include warnings, revocation of on-campus housing privileges, suspension, or the setting of conditions to be met if the student is to avoid further disciplinary action.
14. "Effective participation" is not a defined term. It can cover a wide variety of problematic student behavior inside and outside of the classroom.
15. Decisions to dismiss students for academic reasons remain firmly and exclusively within the province of those senior academic officers and committees responsible for enforcing academic standards. Decisions to dismiss students on other (nonacademic) grounds, however, are usually more complex, and all concerned may benefit when such decisions reflect the experience and expertise of many.
16. Disabilityinfo.gov.

4

AN INCREASINGLY DIVERSE STUDENT POPULATION: A RATIONALE FOR CONSIDERATION OF UNIVERSAL ACCESS AT POSTSECONDARY INSTITUTIONS

Todd K. Herriott

A diverse environment fosters a plurality of perspectives. It creates the possibility of discourse and learning by talented people of various cultures, backgrounds, and experiences. It creates an opportunity for students to come together, challenge each others ideas, learn new perspectives, and grow as individuals.[1]

Access to education in the United States has been seen as a valuable resource. Historically, education in the United States, particularly postsecondary education, was available only to a select few individuals, initially wealthy, white males. In time, the number of people who could avail themselves of higher education increased, either as a result of federal legislation or changes in social attitudes. Access to higher education for women was the one of the first steps towards the diversification of the student population. Racial and ethnic minorities were the next to become the focus of issues of access. Students with disabilities, though present on campus previously, have only recently become a focus of this diversification.

Students with disabilities present unique challenges to the education system in the United States, particularly within higher education. These challenges extend beyond the more obvious issues of physical access to the areas of access to programs and services. Students with disabilities present vastly different learning styles, physical accessibility needs, sensory differences, and a litany of other deviations from the assumed needs and abilities of their non-disabled counterparts. Libraries associated with institutions of higher learning are in a unique position to assist in addressing these challenges due to the central role they play in supporting the larger goal of education. In an attempt to gain a full picture of this phenomenon and to understand its implications, particularly within a library setting, it is important to understand the histori-cal, legal, and social context within which the issue of access arose as well as the response to date by institutions of higher education. This chapter will provide a brief overview of the legal context of disability rights and issues related to the process of providing access. (Chapter 3 offers a more complete discussion of the legal context of this issue.) Additionally, a review of the social perspectives and approaches will be presented. Finally, this chapter will pro-vide a justification as to why this issue should be of concern to libraries, as well as suggested directions for future practices.

LEGISLATIVE INITIATIVES

Initially, the primary focus of discussion regarding accessibility was on the physical access to buildings and facilities afforded to persons with disabilities. The Architectural Barriers Act of 1968, which focused primarily on employ-ment, mandated the removal of what was perceived to be the most significant obstacle for people with disabilities: the physical design of the buildings and facilities they had to use on the job. The act required all buildings designed, constructed, altered, or leased with federal funds to be made accessible. For institutions of higher education, the Architectural Barriers Act of 1968 became the impetus for a review of the physical environment on campuses in terms of access.

In 1973, the Rehabilitation Act was passed with the last-minute addition of Section 504. Ironically, Section 504, which was really nothing more than an afterthought tacked on to what was essentially a spending bill, became one of the most important steps towards the creation of access for persons with disabilities within higher education.[2] Section 504 of the Rehabilitation Act of 1973 was the first true civil rights law for people with disabilities. This act made it illegal for federal agencies, public universities, federal contractors, and any other institution or activity receiving federal funds to discriminate on the basis of disability.[3] The promulgation of regulations was initially stalled by the U.S. Department of Health, Education and Welfare. In protest, disability rights advocates held numerous demonstrations and as a result, regulations were finally issued in 1977.

Section 504 expressly prohibited discrimination of otherwise qualified indi-viduals on the basis of disability. While some colleges and universities in the United States had already made individual commitments to providing better access for students with disabilities, primarily focusing on those with physical or sensory disabilities, there was no national mandate for nondiscrimination until the passage of Section 504.

The Education for Handicapped Children Act of 1975 (now called the Individuals with Disabilities Education Act, or IDEA) guaranteed a free, appropriate education for all children with disabilities. This act had an effect on educational programs as well as on the facilities in which they were conducted. IDEA has resulted in a much greater emphasis being placed on academic preparedness for students in primary and secondary education. Historically, data have shown that students with disabilities are less likely to enroll in some form of postsecondary education than their nondisabled counterparts. One study of graduating high school seniors in the late 1980s reported that only 21 percent of the students with disabilities attended postsecondary institutions as compared to 64 percent of the nondisabled learners.[4] By 1994, when comparing students graduating from high school with disabilities with their counterparts without disabilities, only 63 percent of the disabled students were continuing on with postsecondary education compared with 72 percent of nondisabled students.[5] This gap has continued to decrease over time, as more and more secondary students are encouraged to see a college education as a viable, accessible option.

Part of making a college education an accessible option included the passage of the Americans with Disabilities Act (ADA) of 1990, which awakened widespread public awareness of the civil rights of people with disabilities. The ADA further expanded the mandate of nondiscrimination in both the public and private spheres. This law prohibits discrimination in employment, access to places of public accommodation, services, programs, public transportation, and telecommunications. The intent has been to require the removal of physical barriers that impede access wherever they exist. The ADA has a uniform nationwide mandate that ensures accessibility regardless of local attitudes. The Architectural and Transportation Barriers Compliance Board (Access Board) issued Accessibility Guidelines for accessible design in 1991. These guidelines were adopted with modifications by the U.S. Department of Justice and became the enforceable ADA Standards for Accessible Design.

The issue of legally mandated access extended into the realm of communications with the passage of the Telecommunications Act of 1996. This act required that telecommunications services and equipment and customer premises equipment be designed, developed, and fabricated to be accessible to and usable by individuals with disabilities, if readily achievable. This mandate was applied to all types of telecommunications devices and services, from telephones to television programming to computers. With the growing emphasis on technology for communication, the diverse needs of the public, including those with disabilities, moved from being a secondary thought into a place of primary concern. This focus on accessible technology continued with the addition of Section 508 to the Rehabilitation Act. Section 508 provided the first legislative language for accessible electronic information technology, including the Internet. Section 508 took effect in June of 2001 and was applied specifically to federal agencies and Web sites. Many proponents of accessibility issues predict that the Section 508 standards will ultimately be expanded to include institutions that receive any federal monies, in the same way that section 504 and the ADA expanded coverage to both the public and private sectors, including both public and private colleges and universities.

As the legal protection of persons with disabilities increased, so too did the number of students with disabilities enrolling in higher education. In 1973, only 2.6 percent of all first-year students enrolled in four-year institutions were defined as having a disability.[6] By 1996, 9.4 percent of first-year college students reported having a disability.[7] The dramatic increases in the number of students enrolled who are defined as having a disability are only in part due to the legal protections afforded them by Section 504, the ADA, and other pieces of legislation. While it is arguable that legislation opened the door for students with disabilities to access higher education, the cause for further increases in visibility of students with disabilities on campus can be attributed to a number of programmatic, administrative, and cultural shifts taking place at the campus level.

SOCIAL CONSCIOUSNESS

The ADA began a new, widespread discussion of disability within the context of civil rights. For many years, disability issues were confined to the medical realm where individual differences were given a pathological explanation. While the initial struggles focused on the physical and structural barriers, soon the larger social issues of discrimination came to the forefront. The civil rights movements of the 1950s, 1960s, and 1970s brought the concept of disability as a salient identity into light, similar to that of racial or ethnic identity. Disability rights activists fought to move disabilities from a place of deviance to difference, with disability presented as another just another example of the variety of human experience. This view challenges the societal assumptions and stereotypes associated with disabilities.

Initially, this civil rights perspective was predicated upon the concept of inherent value of each person, which should not be denied. This perspective has sometimes been referred to as the "right thing to do" perspective. Rather than look more in depth into the why's and how's of disability discrimination, it posited a simple value judgment that providing opportunity for access to individuals with disabilities was a good thing. This argument, despite any inherent validity, did little to address the cultural and social underpinnings of exclusion faced by persons with disabilities.

A theoretical movement known as social construction was born out of this shift in perspective. While disability is usually considered an individual characteristic, social justice advocates as well as others who come from a social constructionist perspective argue that it is society, not the individual, that creates disabilities by imposing standards of normalcy that exclude those who are different physically, emotionally, or cognitively. The disability rights organization Disabled People's International[8] made an important distinction between the concepts of *impairment* and *disability,* defining impairment as "the functional limitation within the individual caused by physical, mental, or sensory impairment"[9] and disability as "the loss or limitation of opportunities to take part in the normal life of the community on an equal level with others due to physical and social barriers."[10] This movement argues that disability "becomes an issue at the point where social barriers exclude that individual from participation in everyday activities."[11] In essence, the focus shifts from the simple diagnosis of a particular disability to the manner in which society interprets the presence of disability and uses that interpretation to influence the inclusion or exclusion of the individual from various activities.

Within the context of higher education, social construction is critical of the way in which institutions persist in treating students with disabilities differently from their counterparts. The criticism is of the "single modality" mindset that insists on there being only one appropriate or approved method of doing or being which automatically "disables" any individual who may not fit neatly into the approved method. This view challenges institutions of higher education to reevaluate not just the physical barriers but also the structural and programmatic barriers present.

EDUCATIONAL RESPONSE

Institutions of higher education responded to increased enrollment of students with disabilities with the creation of new policies, and in many cases, whole offices with personnel devoted to addressing issues of institutional access. Issues of architectural access have become a regular consideration of many campus facilities departments during their review of new building plans or in plans that entail the adaptation or retrofitting of existing buildings to create greater physical access. To address issues of access within the classroom context, disability services personnel have become an essential component of most campuses' student affairs divisions, providing not only direct student support, but also serving as a consultant to faculty, administration, and other staff areas on issues of accessibility.

In many ways, the institutional response has been one of reaction: creating specific modifications in reaction to the specific needs presented by an individual student. The process for addressing these students' needs is fairly similar across higher education. Students who are accepted into the institution typically provide some form of documentation or verification of their disability. Disability services personnel then determine what reasonable accommodations are needed based upon the documentation presented on behalf of the student. A large percentage of disability services personnel time is then spent in the coordination of various academic accommodations for students, leaving little time for addressing larger institutional or cultural barriers to accessibility that persist. This response allows for the modifications or accommodations to be individualized and targeted; unfortunately, this process does not typically promote lasting changes. Often this piecemeal approach means that institutions spend a great deal of resources in reacting to the needs of specific students with disabilities. Adaptive equipment or software installed for single student use, while certainly warranted in the absence of other options, is just one example of how this process results in maximum cost for minimum use.

While disability services personnel may be able to effect temporary modification or accommodation to meet the specific needs of a student, it is only through a collaborative, multimodal approach that institutions of higher education can hope to create truly accessible campuses. Faculty and staff from across the institution are often left out of the conversation when it comes to achieving accessibility. Disability services personnel are seen as the campus experts on issues of disability, though that expertise is rarely accessed, either due to the lack of awareness that the resource exists for consultation purposes or because the disability services personnel are focused on coordination of individual accommodations. This dynamic causes a silo effect where areas of the institution act independently of each other, at times resulting in conflicting outcomes.

This type of response is generally focused on compliance with the letter of the law, without providing regard for the spirit or intent of the law. It is often noted that compliance alone does not equal inclusion; simply because students can enter a building or attend a class does not mean that they feel included in the larger campus. The process of accommodation frequently results in a special or different experience for persons with disabilities. This model continues to promote a sense of separation and difference, which seems counterintuitive to the goal of inclusively. The U.S. Supreme Court has previously determined that in educational situations "separate but equal" is inherently unequal. It is with this rationale that a new movement known as universal design began in the United States. This movement seeks to create a more holistic approach to access—one that is less proscriptive and more performance based.

UNIVERSAL DESIGN MOVEMENT

The Center for Universal Design was established in 1989 under a grant from the National Institute on Disability and Rehabilitation Research (NIDRR) as the Center for Accessible Housing, with a mission to improve the quality and availability of housing for people with disabilities, including disabilities that result from aging. In 1996, the center officially changed its name to the Center for Universal Design, which is an officially chartered center of North Carolina State University.[12] A working group of architects, product designers, engineers, and environmental design researchers, as part of a project coordinated by the Center for Universal Design at North Carolina State University, developed the "Principles of Universal Design" and their guidelines.[13] Universal design differs from accessibility requirements in that accessibility requirements prescribe certain standards, whereas universal design is concerned with the largest level of usability and performance possible. The "Principles of Universal Design," published by the Center for Universal Design in 1997, articulate the breadth of the concept and provide guidelines for designers. The seven principles that describe characteristics that make designs universally usable are:

1. Equitable use;
2. Flexibility in use;
3. Simple and intuitive use;
4. Perceptible information;
5. Tolerance for error;
6. Low physical effort; and
7. Size and space for approach and use.[14]

Universal design, as applied within an education setting, is seen as being applicable to not only the physical environment but also the pedagogy of instruction and service delivery. Universal design of instruction, rather than adjusting assignments or making other accommodations after the fact, "anticipates the needs of diverse learners and incorporates effective strategies into curriculum and instruction to make learning more accessible."[15] The "Principles of Universal Design," when translated to classroom instruction, include:

- Using methods that are accessible to people with diverse abilities (e.g., Web-based materials);
- Providing choices in methods to use to complete activities or assignments (e.g., verbal or written tests);
- Eliminating unnecessary complexity (e.g., keeping directions and grading procedures simple and straightforward);
- Using formats that can be accessed in various ways (e.g., through print or using technology);
- Anticipating differences in pace of learning and skills;
- Using methods that require limited physical effort:
- Using seating arrangements that allow students to see each other and provide flexible space options for wheelchairs (e.g., circular seating in an open classroom, rather than providing one open space in the established seating arrangement that then becomes the only seating option for a student using a wheelchair);

- Encouraging communication among students in and out of class to build a learning community; and
- Creating a positive learning environment where all students are held to high expectations and are accorded respect.[16]

These principles not only contribute to the learning of students with disabilities but also help to create positive learning experiences for all students.

Universal design is an approach based upon the belief that the broad range of human ability is ordinary, not special; it thereby removes the focus from the individual to the larger society. Universal design addresses the needs of people with disabilities, older people, children, and others who are nonaverage in a way that is not stigmatizing and benefits all users. By starting with a focus on creating a design for a wide range of users, the overall usability of an environment or product is increased without adding unnecessarily to its cost. This approach also eliminates the need for design modifications later when either abilities or circumstances change. Additionally, a universal design approach avoids the pitfalls of implementing segregated accessibility features that are often viewed as "special" and are typically more expensive and usually not aesthetically pleasing.

APPLICATION TO LIBRARIES

Academic libraries might question the need to consider issues related to access for persons with disabilities in their policy or decision-making process. On face value the extent of the issue may not seem to justify more than cursory exploration, but when explored in greater depth, the strategic advantages become more apparent. The most salient issues can be categorized into three main arguments: efficacy, logistics, and messaging. Efficacy relates to the level of service provided, the overall ability to meet the needs of stakeholders, and cost-effective allocation of scarce resources to maximize impact. Logistics covers the areas of policies, procedures, best practices, and daily operation. Messaging relates to the positioning of a library both within its institution and in the larger field of library and information studies.

In terms of efficacy, libraries simply cannot ignore the facts related to their changing demographics. No longer can it be assumed that only a small percentage of the users of a library will present needs differing from those of the traditional patron. Available data depicting national trends of enrollment for students with disabilities in institutions of higher education show a steady increase in the last two decades, with current numbers indicating a conservative estimate of more than 10 percent of the overall student population defined as having a disability. Additionally, the increases in number of nontraditional students who may have age-related differences in service needs suggest that the scope of the impacted population is worthy of greater consideration.

By taking a more holistic approach, there is a greater likelihood of being able to increase the usability of library resources, thereby increasing the overall satisfaction of both patrons and institutional stakeholders.

Many institutions of higher education are facing difficult budgetary situations, making monetary resources scarcer and increasing the need to get the most out of every dollar spent. The current process of reaction to individual needs as they arise has not proven to be the most effective use of resources, yet due to legal obligations, institutions continue to participate in this piece-meal approach to addressing issues of access. Within library facilities, using a universal design approach allows for the greatest level of flexibility and long-term usability of investments. One example of how universal design can prove to be more cost effective and efficient is in the area of technology. Rather than purchasing multiple licenses of assistive technology software that is then installed on designated accessible computer stations within a library, universal design suggests the use of key-served software that can be accessed from any computer connected to the institution's network. This not only reduces the number of licenses that may need to be purchased, it also decreases the amount of personnel time needed to install and support the software on individual machines and it allows for the greater flexibility for the user. In light of the increased reliance upon technology within information sharing on campuses today, it is important to look at the needs of patrons from a larger picture view rather than through a narrower individual-needs focus.

The next logical argument for consideration is the issue of logistics. While librarians certainly have the greatest level of expertise within their field of library and information science, collaboration with other resources on campus allows libraries to create better-informed policies. Simple suggestions can include the formation of new, or cooperation with existing, taskforces that address issues of accessibility and/or universal design. Out of these forms of collaboration, libraries can access existing resources to augment their staff trainings, develop new and innovative policies in areas such as technology, or provide support for reorganization of staff or facilities. For those institutions that are in the midst of larger-scale changes, such as expansion of existing facilities or the building of new structures, using the concept of universal design in the early planning stages better ensures that the new facilities have the maximum usability. By considering issues of accessibility through the lens of universal design, institutions can shift from reactionary policy making to long-term strategizing.

Finally, library administrators can use this approach to develop the internal and external messages they wish to convey. Libraries can position themselves both politically and academically as cutting edge by showing a willingness to integrate new and innovative approaches in their services and policies. Additionally, libraries can use the opportunity to review existing data sets and evaluations of policy and procedure best practices, or provide the collection of such data for dissemination within the field. Cross-pollination of areas of expertise and experience within the institution creates opportunities for greater integration of library priorities and values to the larger institution. External to the institution, libraries can seek out regional opportunities to collaborate and increase overall efficacy of new approaches to accessibility.

CONCLUSION

For academic libraries, there are numerous benefits to the application of universal design principles, not only for students but also for faculty, staff, and other patrons alike because the approach focuses on enhancing the provision of library services to all users of libraries, not just a select targeted population. Consideration of accessibility, especially from a universal design approach, opens up the potential for libraries to maximize their institutional value and effectiveness. The legal, monetary, and social justifications for responding to the issue of accessibility within higher education are extensive. As academic libraries continue to play an essential role in education, it only makes sense that they serve as role models in making that education accessible to all learners.

> If controversy is any measure, disability has arrived on the American scene. Passage of the ADA in 1990 has provoked public dispute ever since. If nothing else, disability has, it seems at last won a place in the national conversation.[17]

NOTES

1. William E. Kirwan, president, Ohio State University, Spring Commencement address 2001 (unpublished).
2. Janet Shapiro, *No Pity: People with Disabilities Forging a New Civil Rights Movement* (New York: Random House, Inc., 1993).
3. Polly Welch and Chris Palames, *A Brief History of Disability Rights Legislation in the United States.* Pp. 5–12 in *Strategies for Teaching Universal Design*, ed. Polly Welch (Boston, MA: Adaptive Environments Center 1995).
4. James S. Fairweather and Deborah M. Shaver, "Making the Transition to Postsecondary Education and Training," *Exceptional Children* 57 (1990): 264–270.
5. Laura Horn and Jennifer Berktold, "Students with Disabilities in Postsecondary Education: A Profile of Preparation, Participation, and Outcomes," *Education Statistics Quarterly* 1, no. 3 (1999). Available at http://nces.ed.gov/programs/quarterly/vol_1/1_3/4-esq13-a.asp (accessed May 22, 2005).
6. Cathy Henderson, ed., *College Freshmen with Disabilities: A Statistical Profile* (Washington, DC: American Council on Education, 1995).
7. Jose Blackorby and Mary Wagner, "Longitudinal Postschool Outcomes of Youth with Disabilities: Findings from the National Longitudinal Transition Study," *Exceptional Children* 62 (1996): 399–413.

  8. Colin Barnes and Geof Mercer, *Disability* (Cambridge, UK: Polity Press, 2003).
  9. Ibid., 66.
 10. Ibid.
 11. Ibid.
 12. Center for Universal Design, North Carolina State University, Raleigh, NC (1997). Available at http://www.design.ncsu.edu/cud/center/aboutus.htm (accessed June 1, 2005).
 13. Universal Design Education Online (Center for Universal Design, North Carolina State University; IDEA Center, University at Buffalo; Global Universal Design Educator's Network). Homepage. Available at http://www.udeducation.org/learn/aboutud.asp (accessed June 1, 2005).
 14. Center for Universal Design, North Carolina State University, Raleigh, NC (1997). Available at http://www.design.ncsu.edu/cud/univ_design/princ_overview.htm (accessed June 1, 2005).
 15. Stan F. Shaw, Sally S. Scott, and Joan M. McGuire, "Teaching College Students with Learning Disabilities" (November 2001), ERIC Digest (ED459548). Available at http://www.ericfacility.net/ericdigests/ed459548.html (accessed June 1, 2005).
 16. Ibid.
 17. Diane Coleman, "Introduction," in *The New Disability History: American Perspectives*, edited by Paul Longmore and Lauri Umansky (New York: New York University Press, 2001), n. p.

5

DISABILITY SUPPORT SERVICES, VICTORIA UNIVERSITY OF WELLINGTON

Ava Gibson

Great service is not an impossible dream.[1]

Disability Support Services (DSS) facilitates equal access to Victoria University through the ongoing removal of barriers to education for students with impairments, with medical conditions, or who are Deaf. DSS enables students to fulfill their academic potential and participate in all aspects of university life. Together with the student and appropriate others, the unit identifies students' needs and the barriers that they may face in their course or activity. DSS provides staff with a formal evaluation of the accommodations, support, and services that are required for a student and with assistance to implement these recommendations effectively. DSS also funds and coordinates the provision of specialized services, furniture, or equipment.[2] Examples include training and advice on adaptive technology, the provision of sign language interpreting and note-taking services for lectures and tutorials, mobility parking, physical access arrangements, and alternative formatting.

HOW DSS WORKS

The social model of disability informs the unit's practice. The New Zealand Disability Strategy, which "provides an enduring framework to ensure that government departments and agencies consider disabled people before making decisions,"[3] states, "disability is not something individuals have. What individuals have are impairments. They may be physical, sensory, neurological, psychiatric, intellectual or other impairments." Instead, "disability is the process which happens when one group of people create barriers by designing a world only for their way of living, taking no account of the impairments other people have."[4] By this definition, the interaction between the student with the impairment and the tertiary environment can create disability.[5] Disability has parallels with other attitudes and behaviors that create discrimination, such as racism and sexism. The social model is a useful tool for identifying where change is required in order to create a more inclusive environment for people with impairments.

DSS staff serve as advocates for students as individuals to ensure a particular student's needs are met, and for students with impairments collectively through DSS's membership on various committees and input into policies. The staff also provide information and training opportunities within the university community to further understanding and awareness on disability issues. They work in partnership with disabled people to deliver this understanding and awareness.

DSS faces a difficult situation in working with individual students to ensure their needs are met and in working towards change in the wider university to ensure a more inclusive environment is created. Two central questions become, (1) "How much should we do?," and (2) "What are other responsibilities?" Some disabled people have remarked that with the establishment of a specific unit for disabled people on campus, disability has been further ghettoized, with everyone referring anything to do with a student with an impairment to the DSS. Fortunately, this situation rarely occurs, but it continues to be an issue as we question what is most effective for us to do. Students should not be the pawns in a philosophical debate.

Along with a philosophy of inclusion, we hold to the principle that all interactions with people with impairments must be characterized by respect for their rights, dignity, privacy, confidentiality, and equality. DSS is part of the Student Services Group, which provides a range of quality services aimed at enhancing the educational outcomes and the total university experience of students.[6] The Student Services Group believes in a holistic approach and that service provision must address the personal needs and development of the total student, be delivered in a manner that is seamless and meaningful, and be integrated with the academic mission of the university. Thus, DSS provides a range of personal support, assists with planning, and coordinates with a number of different areas in the university.

THE STUDENTS WITH WHOM WE WORK

Students with impairments are underrepresented in tertiary education. In 2001, Statistics New Zealand found that there were fewer people with impairments with school or postschool qualifications compared to the general population. For those over 15 years, the highest qualifications of 34 percent of people with impairments were school qualifications, with 27 percent attaining postschool, compared with 42 percent and 34 percent, respectively, for those people without impairments.[7] In 2001, the participation rate in tertiary education for people with impairments was estimated at 2 percent, whereas the rate of participation by nondisabled people was estimated at 17 percent. Inclusion and equity are a right for all students. Through its obligations in its Charter, Profile and Statement of Objectives, the university acknowledges the disadvantage that exists for students with impairments. A commitment has been made to increase both the number and success of students with impairments at Victoria University, in order that numbers reflect the community from which the university draws.

In 2004, 498 students actively used DSS services, with 539 students registering with the unit. This was a 16 percent increase on 2003 figures. Ninety students accessing DSS services had a temporary impairment, with 123 having multiple impairments. The additional 41 students who did not actively use DSS services are likely to have registered with us in case they required services during the year.

A total of 344 students identified on the Application to Study form that they had an impairment, injury, or chronic medical condition, with a further 20 students identifying as Deaf, being a total of 364 students. Of these students, 230 students also registered with DSS. We cannot give a definitive reason as to why 134 students chose not to register with us. Many reasons are probable. Lack of barriers in the environment is one. For example, in 2004 10 Deaf[8] students registered with DSS, compared with the 20 who identified themselves on the Application to Study. The 10 students who did not use the service are likely to be students enrolled in Deaf Studies, which is taught in New Zealand Sign Language. Consequently, no communication barrier is present. Another possible reason is that many students with mobility impairments may not face barriers as the physical environment becomes increasingly more accessible. They may contact us only if a barrier is faced. This is similar for students with a recurring illness or impairment who will contact DSS if they have a period of ill health. Some students with impairments may choose to work directly with staff themselves, rather than go through an intermediary like DSS. Other reasons include students not believing we are able to assist them, or not feeling they are as deserving of services as others. There will also be students who do not enroll at all, as they either are unaware of our existence or of what we can provide.

Some 4 percent of the domestic student population either registered with DSS or indicated they had an impairment on the enrollment form. One in five New Zealanders have an impairment, and it is likely that one in eight have an impairment in the population from which university students are drawn. Brett Challacombe-King and Katie Taylor found in their research on transition from secondary school that neither the schools nor the Ministry of Education currently keep statistics on the number of students with impairments likely to attend tertiary education within our catchment area.[9] DSS worked with 49 prospective students in 2004 who were considering attending university in the future, with many other prospective students accessing our printed material on our Web site.

RELATIONS WITH THE UNIVERSITY LIBRARY

The library has a history of being proactive in meeting the needs of students with impairments. When the first Coordinator of Students with Disabilities began in 1994, the reference librarians on the entry level of the library were the first point of contact for students, and all students with specific needs in relation to library services were introduced to the staff. The head of the reference section attended meetings of CAN-DO, a support and advocacy group for students with disabilities, to listen and act on any concerns students raised.

In late 1992, a proposal from the library was included in an approach to the Sutherland Trust for funding for projects on campus to assist students with impairments. In June 1993, the trust announced a grant to Victoria University of Wellington, and part of that grant was allocated for a separate room inside the library. University staff and representatives from CAN-DO were involved in the planning, and construction started later that year. The opening ceremony was held on March 1, 1994, and was well attended by the Wellington disability community, who celebrated the opening of the room, the first of its kind within New Zealand. It contained adaptive technology and equipment, ergonomic furniture, a microwave and facilities for hot drinks, and two rooms in which the students could rest.

The Sutherland Room was successful on several counts. It not only met its intended purpose of providing a place to study and rest for students with impairments, but also became a safe, supportive place on campus for students with impairments to go to, and from it social networks and a sense of identity have formed.

During 2000, a new project to renovate and expand the Sutherland Room was begun, with the cooperation of DSS, Student Computing Services, Facilities Management, the library, and student users. The Sutherland Room continues to be a good example of cooperation to achieve a positive result for end users. DSS determines which students have access to the room (programmed identification cards allow students to swipe into the room) and provides furniture, equipment, and specialist software that may be required. The library owns (paying the occupancy charge) and monitors the room. Student users fundraise for small-cost items. Student Computing Service provides the computers.

Victoria University exists on a multicampus site and there are now five libraries: Central, Architecture and Design, Law, Commerce, and WJ Scott Libraries. Variations on the Sutherland Room exist on each campus. Victoria University of Wellington's Pipitea Campus is the campus on Lambton Quay formed by three prominent Wellington landmarks: Rutherford House, Government Buildings, and the Wellington Railway Station West Wing. There Mahi Nga¯tahi consists of a separate social space with a wheelchair-accessible kitchenette (open to all students), a separate study space, a room to rest, and the "'Dragons Lair," a room with a computer with voice-activated software. There are no general computers in the space, as DSS works with the Student Computing Services to make the numerous computer labs at Pipitea accessible. As the Commerce Library is very small with limited opening hours, Mahi Nga⁻tahi is not contained within the library. However, there is a book reading room, with Openbook software, located in the library.

Disability Liaison Person

The library, like many places within the university, has a Disability Liaison Person. The liaison person is promoted in publications and on the library's Web site as the contact person for students with impairments within the library. The Disability Liaison Person is also a point of contact for DSS staff when addressing issues of general relevance to the library. They attend the Advisory Committee on Students with Impairments and the Orientation morning for students with impairments at the beginning of the year. They have a key role in addressing equity issues at the library for people with impairments.

Equity Training

DSS coordinates the provision of Disability Equity Training to all staff at the university. In 2000, the library committed itself to ensuring that as many staff as possible had attended the training. Three training workshops of seven hours each were provided to library staff to ensure the majority were trained. The library also had several staff attend a course in conversational sign language. Library staff have continued to have a presence at Disability Equity Training.

LIBRARY SERVICES—WHAT IS IMPORTANT?

In order to improve services to students with impairments within the library, this section outlines what I believe would occur ideally in a library. The suggestions are divided into four categories: policies and procedures, staff development, access to facilities and equipment, and specific services. In reality these are not stand-alone categories but are interwoven. I have also provided ideas on how I believe these suggestions could best operate within the available environment. A partnership approach, as suggested in this chapter and elsewhere, is the most effective way to provide library services to students with impairments.

Policies and Procedures

It is important that policies and procedures exist to guide the interaction between library staff and students with impairments. The staff need to understand this and to make these policies and procedures easily accessible to students with impairments (e.g., available on the library Web site).

Policies would include ensuring both students and staff are aware of their rights and responsibilities under legislation (e.g., Human Rights Act, Privacy Act, and Health and Safety Act) and under university policies (e.g., a policy on meeting the needs of students with impairments). They would also provide students with information on:

- What adjustments to services and facilities are already available to students with impairments;
- What can be done for them on an individual basis; and
- The procedures to access these services or facilities.

A complaint procedure for any complaints that arise directly from disability would also be included.

Students need to be involved in both the development and review of relevant policies, procedures, services, and facilities available in the library. They could do so, for instance, through direct feedback, surveys, or focus groups.

Staff Development

Induction for new staff would include information on what the library and the university provide for students with impairments and would ensure staff are aware of relevant legislation, policies, procedures, and current practices.

Disability Equity Training would be a key component of staff development to ensure staff have the knowledge and skills to work effectively with people with a variety of impairments. In the consultation process for the New Zealand Disability Strategy, attitudes were identified as the biggest barrier for people with impairments. Without Disability Equity Training, there is no avenue to reflect on and address personal attitudes towards disability. Training also provides an opportunity to understand the experience of people with impairments and implications of those experiences for people with different impairments on library services, discuss communication and information strategies, be clear on staff obligations, study best practice in library services, and review personal practice to ensure that it is inclusive for all people with impairments.

Designated, trained contacts at each library site, who are actively promoted to students and staff, are important. It is vital that these people have effective channels of communication to management level within the library and to DSS. They would also have a role in communicating issues to others within the library. Contact people require additional time for ongoing development on disability issues and library services. The role would be formally acknowledged through human resource processes. For example, it could be included in role descriptions, work plans, and performance reviews, rather than an additional thing for which a staff member volunteers.

With staff trained to meet students' requirements, the library is more likely to provide a safe environment for students to discuss their requirements. Students should be invited to do so, and where possible share responsibility for developing solutions and advising staff of any difficulties they face. Diversity among employees is an asset in the workplace, so hiring people with experience of disability can add value to library services.

Access to Facilities and Equipment

Students with impairments must have equitable access to the library and its facilities. Ideally the library would comply with or exceed the standards in *NZS 4121:2001 Design for Access and Mobility: Buildings and Associated Facilities.*[10] This includes, for example, accessible toilet facilities, talking elevators, adequate signage, lighting, and good color contrasts. Where this is not possible or unreasonably difficult, an alternative means of participation must exist. When any upgrade or changes are to be made to the library, planning should incorporate improvements to facilities and access for people with impairments.

Adaptive technology (e.g., magnifiers, scanners, and screen readers) need to be readily available to students who have difficulty accessing information in print. The adaptive technology needs to be situated in the best possible location for students, which is often in an adaptive technology room in the library, although the technology might also be part of computer labs or placed in stand-alone locations.

Computers provided in the library need to be in accessible labs and be able to be set up to meet users' requirements. Ergonomic furniture (e.g., desks to work at while standing, kneelers, and adjustable chairs) are also required. It is also beneficial to have a room available for people to rest.

Specific Services

Libraries are all about information and for some people with impairments, information needs to be available in alternative formats. For example, accessible electronic formats for students who have difficulty accessing print but use adaptive technology (e.g., screen readers or videos that are captioned for students who are Deaf, hearing impaired, or have a concentration or learning difficulty). Resource sharing with other university libraries can occur so that loans of books in Braille or on tape can be made with ease. It is ideal if when purchasing books, the library found out what other formats the book is available in. Increasing the supply of electronic books can also be advantageous. When designing a Web site, online public access catalog system, or other Web-based material, it is important to give attention to accessibility issues and to ensure all can use it, including people who use screen readers or who do not use a mouse.

Individualized services for students could include flexible lending and extension policies; a system of telephoning, e-mailing, or dropping off a book list for collection later; personal induction sessions on using the library; and assisting students in using the catalog, finding resources, or using equipment. Use of the "equity in action"[11] card or a specific library assistance card could be useful for students. Another alternative is for information that students provide about their needs in relation to the library being embedded in their library card or student identification card, saving the student valuable time in explaining their requirements repeatedly.

Proactive budgeting to meet the needs of students with impairments should occur. Given the funding system for students with impairments within New Zealand's tertiary education system,[12] a small budget held within the library to fund low-cost support for students with impairments is ideal, with continued liaison with DSS and other areas (e.g., areas responsible for computing services or building maintenance) to plan for larger expenditure items.

WHAT DOES DSS WANT TO KNOW
ABOUT LIBRARY SERVICES?

Services to all students need to be regularly reviewed, ensuring that they meet the current and emerging requirements of students with varying impairments. DSS conducts annual surveys on the quality of its services to students. The unit usually includes one question on another area of the university so that the feedback can be incorporated into its advocacy work. It is hoped that these other areas include a section on students with impairments in any survey they conduct.

As well as through the survey process, DSS receives feedback directly from students during their appointments, through feedback boxes, and through attendance at meetings. We also deal with frustrations and complaints. Getting constructive feedback that can assist in identifying what is going well and why, and where improvements are needed, is difficult. It requires going beyond the survey questionnaire to build a relationship in which students feel able to say what they think and become real partners in making services as effective as possible.

On an operational level, DSS looks for two types of information when seeking feedback:

1. Immediate things that require resolution or improvement to enhance the current experience of students; and
2. Issues that require more long-term strategic planning.

DSS needs to be clear as to why it is asking for information and ensure that the information is used for its intended purpose and that it is not asking for feedback for the sake merely of seeking feedback. People with impairments are over-surveyed and often receive no benefit from their input.

CONCLUSION

There is continuous dialogue between DSS and library staff to improve services to students. For example, recent dialogue has included the library Web site and its coverage of disability services, the library's strategic plan, library renovations, the design of elevators, and collection development (e.g., the purchase of electronic books and systems are established to ensure students' individuals needs are met).

Communication could always be improved, and it has been pleasing in recent months to strengthen the dialogue and make library services to students with impairments a greater priority, We have work to do in order to engage students more in the process of reviewing and suggesting areas for improvements. In the future, any use of a disability—or impairment-focused—service quality questionnaire should involve DSS staff.

Later this year (2005) we will be reviewing services in line with *Kia Ōrite—Achieving Equity: The New Zealand Code of Practice for Creating an Inclusive Environment for Students with Impairment*. This code of practice should provide useful information for the library and DSS.

The key to ensure high-quality library services that meet the present and future needs of the diversity of students with impairments is the development of a close relationship between library users and the staff who work with the students in the library. DSS has an important role in facilitating this connection and fostering this partnership.

Great service is the inspiration to excel.[13]

NOTES

1. Leonard L. Berry, *On Great Service: A Framework for Action* (New York: The Free Press, 1995), 59.
2. The university receives a targeted Special Supplementary Grant to assist with meeting the high cost of needs of students with impairments. The size of the grant is determined by the number of full-time equivalent domestic students who are enrolled.
3. Ministry of Social Development, Office for Disability Issues, *NZ Disability Strategy* (Wellington: Ministry of Social Development, n.d.). Available at http://www.odi.govt.nz/nzds/index.html (accessed April 20, 2005).
4. Ministry of Health, *The New Zealand Disability Strategy: Making a World of Difference, Whakanui Oranga* (Wellington: Ministry of Health, 2001), 1.
5. In New Zealand, tertiary education falls under the jurisdiction of the Tertiary Education Commission (TEC) Te Amorangi Matauranga Matua, which is a crown entity established under Section 159C of the Education Act of 1989. The TEC funds all postcompulsory education and training offered by universities, polytechnics, colleges of education, wananga, private training establishments, foundation education agencies, industry training organizations, and adult and community education providers.

6. Victoria University of Wellington, *Student Services Strategic Plan* (Wellington: Victoria University of Wellington, 2004).

7. Statistics New Zealand, *Disability Counts* (Wellington: Statistics New Zealand, 2001).

8. Deaf with a capital "D" refers to those people whose identity themselves as members of the Deaf community and as a cultural and linguistic group. They usually share the common language of sign language, and they often do not consider themselves as having an impairment.

9. Brett Challacombe-King and Katie Taylor, "At the Mighty Steps of Academia: What Foils the Young Disabled Person?" (paper presented at Standards Plus conference on Exploring Pathways to Tertiary Education, Auckland, New Zealand, 2004). Available at http://www.imaginebetter.co.nz/coa2004_proceedings.shtml (accessed May 10, 2005).

10. All buildings built since 2001 must comply with the Code. Any renovated building must comply with the standard. *NZS 4121:2001: Design for Access and Mobility: Buildings and Associated Facilities* is available from Standards New Zealand. Available at http://www.standards.co.nz/web-shop/?action=viewSearchProduct&mod=catalog&pid=4121:2001(NZS) (accessed September 26, 2005).

11. Victoria University has an "equity in action" card that all students who register with DSS receive. It can be used for all nonacademic registration without any explanation required, making it particularly useful for students with invisible impairments.

12. The Tertiary Education Commission pays each university a targeted Special Supplementary Grant to meet the high-cost needs of students with impairments. The amount of the grant is based on the overall domestic equivalent full-time student numbers. At Victoria University, this additional funding goes to DSS, which allocates it based on student needs. All schools and central services are expected to have their own budget to cover small-cost items.

13. Berry, *On Great Service: A Framework for Action*, 267.

6

PERSPECTIVE OF LIBRARY DIRECTORS

> Providing support to students with disabilities is the responsibility of student support, not academic support.
>
> —*anonymous director*

Library literature, as chapter 7 notes, covers various aspects of library services to students with disabilities. However, those writings do not provide commentary directly from library directors at academic institutions that primarily or exclusively serve students with disabilities and at institutions that serve a broader mix of students. Because the research for this book occurred in both New Zealand and the United States, we offer the perspectives of some senior administrators in both countries. The intention is to let the directors or their designees discuss their libraries and institution's approach to serving students with disabilities. From our discussion with a number of librarians, it is clear that three approaches prevail:

1. The library serves as a proactive partner with the office of disability services in identifying and meeting the information needs and expectations of students with disabilities;

2. The library lets the office of disability services assume the leadership role; a member of the library staff either works actively with that office or is assigned to be a coordinator, but is not actively engaged with the office or disability students; and

3. The library fails to assume any responsibility or role, other than meeting legal requirements for physical access. The library may or may not meet programmatic responsibilities as specified in the law.

None of the following examples falls into the third category.

The contributors to this chapter include:

- Larry Hardesty, Dean, University of Nebraska at Kearney Library (Kearney, Nebraska);
- Rush G. Miller, Hillman University Librarian and Director, University Library System, University of Pittsburgh (Pittsburgh, Pennsylvania);
- Sarah Hamrick, Director of Information Services, Gallaudet University (Washington, D.C.);
- Jennifer Lann, Director of Library Services, Landmark College (Putney, Vermont);
- Helen Renwick, Associate University Librarian, University of Auckland (Auckland, New Zealand);
- Philip Jane, Central Library Manager, University of Canterbury (Christchurch, New Zealand); and
- John Redmayne, Librarian, Massey University (Palmerston North, New Zealand).

KEARNEY STATE UNIVERSITY LIBRARY

Both academic libraries in general and my own specific library deal with students with various disabilities. For example, there are students who are wheelchair bound and who face both visual and auditory challenges. In my experience, for those with visual and auditory challenges, the institution arranges for someone to assist them. Sometimes this has meant someone to accompany them to class and to ensure class lectures are made available to them in a form they can use. The library has special equipment so that, for example, anyone with a disability can read the computer screens. In Texas, the state provided library equipment for students with various challenges; In Nebraska, I recently assumed my current position and thus do not know how we acquired the equipment we have.

Turning to the questions "In meeting disability needs and expectations, does service relate largely to legal requirements or is service quality a more expansive topic?" and "To what extent should disability law be the sole criterion on the offering of services?," generally I have found library staff willing to provide whatever service is needed to help students with various challenges. By and large, library staffs consist of service-oriented individuals who are willing to help students to the best of the staff's ability.

In response to the question "How well trained are librarians to deal with different disabilities in library services?," I doubt librarians, in general, have much training in how to deal with students with various disabilities. I do not know if schools of library and information studies (LIS) are the best place to offer such training since graduates of LIS programs go into so many different facets of librarianship. The training might best be offered through various state agencies to librarians on the job.

Next, "How do libraries identify which services to offer disability students?" Within academic institutions I think our admissions offices work to identify those with the most salient challenges, and these staff members try to work with and alert the rest of the campus to the presence of students with particular needs. I believe this is simply a federal legal requirement.

Finally, serving students with particular challenges can often be a challenge. For example, we need to be mindful of visual challenges in creating Web pages. We need to make aisle widths in the stacks adequate to accommodate students in wheelchairs. At the same time, a significant portion of the collection is not available to them without assistance simply because the materials are placed too high on the stacks. To make all the collection available to students in wheelchairs would be very expensive. We offer paging services and so forth, and do the best we can. My background has largely been in small private institutions, and relatively elite institutions at that. Therefore, I have not worked directly with a lot of students, faculty, or others with severe limitations. I suspect, but without direct experience, proportionally more students with disability challenges attend the larger state institutions. Nevertheless, wherever I have been, the admissions and the human resources offices have tried to keep the library informed of legal requirements, and the library staffs have tried to work with people with various disabilities.

UNIVERSITY OF PITTSBURGH LIBRARY SYSTEM

Staff from the Office of Disability Services (ODS) refer and often accompany students with disabilities to the university libraries. However, many students as well as community users with disabilities come to the libraries directly and then library staff assist them. The libraries have developed a solid working relationship with ODS, which has equipped and maintains a laboratory in the main library.

The libraries are diligent regarding the legal requirements for provision of service to students with all kinds of disabilities. The staff work closely with the ODS on campus to review and revise these services either overall or for dealing with individual cases. Fundamentally the library staff are trained to provide any and all service required to meet the library and information needs of these students. Our view is that we will not only abide conscientiously by the requirements of law, but also strive to give all users whatever additional assistance they require or request from us if it is within our capacity to do so.

Staff from the ODS meet with all public services staff on a regular basis to review the resources available to students at various offices/sites on campus and have discussed how and when to refer them. In addition, they have discussed how best to provide assistance to users with disabilities. The University Library System has been proactive in providing these services for decades, and especially within the past eleven years—my tenure as university librarian.

In identifying services to offer students with disabilities, the library staff work closely with the ODS, which encourages us to contact them with questions at any time, and often this is done. Someone from that office will come to the library to offer users additional assistance where needed.

The library has to offer services proactively to meet the special needs of students and other users with disabilities. This service must go beyond simply offering equipment and facilities, and must involve an active partnership with ODS constantly to review and revise services needed as new cases arise. In addition, the library must be committed to ensuring access to its resources and services to anyone regardless of the accommodation that is required. The staff of the university's libraries is trained and committed to such service.

GALLAUDET UNIVERSITY LIBRARY

Service to students with disabilities is one of many challenges academic libraries face in the twenty-first century. Technological and legal developments have provided the means for more individuals with disabilities to study and learn alongside their peers in the classroom and on campus than ever before. Many of these students need specialized library services, and librarians are employing a variety of strategies to satisfy those needs and provide students with disabilities access to the best library services possible.

Gallaudet University is the world's only liberal arts university for students who are deaf or hard of hearing. The majority of students enrolled there have some level of hearing disability, and for that reason the campus is entirely accessible to people who are deaf. All faculty, staff, and students communicate in both printed/written English and American Sign Language. Because deafness is the norm at Gallaudet, it is not considered a disability. Gallaudet's Office for Students with Disabilities (OSWD) has responsibility for providing accommodations for students with other disabilities, and the University Library works closely with staff in OSWD to ensure that library services are fully accessible. All students must register with OSWD in order to receive accommodations.

At Gallaudet service quality for students with disabilities is not measured strictly by legal requirements (see chapter appendix). Every effort is made to provide students with the services they need, and sometimes that means going beyond the letter of the law. Gallaudet students have differing communication preferences (e.g., varying forms of sign language and speech reading), and for that reason staff have found that the best means of providing virtually every service, including library instruction, is one-on-one. Traditional instruction sessions are held in classrooms, but students are encouraged to make an appointment with a librarian for personal assistance. Students with disabilities are given the same attention. One librarian has primary responsibility for providing information to students and staff about the mechanics of accessible services, but all staff participate actively in the service itself, and all staff have the information needed to provide those services.

Gallaudet's services to students with disabilities are somewhat unique because of the nature of the student body. Services to people with disabilities vary widely in academic libraries across the United States. Many libraries offer a full range of services and programs. Others offer very little, if that. Those that do provide accessible services work closely with campus offices for students with disabilities, and in many cases, as in Gallaudet's, the library offers accessible services only to those students who have requested services from the campus office for students with disabilities. Students who have not registered with the institution's central office charged with providing accommodations are not eligible to receive them from individual units. This process of self-identification is essential for students to receive services, yet many are reluctant to label themselves disabled. This is especially true for students with learning disabilities, who pose a significant challenge for academic libraries. Unless a student identifies himself or herself as having a learning disability and specifies exactly what accommodations he or she needs, there is no way for the library to provide accessible service.

Many students are reluctant to identify themselves as learning disabled because of the stigma they believe is attached to the label, and some have not been tested and are not aware they have a disability at all. Academic librarians are now seeking ways to make services accessible to students with learning disabilities. This is a relatively new challenge that is being faced by faculty in the classroom as well.

In the early 1990s there was a surge of interest in service to students with disabilities when the Americans with Disabilities Act (ADA) first took effect. Librarians were aware that the new law required them to provide students with disabilities equal access to services and collections. As campus administrators addressed some of the physical aspects of accommodating students with disabilities (e.g., providing access to buildings), librarians addressed the service aspects. Many libraries appointed ADA coordinators, staff members who were charged with the responsibility to ensure that their libraries provided appropriate "reasonable accommodation" for students with disabilities. During that period attendance at meetings of the American Library Association's Academic Librarians Assisting the Disabled Discussion Group (a unit of the Libraries Serving Special Populations Section of the Association of Specialized and Cooperative Library Agencies) surged. Much of the focus of those interested in services to students with disabilities during that period was to learn how to satisfy the somewhat vague requirements of the ADA. Now, more than ten years after ADA, attendance at the renamed Academic Libraries Accessibility and Disability Services Discussion Group is very low, and the discussions often focus on strategies to ensure equal access to collections and services with little or no funding. The Association of College and Research Libraries has no section, committee, or discussion group devoted to library services for students with disabilities.

According to the Heath Resource Center at George Washington University, the National Postsecondary Student Aid Survey (NPSAS) 2000 found that 9.3 percent of undergraduate students at colleges in the United States have some form of disability. For purposes of its survey the NPSAS defined disability as "a long-lasting condition such as blindness, deafness, or a severe vision or hearing impairment"—"a condition that substantially limited one or more basic physical activities such as walking, climbing stairs, reaching, lifting, or carrying," or "any other physical, mental, or emotional condition lasting six months or more."[1] This is a significant percentage of the student population, yet there is relatively little in the standard library literature about services to college students with disabilities. A simple search in *Library Literature* yields only fifteen articles directly related to students with disabilities in college and university libraries.

Most librarians who are responsible for services to students with disabilities have little or no formal training in that area. Some schools of library and information studies now address the topic as one component of a broader course, but little specific information is given. Librarians often rely on staff in their campus's office for students with disabilities for information and support, including training to use the hardware and software required to make collections accessible.

It is difficult for academic librarians to measure the quality of their services, and one reason is that a significant percentage of students do not take advantage of those services. Some academic librarians make little or no attempt to provide services to students with disabilities because they believe there are none at their institutions. This may be true, but it is very possible that students with disabilities are not using the library because accommodations are not provided.

Library services to college students with disabilities have certainly improved since passage of the Americans with Disabilities Act, but there is much room for improvement.

LANDMARK COLLEGE LIBRARY

The Landmark College Library primarily serves students with a language-based learning disability and/or attention-deficit hyperactivity disorder (ADHD), although a minority of students have nonverbal learning disabilities, Asperger's Syndrome, or traumatic brain injury. Since the entire student body has documented learning disabilities and/or ADHD, the college does not have a special disability services department. According to year 2000 numbers from the American Council on Education, 2.4 percent of first-year college students have a diagnosed learning disability.[2] Estimates for the number of college students with ADHD vary from 2 to 4 percent.[3] Further, it is a reasonable assumption that there are even more students who have not yet been diagnosed.

Given the prevalence of learning disabilities (LD) and ADHD among U.S. college students, chances are that most academic libraries encounter some students with LD/ADHD with or without formal confirmation of that diagnosis. The situation at Landmark College Library is not as different as one might expect. Even though we know that all of our students have some learning difference,[4] we rarely know a student's particular learning profile ahead of time. A student with dyslexia has some different challenges than a student with ADHD, for example, and, just like at other academic libraries, most students do not announce their learning difficulties at the reference desk. Therefore, we rely on a universal design approach to instruction when we serve our students. In other words, the instructional practices that work optimally for all students are particularly important for students who learn differently. It is an approach that the rest of the college faculty and staff embrace as well.

A relatively small amount of the literature examines the challenges that students with learning disabilities and ADHD face with research assignments. Nonetheless, the literature about the average college student's difficulties with research offers some useful insights. A common theme is that many beginning college students are anxious about doing research. This anxiety is not a surprise, considering that college-level research projects require a substantial amount of many different kinds of work. Research projects demand that students synthesize the information they find, and synthesis is a sophisticated skill that is all the more difficult to attain when one attempts to synthesize unfamiliar material. The ability to synthesize information is predicated on the ability to synthesize skills; the latter must precede the former in the student's development. To compound the challenges offered by these two types of synthesis, many college students receive inadequate instruction about the research process beyond instruction in library tools.

Three major research challenges daunt many first-year college students:

1. Gaps in background knowledge;
2. Skills deficits; and
3. Unfamiliarity with the research process.

Students with learning differences struggle with these challenges to a greater degree and are therefore more likely to be stymied by them. As a result, applying a universal design approach for instruction offers benefits for the widest range of students, but particularly for those with learning differences. Ron Mace of the Center for Universal Design at North Carolina State University defines universal design as "the design of products and environments to be usable by all people, to the greatest extent possible, without the need for adaptation or specialized design."[5] Universal design, when it is applied to instruction, meets the special needs of those who learn differently by addressing the varied learning needs of everyone via best teaching practices.

It is a perennial complaint that young adults lack adequate cultural literacy,[6] resulting in remarkable gaps in what many would consider common knowledge. For students with learning differences, the potential for gaps in background knowledge is greater. These students may have struggled in K-12, received poor grades, or even been passed without mastery. Their parents may have assisted them with their homework to an inappropriate (but understandable) degree. These hypothetical but common scenarios illustrate how a student with a learning disability or ADHD might receive an incomplete formal (not to mention informal) education before entering college.

Background knowledge provides a foundation on which to build new ideas that we encounter when we do research. Without that foundation, the builder of knowledge does not know where to put the new bricks, or even which bricks would be appropriate to add. To learn something new, we need new information to reach our long-term memory. Social cognitive theory asserts that new information needs to make a connection to information that we already know in order for it to enter our long-term memory, and that this connection, or mortar between old and new bricks, is a literal connection, made between neurons.[7]

A universally designed instruction (UDI) practice for addressing gaps in background knowledge involves explicitly linking new information to familiar information via *connectors*.[8] Instructional librarians can indicate how a new piece of information relates to something that the students just learned in that research visit or recently in their course. Librarians can also use analogies to examples or concepts that are familiar to all students. Another helpful technique involves the use of *activators*,[9] in which students brainstorm what they already know or suspect they know about their research topic or about the research process. This activates their thinking and, just as importantly, gives the instructor a clearer sense of what the students already know. Additionally, periodically summarizing (using *summarizers*)[10] helps to reinforce the connections between old and new information.

Just as gaps in background knowledge threaten the beginning of the research process, skills deficits can derail the process at any stage. Many new college students who read and write well are unaccustomed to the level of reading and writing that discipline-specific, college-level research requires. In high school, they may not have been required to synthesize information in such as way as to create a sum greater than its parts, and so their completed assignments resemble a string of loosely connected book reports. Of course, reading and writing presents a significantly higher hurdle for students with dyslexia. Difficulty with either skill also makes sufficient paraphrasing (a sophisticated skill that is not always taught very explicitly) all the more daunting.

A UDI approach that addresses reading deficits provides what Sally S. Scott, Joan M. McGuire, Mary D. Sarver, and Stan F. Shaw, from the Center on Postsecondary Education and Disability at the University of Connecticut, call "perceptible information," in which information is made available via multiple formats (e.g., verbally, visually, kinesthetically, and potentially with assistive technology, such as text readers or books on tape).[11] Another way to make information more perceptible is by offering a variety of reading levels that can be presented in terms of *intended audience:* the general public versus professionals or advanced students. In situations when only scholarly sources are appropriate, librarians can recommend that students use more student-focused reference works or reliable popular sources such as translation guides to the more scholarly texts, even if the students may not cite the more accessible sources. When possible, librarians can encourage faculty to micro-unit the research project to allow for multiple points of assessment that demonstrate the UDI principles of *tolerance for error.*[12] Librarians can also encourage students to make use of appropriate campus-wide support services, such as librarians, the writing center, their tutor, and/or their instructor or class teaching assistant.

Another significant skill deficit that beginning college students may demonstrate is that of critical thinking. Psychologist William Perry theorizes that college students pass through stages of adolescent development that impact their readiness for and sophistication of critical thinking.[13] In the stage of *dualism,* students fail to think critically because they passively receive knowledge from those they believe are absolute authorities and thus can perceive only one truth. Their world of meaning is divided into two opposing realms, such as "right versus wrong" or "we versus they."[14] Students begin to develop critical thinking skills in the stage of *multiplicity,* and yet they perceive all viewpoints as equally valid, thereby failing to see the need to critique opposing arguments or to support their own claims with outside information. It is at the stage of *relativism* that students are developmentally ready to think critically, because they understand the need to evaluate information and its sources. They then understand the value of following discipline-specific research strategies.

Students with LD may face obstacles in their developmental path, which can include self-esteem issues, increased stress, social adjustment difficulties, and comorbid (i.e., coexisting) conditions, including substance abuse and depression.[15] As college freshmen, they may be more dependent than their peers on their family, given their parents' extraordinary investment of time and support for their child's K–12 education.[16] Critical thinking may challenge students with learning differences in less developmental ways as well, given these students' potential deficits in attention, language processing, and long-term and active working memory.[17]

Fortunately, this lack of developmental readiness need not prevent students from applying critical thinking to their research projects. Lev Vygotsky's concept of the "zone of proximal development" asserts that students can learn beyond their stage of development if they have explicit guidance from an instructor.[18] By making the steps for critical thinking simple and obvious, instructors can offer procedures or strategies to make explicit what these students will hopefully do implicitly someday. Many librarians translate the critical thinking skill of source evaluation into a procedure by having students ask a series of questions about an information source that the librarians themselves might no longer consciously ask. Librarians and other adept critical thinkers seem to know instinctively whether or not a source is reliable, because they have internalized critical thinking strategies so that they are now a skill. (To borrow Vygotsky's phrase, skills are strategies "go[ne] underground."[19]) Such strategies can be made routine through multiple opportunities for practice, and routines may be particularly helpful for students with nonverbal learning disabilities who crave predictability and structure.[20] Strategy routines also help students with learning differences work around the attention, language, and memory hurdles that may lie in their path to critical thinking readiness.

Research projects also require nonacademic skills (e.g., executive functioning), which, like critical thinking skills, may not be fully developed in the new college student.[21] Russell Barkley defines executive functions as "those types of actions we perform ourselves or direct at others so as to accomplish self-control, goal-directed behavior, and the maximization of future outcomes."[22] Public service librarians are familiar with students who procrastinate to the point of giving themselves less than twenty-four hours to research and write a research paper. Other students manage not only their time but also their materials poorly and misplace key citation sources. Management of one's emotions is also critical; anxiety and fatigue can either slow or completely stall progress on a research project. Skills deficits and possible comorbid disorders, such as generalized anxiety disorder, can increase the paralyzing power of negative emotions. Carol C. Kuhlthau's "Model of the Stages of the Information Process" provides a useful guide to the many different emotions that may accompany various steps of the research process, from "task initiation" to "search closure."[23]

As students become more familiar with the entire process of scholarly research, from task initiation to project closure, they may be less prone to becoming derailed from their project by runaway emotions, procrastination, and disorganized materials. Gloria Leckie illustrates the obstacles to this holistic understanding of the research process.[24] She indicates that college faculty and students have different models of the research process. Faculty's "expert research model" gives them a depth of background knowledge of their field, which includes ease with disciplinary jargon as well as key theories and theorists. Faculty are more likely to follow citation trails on very specific topics, or to already know what the literature says before they review it again in order to write about a topic. They are familiar and comfortable with the fact that research can be nonlinear, recursive, and full of not only "ambiguity" but also "serendipity."[25] Finally, faculty tend to assume that their students share their research model.

In contrast, the "novice research model" fails to provide students with the deep and extensive background knowledge of the field they must attempt to research. They lack the "long process of acculturation" to the discipline that their professors have had and are either assigned broader research topics than their instructors typically research, or they are expected to narrow it themselves with fewer tools to do so.[26] Libraries and librarians can seem intimidating, especially for students with learning differences for whom libraries can represent a confusing conglomeration of what they do not know, full of "experts" who they fear may judge them as stupid for asking a supposedly stupid question. Faced with this foreign environment and a daunting assignment, many students may employ a "coping strategy" instead of their instructor's "information-seeking strategy."[27] As part of this coping strategy, students may engage in what Beth L. Mark and Trudi E. Jacobson coined "print and run,"[28] but they lack the skill to do so in such a way that gives them quality sources. Jane Keefer provides the metaphor of the "hungry rats," alluding to Bruner's, et al., classic 1955 experiment in which hungry rats were much less adept than their satiated control group at navigating a maze for cheese, because in their state of "overdrive," they rushed and were less able to notice external cues or to learn from their errors.[29] In this overdrive mode, students want only to satisfy their instructor's expectations rather than their own sense of what they want from their project. They tend to avoid sources that disagree with their assumptions about their topic, either to save time and effort or because of a lack of developmental readiness to synthesize opposing viewpoints.[30]

Fortunately, there are UDI solutions to students' inexperience with scholarly research. The activators, connectors, and summarizers, described as approaches to addressing background-knowledge gaps, can also be customized to address this unfamiliarity. Students may have a tension between those aspects of research that they already know and are weary to have reviewed, and those aspects that they do not yet know or know adequately. Activators can engage them to explore what they already know and anticipate about the research process, and connectors can be used to compare aspects of the research process to more familiar activities (e.g., comparing Google to Wal-Mart,[31] and databases to more specific stores, such as Tower Records). Summarizers review and are particularly helpful if the students themselves participate in the summarizing. "Advance organizers," which are a counterpart of summarizers, briefly preview what students are about to learn. Multisensory techniques can be employed to make the research process as *perceptible*[32] as possible to as many students as possible.

As with skills deficits, multiple points of assessment can help an instructor pinpoint the step(s) in the research process that challenge a student the most and prevent that challenge from ruining the entire project. Of course, librarians may be limited in how much they can influence faculty to adopt flexible assessment, but perhaps individual faculty may be receptive, or progress can be made at the curricular level if librarians serve on curriculum committees. The UDI approach of "flexible assessment"[33] may appeal to faculty who are hesitant to squeeze a large term paper into an already full syllabus: research projects need not be large papers; they can be a series of short papers or be a speech, a video, or a Web site. The option of alternative formats allows students to choose a format that may be the least hampered by their area of disability, so that they may be able to demonstrate their knowledge and understanding more accurately.

Even without faculty cooperation, librarians can provide a context of *tolerance for error*[34] by making explicit that research is both a skill one develops and a multistep process involving people (e.g., librarians, the instructor, and staff at the writing center) to assist students with each step. It may help reduce student anxiety to acknowledge that research is naturally recursive and that it is not a sign of failure when students need to refine their searches. As Leckie indicates, research requires "patience and faith,"[35] and librarians can model this state of being while recognizing how disconcerting the initial uncertainty in research can be. That recognition can be tempered with the excitement and hope we may also feel when pursuing research. Librarians can acculturate students to the process of research, as well as give them the tools (e.g., reference works) to help them acculturate to the subject discipline of their assignment.

Librarians can create an "instructional climate" of enthusiasm and respect and promote a "community of learners" among students and between students and themselves.[36] Everyone deserves and values respect, but it is particularly important for students who may have been denied respect in other instructional climates. Students with learning differences may exhibit learned helplessness, or if they escaped that debilitation, they are still quick to notice disrespect, even in the form of well-intentioned condenscension.[37] Either because of a comorbid disorder, (e.g., the aforementioned anxiety disorder, as well as oppositional defiant disorder and bipolar disorder), or as a concomitant difficulty, some students with learning differences experience problems in social interactions. Librarians who work with such students should keep in mind the possibility that a student is acting out of a social deficit rather than out of personal disrespect. This mindset helps us to maintain an appropriate balance between respect and clear boundaries.

Not only do librarians set the instructional climate for students, the library itself does as well. Two other "Principles of Universal Design for Instruction™" can be applied to the library: "Low physical effort" and "Size and space for approach and use."[38] With "low physical effort," an instructor seeks to "minimize nonessential physical effort" to maximize learning.[39] The Landmark College Library provides a Digital Text Library that contains digitized copies in Kurzweil text-to-speech software format of all required course texts, to save students from having to spend valuable reading time scanning the texts themselves. All Landmark College students have Kurzweil software available on their notebook computers and the library's public computers include this software as well. Unfortunately, the library cannot offer this scanning service for any text a student finds when doing library research, but we can assist students in finding comparable texts in full-text article databases and e-book databases. To address "size and space for approach and use," we have tried to arrange our instructional computer lab so that students can see their computers, the screen on which the librarian's computer screen is projected, as well as the librarian and fellow students. Without that line of vision, students, especially those with ADHD, might be more distracted.

Other size and space concerns have more to do with setting a welcoming instructional climate than with ensuring that all students can physically interact with the space successfully. When students entered the Landmark College Library six years ago, they walked under a substantial and inviting skylight, but they were also sandwiched between a tall, imposing reference and circulation desk on one side, and rows of stacks of intimidating-looking reference books on the other. One student admitted that these reference books seemed to "loom overhead" and threaten to topple on him. Behind the first two rows of reference were many rows of periodicals back issues. The former library director, Lisa Griest, recognized that the space needed to be altered in order to more efficiently meet students' needs while creating a more inviting atmosphere.

By moving those back issues into library basement storage, and shifting the reference collection to line the walls of a wing next to the reference desk, it was possible to open up half of the first floor of the library. The Learning Disabilities and ADHD Research Collection lines the walls of one half of this opened space, and a Technology Learning Center, with powerful computers and a suite of media software, occupies the other half. Dividing the two areas is a low, diagonal wall lined with periodical shelving that houses current issues of both journals and magazines. Due to the skylight, plants and even trees thrive in the space, softening the potential austerity of the books. We replaced creaking wooden chairs with upholstered wood-framed chairs designed to be attractive and comfortable but also durable. After testing the chairs with students, we decided to have half of the chairs resemble normal chairs and the other half be the company's "three-position chairs" that allow the sitter to sit normally, lean forward, or lean back in three changeable but stable positions. Each year a new student asks, "These are ADHD chairs, aren't they?," because they allow a student to rock and fidget in a controlled way.

Another space in which UDI principles apply is the virtual space of the library's Web site. The Landmark College librarians periodically redesign the Web site to follow the UDI principle of "Simple and intuitive,"[40] and, in the 2003/2004 academic year, the library had to do so within the constraints of the college's Web site redesign. In the upcoming academic year, the library intends to conduct usability testing with students. The librarians are constrained by font and color (elements that affect readability, particularly with students with learning differences), but fortunately the Landmark College Web site adheres to font and color guidelines for people with cognitive disabilities, in that the font is san serif and enlargeable, and the colors contrast distinctly.[41] For the other aspects of the library's Web site, we can make sure that what seems "simple and intuitive" to librarians is also simple and intuitive to students with various learning differences.

The library used to rely on more anecdotal assessment to review and improve the services available to students. We interpreted as an affirmation the growing evening occupancy and class visit counts, as well as spoken feedback from faculty about their classes' library research visits, but we now realize the need for more extensive and formal assessment. Consequently, over the past few years, the library has begun to assess formally its class research instruction with both faculty and student evaluations. In spring 2005, the librarians expanded their assessment focus by surveying regular library users and nonusers about service quality (see chapter 9). The SERVQUAL adapted instrument enabled the staff to assess library services more comprehensively and to address the unique needs of students. The goals were twofold: (1) to confirm that the way the library interprets UDI is optimal for students; and (2) to pinpoint areas in which the library can improve its services. If Landmark College students view their library's interpretation of universal design for instruction principles as ideal library service, perhaps their peers—with and without learning differences—would benefit from this approach in other academic libraries as well.

UNIVERSITY OF AUCKLAND LIBRARY

The University of Auckland provides support for students with a disability through its Disability Services team, whose "goal is to enable and encourage students with disabilities to access university study and to reach their academic potential," and any individual concern or request is accommodated if possible.

The university's Disability Services comprises seven staff (some part-time), including two coordinators who assist students. They administer five rooms in the General Library that have been set aside for students with a disability. Two of these rooms are simply individual study carrels, whereas the others contain computers with voice-activated software (other software can be installed if required). One room also contains a CCTV and magnifier. These rooms must be booked and this is organized through Disability Services. In addition, there is a low-height photocopier in the nearby Kate Edger Information Commons, which is part of the library.

The coordinators provide assistance with searching for and retrieving books from the shelves; fetching, carrying, and lifting books; and photocopying material. Additional assistance is provided for visually impaired students. Disability Services administer designated resting rooms around the university, one of which is in the General Library.

A survey of students, which is conducted every two years under the auspices of Disabilities Services, is posted to all those who identify with having a disability or who use Disability Services. Over 80 percent of respondents reported that they were "satisfied" or "very satisfied" with the Library Support Service.

Other than the Disability Services team, the inquiry services librarian is the point of contact when the need arises. Students contact Disability Services in the first instance, and they then contact the library. The library, in turn, also refers students to Disability Services where appropriate.

Some of the services the library provides specifically for this student group include:

- Access—there is an elevator for those with a disability;
- Resource Rooms—these are available for private study;
- Proxy borrowing—this enables students with a physical disability to authorize another registered library member to borrow on their behalf;
- Special assistance—reading call numbers, retrieving books from the shelves, assisting with searching the library's catalog, giving verbal or written directions to aid locating items in the library, phoning other libraries to check if a book is available, issuing and renewing items, accepting phone inquiries as to the availability of books on the shelf, and assisting with completing online forms; and
- Library skills—the Information Skills group within the library provides individual or group tuition on using the library's online public access catalog, the databases, and the Internet. In addition they also give specialized library tours on request.

Although the staff currently do not receive training in dealing with people with disabilities, they are responsive to individual needs as they arise.

UNIVERSITY OF CANTERBURY LIBRARY

The University of Canterbury Library works closely with the institution's Disability Support Service to improve and extend library services that are offered to users with disabilities. While the Disability Support Service is a unit with a small number of staff, personal relationships between them and library staff are fairly close and developing continuously. Until the support service was established, library staff would have provided more individualized services for users with disabilities, on a case-by-case basis. The Disability Support Service has assumed the primary role of user interface and advocate. The library provides space for specialized equipment that Disability Support Service provides for users, such as large screen computers and dedicated printers.

Areas in which library staff contribute include aspects of physical access to some very difficult buildings and access to materials within the buildings. Library buildings often have difficult external and internal access, and it is the front-line staff who deal on a daily basis with the difficulties this poses to users with disabilities. While the use of space within buildings conforms to the legislative requirements, this still means that users with disabilities are often severely restricted in the materials they can access.

Examples of initiatives that the library has undertaken include relocating seating and widening a doorway to a specific study facility, in order to allow access for oversized wheelchairs. The library also provides study furniture of a different height, which allows wheelchair users to fit comfortably. The specific problems facing wheelchair users have been considered when upgrading or designing new service desks, as well as considerable liaison over location and design of after-hours returns boxes. Prior to advances in computer technology, the library provided access to a Kurzweil talking machine.

Nowadays the library assists by providing "proxy" membership for able-bodied staff, who can borrow on behalf of the user with a disability. Staff members are also aware that flexible borrowing is extended to allow copying materials that may take longer than an existing loan period may allow. Off-campus services that have recently been implemented to allow requested material to be retrieved, copied, scanned, and posted or electronically delivered have been extended to registered users of the Disabilities Support Services.

Some users have disabilities that are not immediately obvious, and this can pose some unintended difficulties for library staff. It is appreciated that individuals may not want to be labeled. However, from the point of view of providing quality service, or extensions of services that may be able to be offered, it is important that library staff can unobtrusively identify all users with disabilities. Blind users will readily bring a seeing-eye dog into the library. This has also been extended to users who have social phobias and are accompanied by a "comfort" animal.[42] It is becoming more common for library staff to undertake extensive work with socially dysfunctional people.

For Web access, the library is conforming to standards in order to create maximum accessibility. This entails using colors that are distinguishable by people with the common forms of color blindness, and conforming to "Bobby Priority 1" standards (see note 26, chapter 7).

As a major service provider on the university campus, the library is acutely aware of needing to be able to provide services tailored to the needs of users with disabilities. Although the Disability Support Service now provides much of this, the library still works closely with that office to improve services. At this time, there have not been any specific surveys or focus group interviews that target the needs and expectations of this group.

MASSEY UNIVERSITY LIBRARY

Massey is a multicampus, multicity university of some 23,000 EFT (equivalent full-time) students. This number equates to a headcount of 41,000 students; 48 percent of the students are extramural. Massey has the largest number of Maori students, by headcount (3,900) of any New Zealand university. There are two libraries in Palmerston North (Turitea and Hokowhitu), and libraries at the Albany (Auckland) and Wellington campuses. There is also a small education library at the Ruawharo site in Napier.

Massey University has followed the model of central disability services, which is an advocate for the students with the various units on each campus. The university administration section of each campus has a disability coordinator, and the library works with the coordinator in terms of services provided. Each campus also has a disability committee (usually chaired by an academic, but with the coordinator as a member), and library representatives sit on these.

The coordinator, who will talk to library staff about the particular needs of the student, identifies students who need support at the time of enrollment. Students who do not self-identify may be missed, however. Each student is issued a swipe card for access to the library via an alternative (usually staff) entrance, where the main entrance is difficult (Turitea is up a ramp to a second floor, through a very narrow entrance; Hokowhitu has steps with an unwieldy outside elevator). The Turitea, Albany, and Wellington libraries all provide spaces for these students with a range of equipment, including computers with software for the aurally and visually impaired, printers, and a large monitor for accessing the library catalog. The disability coordinator provides and maintains the equipment. At Turitea and Wellington the spaces are separate rooms, and specialist toilet facilities are nearby. Library staff will accompany students to the shelves for assistance or will retrieve items from the shelves for them. They also offer a personal tour of the library when the student first arrives, both for familiarization and so that the student can meet the staff member (as a useful contact if issues arise in the future). Although usage of the spaces and rooms is low, it is regarded as an essential library service.

There are a number of problems with the current buildings, which will not be remedied until we get new or refurbished buildings as part of the university's capital building plan. Because space is at a premium some stacks are too narrow for wheelchair access. The Wellington library, a former polytechnic, is especially bad, with floors and half floors added over a long period of time. Some areas in this library are not accessible even by elevator. Retrieval on behalf of the student is the solution in such a case, but this is not satisfactory long term. The Wellington library is at the top of the list of library rebuilding. We do make minor changes where we can. Recently, a photocopier with a lower height (and with the bottom tray removed) was installed at the Albany Library for students in wheelchairs, and the new lending desk at Turitea will have a lower counter at one end for similar reasons.

We have advised the disability coordinator that we will consult with him and the students, as a specific focus group, as the library building program develops. Students with a disability would like larger spaces, with comfortable casual seating and basic kitchen facilities, in addition to the equipment and study space. We will consider this. We had wondered about the concept of the "room" and whether "mainstreaming" these facilities would be preferable, but we have been advised that this is not so. For those students with a psychological disability, in particular, the rooms provide some privacy and quiet.

We suspect (but have no data) that the percentage of students with a disability studying extramurally may be higher than for internal students. This is an area where we need to be more proactive. We do provide some special services (e.g., photocopying material in a larger font), but this is very much at the request of the students. The extramural library handbook does not mention services for students with a disability and we will revise the next edition so there is a contact point. The Web site also needs to be amended. On the other hand, given the personal nature of the distance library service, staff do become aware of some students with special needs, for example those with an obsessive or compulsive disorder. This is generally handled with some discretion and compassion.

Students with a disability who are enrolled for internal papers (courses) but have difficulty with regular attendance at a campus are provided with the distance service at the discretion of library staff, even though they may not strictly fit the criteria (of at least 50 percent of their enrolled papers being designated extramural). This service provides books and photocopied articles delivered by courier to their home address and free of charge.

The library has had a formal (internal) policy for some years. Although it was amended in November, 2003, the policy still needs further change. At any rate, the chapter appendix reprints part of the policy.

CONCLUSION

As the opening and closing quotations for this chapter illustrate, directors and libraries differ in the extent to which they proactively serve students with disabilities. Access and the services provided might be within legal requirements for students with physical disabilities (i.e., for physical accommodation); however, they might fall short of meeting student programmatic needs and expectations. In some cases, an institution's faculty are far ahead of the library and the disability office in working with students to provide the types of accommodations they need to meet program and institutional outcomes. On the other hand, some libraries are more service oriented in meeting the needs of a broader group of students. However, as Sarah Hamrick of Gallaudet University Library notes, "most librarians who are responsible for services to students with disabilities have little or no formal training in that area." Clearly, professional associations and schools of library and information studies ought to play a significant role in reversing this situation, especially since the legal framework extends to meeting programmatic needs and requirements. They can help make students and program graduates aware of appropriate guidelines, especially those for making library Web sites more accommodating and easily navigable.[43]

Some questions and issues arise from the directors' reports. First, "When does the library assume responsibility for dealing with the customer rather than letting the university's disability service take the lead?" Clearly, there is a point at which most libraries will assume responsibility, but it varies from library to library. For some matters the expertise of the disability services will be essential, but for relatively trivial service tasks (e.g., fetching books from a high shelf for a student in wheelchair), why is it necessary for the student at some institutions to contact disability services, which will then make arrangements for someone to help the student in the library? This *double-handling* is to no one's advantage. Inadequate funding can complicate almost any task in a library, but the service-oriented library deals with immediate service issues rather than letting a bureaucracy take over.

Second, "Is library skills training done by library staff, or is it 'outsourced' to the disability service?" It would seem strange for any library to see this fundamental task handled by anyone except library staff. Third, "Do library staff have all the information they need to assist customers with disabilities?" Privacy laws can limit the flow of personal information about students, so the library may have to find ways to assist customers without using data from the disability service. Necessary information could be embedded in the students' library card. Even so, will the staff member be able to handle customers with disabilities as described by Jennifer Lann of Landmark College?

And, finally, "How does the senior library management collect information about the service quality expectations of customers with disabilities?" For example, do they ask for feedback from front-line staff dealing with these customers, and do they conduct surveys or focus groups? How often do they communicate directly with customers?

> We only do what is legally required of us.
>
> *—anonymous director*

APPENDIX: LIBRARY POLICIES: SERVICES
FOR USERS WITH DISABILITIES

This appendix reprints a portion of the statements from the libraries at Gallaudet University and Massey University for services provided to individuals with disabilities. The complete text for Gallaudet University Library is available on the library's homepage (http://library.gallaudet.edu/li/policies/disability-services.html). For Massey University, please contact the library director.

The Gallaudet University Library staff seeks to provide all patrons with equal access to library resources and services. The Gallaudet University Library staff is available to provide accommodations in services for people with disabilities. Provisions are available for the patrons to receive appropriate accommodations while maintaining their right to confidentiality.

GALLAUDET UNIVERSITY LIBRARY

Facility Accommodations

- Automatic entrance doors and elevator
- Public telephones are wheelchair accessible with amplification and TTYs

Services

- Orientation about Library services and resources
- Appointment for in depth reference assistance
- Book retrieval
- Help with renewals
- Photocopying

Adaptive Equipment and Materials

- Photocopy machines with enlargement capabilities
- Captioned videotapes and DVDs
- Closed captioned televisions
- Separate room for watching video materials with sound headphones
- Zoom text Xtra 7.1 screen magnifier on two PCs
- Large computer monitors
- CCTVs with magnifiers for reading print on paper
- Selection of large print materials

Retrieving Materials

Staff will retrieve books and other materials as time and level of business permit. Particularly on evenings and weekends, retrievals may be limited to five items. Patrons who need large amounts of materials should leave requests at the Library Service Desk. Here is the Gallaudet University Library Disability Services Retrieval Request Form (see http://library.gallaudet.edu/li/policies/disability-retrieval.html).

Photocopying

All Library users must pay for their own copies with a copy card. Staff will assist with photocopying or make a limited number of copies as time allows. Items that cannot be copied immediately may be left for pickup within 24–48 hours. Users with large copying jobs should leave written requests at the Library Service Desk. Here is the Gallaudet University Library Disability

Services Photocopying Request Form (http://library.gallaudet.edu/li/policies/disability-photocopying.html). Gallaudet University abides by all laws pertaining to U.S. copyright law; staff may not make photocopies that violate the U.S. copyright law (see Gallaudet University Copyright Policies and Information; http://library.gallaudet.edu/li/policies/copyright.html).

Reference Services

Users who need in-depth, uninterrupted help doing research should make an appointment with the Library liaison for persons with disabilities. The librarian can recommend search strategies and information sources. Users who need help reading citations, abstracts, and other materials must provide their own readers.

To Arrange For Accommodations

Students

Students should register with the Office for Students with Disabilities (OSWD; http://depts.gallaudet.edu/OSWD/index.htm) and obtain an OSWD identification card. Students should then make an appointment with the Library liaison, who will determine the appropriate accommodations for library services needed.

Waiver

The Library follows Gallaudet University confidentiality rules (see OSWD, Confidentiality in Higher Education; http://depts.gallaudet.edu/OSWD/confidentiality.htm). Under these policies, only the Library liaison for people with disabilities has information about a student's needs. However, a student may sign a waiver that permits the liaison to release the student's name and information about accommodation needs to other Library staff members. This allows more staff members to help the student and provide service more quickly and conveniently. Here is the Gallaudet University Library Disability Services Permission to Release Information Form (waiver; http://library.gallaudet.edu/li/policies/disability-waiver.html).

Faculty and Staff

See contact information below.

Visitors

See contact information below.

Library Contact

[Name and contact information provided]

For General Library Information

[contact information provided]

Following are a series of icons covering, for instance, "Library Information," "Library Resources," "Deaf-related Resources," and "Internet Resources."

MASSEY UNIVERSITY LIBRARY

The obligation for the Library to accommodate the needs of students with disability is based on university policy as well as legal responsibilities. The Human Rights Act of 1993 protects against direct and indirect forms of discrimination, and also states that individuals should receive appropriate support to enable them to achieve their potential. Massey University subscribes to the guidelines in *Tertiary Students with Disability: A Resource Guide for Staff*, which outlines the responsibility of the University to create an environment dedicated to the equality of educational opportunity for all.

Library support for students with disability includes a Campus of Massey (Palmerston North–Turitea):

Access

Ground floor (Level 1) entry is from the concourse through automatic doors, or from the back of the Library entering from the car park area (ramped access within the loading bay). Both entrances are operated by a swipe card which is available from the Disability Office (ext. 4320). A ramp and stairs provide entrance to Level 2. Within the Library, lifts are available in the south and car park wings.

Toilets

Accessible toilets for students with disability are provided on the ground floor in the north (Registry end) and car park wings of the building.

Equipment

The Library has a resource room (Room no. 2.29) which contains specialized equipment and ergonomic furniture for the use of students with disability. The key is held at the Information Desk and is available during all opening hours. The Library has three desks specifically reserved for the use of people with disability (Level 1 at the north end of the building).

Assistance with access, collecting books, retrieving and carrying items

Library staff from the Lending Desk are able to provide this assistance. Arrangements made in advance are appreciated. At busy times (e.g., over the lunch period) students may be asked to wait a short period until a staff member is free.

Assistance with personal requirements

Library staff are not expected to help in this area.

Photocopying

Staff in the photocopying room can provide assistance for students who have difficulty using the self-service copiers. Students are asked to telephone first. . . .

NOTES

1. *Postsecondary Students with Disabilities. Recent Data from the 2000 National Postsecondary Student Aid Survey* (Washington, D.C.: The George Washington University, HEATH Resource Center, n.d.). Available at http://www.heath.gwu.edu/PDFs/Recent%20Data.pdf (accessed November 24, 2004).
2. Cathy Henderson, *College Freshmen with Disabilities: A Biennial Statistical Profile* (Washington, D.C.: The George Washington University HEATH Resource Center, 2001). Available at http://www.heath.gwu.edu/PDFs/collegefreshmen.pdf (accessed November 22, 2004).
3. Lisa L. Weyandt, Wendy Iwaszuk, Katie Fulton, Micha Ollerton, Noelle Beatty, Hillary Fouts, Stephen Schepman, and Corey Greenlaw, "The Internal Restlessness Scale: Performance of College Students with and without ADHD," *Journal of Learning Disabilities* 36 (2003): 382.
4. The term *learning differences* serves as both shorthand for learning disabilities and/or ADHD, as well as an acknowledgement of the preference of some students and learning disabilities theorists (e.g., Mel Levine) to frame learning disabilities more positively.
5. North Carolina State University, Center for Universal Design, "What Is Universal Design?" (Raleigh, NC: North Carolina State University, Center for Universal Design, 1997). Available at http://www.design.ncsu.edu/cud/univ_design/ud.htm (accessed November 22, 2004).
6. Edward D. Hirsch, Jr., *Cultural Literacy: What Every American Needs to Know* (Boston: Houghton Mifflin, 1987).
7. James E. Zull, "The Art of Changing the Brain," *Educational Leadership* 62 (2004): 68. See also Preston D. Feden and Robert M. Vogel, *Methods of Teaching: Applying Cognitive Science to Promote Student Learning* (Boston: McGraw Hill, 2003).
8. Christina Herbert, "Making College Classrooms Accessible to Students with and without Learning Disabilities," in *Promoting Academic Success for Students*

with Learning Disabilities: The Landmark College Guide to Practical Instruction, edited by Stuart Strothman (Putney, VT: Landmark College, 2001), 11.

9. Ibid., 15.

10. Sally S. Scott, Joan M. McGuire, Mary D. Sarver, and Stan F. Shaw, "Universal Design for Instruction: A New Paradigm for Adult Instruction in Postsecondary Education," *Remedial and Special Education* 24 (2003): 377.

11. Ibid., 375.

12. Ibid.

13. William G. Perry, Jr., "Cognitive and Ethical Growth: The Making of Meaning," in *The Modern American College,* edited by Arthur Chickering (San Francisco: Jossey-Bass, 1981), 79–80. See also Solvegi S. Shmulsky, "Developing Critical Thinking in College," in *Promoting Academic Success for Students with Learning* Disabilities, 109.

14. Perry, Jr., "Cognitive and Ethical Growth," 79.

15. Kenneth Gobbo, "College Student Development Programs and Students with Learning Disabilities," in *Understanding Learning Disabilities at the Postsecondary Level: A Landmark College Guide,* edited by Lynne C. Shea and Stuart W. Strothman (Putney, VT: Landmark College, 2003), 114.

16. Ibid., 115.

17. Shmulsky, "Developing Critical Thinking in College," 110–111.

18. Lev S. Vygotsky, *Mind in Society: The Development of Higher Psychological Processes* (Cambridge, MA: Harvard University Press, 1978), 86.

19. S. G. Paris, B. A. Wasik, and J. C. Turner, "The Development of Strategic Readers," in *Handbook of Reading Research,* Volume II, edited by R. Barr, M. L. Kamil, P. B. Mosenthal, and P. D. Pearson (New York: Longman, 1991), 611.

20. Dorothy M. Vaca, "Confronting the Puzzle of Nonverbal Learning Disabilities," *Educational Leadership* 59, no. 3 (2001): 30.

21. U.S. Department of Health and Human Services, National Institute of Mental Health, *Teenage Brain: A Work in Progress* (Bethesda, MD: National Institute of Mental Health, 2001). Available at http://www.nimh.nih.gov/publicat/teenbrain.cfm (accessed December 3, 2004).

22. Russell Barkley, *ADHD and the Nature of Self-control* (New York: Guilford Press, 1997), 57.

23. Carol C. Kuhlthau, "Kuhlthau's Model of the Stages of the Information Process" (Arcata, CA: Humboldt State University Library, 1999). Available at http://library.humboldt.edu/~ccm/fingertips/kuhlthau.html (accessed September 28, 2004); and adapted from: Carol C. Kuhlthau, *Seeking Meaning: A Process Approach to Library and Information Services* (Norwood, NJ: Ablex Publishing Corp., 1993), 45–51.

24. Gloria J. Leckie, "Desperately Seeking Citations: Uncovering Faculty Assumptions about the Undergraduate Research Process," *The Journal of Academic Librarianship,* 22 (May 1996): 201–208.

25. Ibid., 202.

26. Ibid., 203.

27. Ibid., 202.

28. Beth L. Mark and Trudi E Jacobson, "Teaching Anxious Students Skills for the Electronic Library," *College Teaching* 43 (1995): 28–31.

29. Jane Keefer, "The Hungry Rats Syndrome: Library Anxiety, Information Literacy, and the Academic Reference Process," *RQ* 32 (1993): 336–337.

30. Leckie, "Desperately Seeking Citations," 204.

31. Rebecca S. Graves, "Re: Sequencing Info. Lit. in College?," Information Literacy Instruction Listserv (ILI-L) listserv (August 23, 2004). Available at http://lp-web.ala.org:8000/ (accessed November 30, 2004).

32. Scott, McGuire, Sarver, and Shaw, "Universal Design for Instruction," 375.

33. Herbert, "Making College Classrooms Accessible to Students with and without Learning Disabilities," 18.

34. Ibid., 375.

35. Leckie, "Desperately Seeking Citations," 203.

36. Scott, McGuire, Sarver, and Shaw, "Universal Design for Instruction," 375.

37. Michael A. McNulty, "Dyslexia and the Life Course," *Journal of Learning Disabilities* 36 (2003): 376.

38. Scott, McGuire, Sarver, and Shaw, "Universal Design for Instruction," 375.

39. Ibid.

40. Ibid.

41. Kanta Jiwnani, "Designing for Users with Cognitive Disabilities" (College Park, MD: University of Maryland, April 2001). Available at the University of Maryland Universal Usability in Practice Web site, http://www.otal.umd.edu/uupractice/cognition/ (accessed December 3, 2004).

42. The library does not have any policy on dogs within any of the libraries. The general practice is to exclude all dogs, unless they are obviously a guide dog or "comfort animal." In either case, the animal has to be clearly identifiable as such, rather than just accompanying their owner. We have had no problems with seeing-eye dogs; they are usually very clearly identified. Through the University Disability Support Services, the person with the comfort dog was informed that his or her dog would need to be clearly identified.

43. W3C® [World Wide Web Consortium], "List of Checkpoints for Web Content Accessibility Guidelines" (Cambridge, MA: World Wide Web Consortium, 2004). Available at http://www.w3.org/TR/WAI-WEBCONTENT/checkpoint-list.html (accessed November 30, 2004).

7

LITERATURE REVIEW

Peter Hernon

> The communities our libraries serve are already diverse, and all indications
> point to more diversity rather than less in the years to come.[1]

The relevant literature on academic librarianship tends to address topical areas
such as adaptive technologies; Web accessibility; the provision of, and compliance with, laws (e.g., the Americans with Disabilities Act [ADA]); equity issues;
types of services provided to students with disabilities; the promotion of library
services to students with disabilities so that they can understand which ones
are available and how to gain access to them; and the need for library staff
to receive sensitivity training, for library and information studies (LIS) students
to be knowledgeable about relevant laws and technologies, and for libraries to
develop disability policies. Such policies identify contact individuals and cover
physical access (e.g., for those in wheelchairs), equipment, services, and staff
training in disability awareness and sensitivity, as well as the level of service
provided to those with disabilities (see chapters 2 and 6). The policies also
cover complaint (and, one would hope, compliment) procedures.

The literature, especially that portion appearing on the World Wide Web,
is international in scope,[2] and it highlights local services, accomplishments,
and upcoming plans. Through local announcements, annual reports, newsletters, and presentations, some academic libraries indicate a commitment to
improving the adaptive technologies they provide through the installation of
multimedia workstations, additional software purchases and updates (e.g.,
Dragon Naturally Speaking voice-activated software), and new equipment
(e.g., Braille printers and power adjustable tables). As part of a renovation

project, a particular library might be in the process of rewiring the facilities to provide state-of-the-art computing, telecommunications technology, and improvements in access as part of better compliance with the ADA. As well, some libraries reported that they have upgraded their online public access catalog (OPAC) to conform to requirements of Section 508 of the Rehabilitation Act as amended in 1998. They might use Cascading Style Sheets (CSS) and HTML code that adhere to disability guidelines.

The literature observes that it is the responsibility of higher education institutions to ensure that those students who have disabilities have equal opportunity in receiving a high-quality education. The physical environment of the campus, administrative services, library facilities and services, other support services, and the delivery of courses should be accessible to all students. It is important to remember that people who have disabilities number more than 500 million, two-thirds of whom reside in developed countries.

Some authors argue that the library profession needs to attract diverse populations to the workforce and to mentor them, but these discussions tend not to mention the disability population. The literature also discusses learning styles and how to match these styles to types of instruction; the provision of special services for groups with disabilities (e.g., the deaf and blind communities); Web design and layout; and what individual libraries are doing to meet to needs of students with disabilities.[3]

Only a small portion of the international literature includes research, some of which is now dated.[4] The purpose of this chapter is to discuss selected portions of that literature on academic librarianship and to set the stage for subsequent chapters. Linda Lucas Walling provides an excellent, but brief, overview of some relevant books and articles, especially those covering adaptive technologies and the need for the LIS student population and workforce to be knowledgeable about serving the entire student population.[5]

SOME GENERAL WRITINGS

Margaret McCasland and Michael Golden noted that the ADA "motivated libraries all over the United States to evaluate their accommodations and services to patrons with disabilities."[6] They then show how Texas Tech University Libraries has responded to meet the needs of those patrons. Mary Beth Applin discussed the ADA and ways in which librarians might improve the quality and consistency of service they provide, such as through an annual staff training program devoted to the library's disability services, policies, and procedures. She also maintained,

Many libraries do not worry about serving a person with a disability until the need arises. By then, people are scurrying for information, trying to find someone who knows what the library's policy is, what services the library has available and/or what the library should do if it cannot accommodate a need.[7]

The purpose of her article is to discourage continuation of such practices.

In another paper, Applin identified barriers to library service, such as "the specialized equipment necessary for providing adequate services is costly and therefore deemed unaffordable." She notes,

Libraries are not anxious to purchase expensive items which may only be used for a short time by one or two persons. Another obstacle is that librarians are typically inexperienced or uneducated when it comes to working with people with disabilities. Most libraries offer little or no training to their staff concerning the special needs of the disabled population.[8]

Consequently, she recommended an annual staff-training program. She also discussed other ways to cope with these obstacles, including the creation of a library disability liaison and a campus-wide Web access policy.

Vincent P. Tinerella and Marcia A. Dick highlight that, since the early 1990s, Northern Illinois University library has hired students with disabilities "as one method of enhancing the undergraduate experience of the university's special-needs students." The purpose is to create and implement "a flexible, comprehensive program designed to help students with limitations, tailoring the assistance provided to individual students based on each student's particular special need."[9]

Jennifer Church, Sharon Drouin, and Katherine Rankin provide an excellent bibliography of electronic resources "on disabilities in general, assistive technology, associations and organizations, government resources, and sites centered on specific disabilities, as well as Web page accessibility."[10] Their list complements the appendix in chapter 2.

Library Technology Reports introduces the topic of "information access for people with disabilities" to the general reader—a library manager unfamiliar with what they might do. The paper shows the types of services that some libraries provide, informs readers about the types of plans their libraries might create, and highlights tips and steps they might take to improve information access, explain different technologies and their applications, and so on.[11]

OVERVIEW

Axel Schmetzke of the library at the University of Wisconsin–Stevens Point maintains a most useful Web site, the "Web Accessibility Survey Homepage," which

aspires to be a clearinghouse for studies involving the collection of accessibility data pertaining to web sites and online resources in education, particularly in higher education.... The audience ... [includes] producers of online resources, including web designers, college and university instructors, administrators, and policy makers; distance educators; librarians; and disability professionals.[12]

Linda Lou Wiler and Eleanor Lomax conducted "an exploratory study of academic libraries in the Southeastern United States and their compliance to the Americans with Disabilities Act." Their findings raise "questions about the perception in [responding] libraries of disabilities, discrimination, compliance and the libraries' understanding of the spirit of the law." They believe that "libraries with their intellectual resources and dedication to service should be in the forefront of assisting those individuals with disabilities. At present this aim is not always being met." In conclusion, they ask, "Are libraries up to the challenge?"[13]

Although his findings are dated, Scott A. Carpenter showed the extent of accommodation to people with disabilities in the academic libraries of one state.[14] Because the picture undoubtedly differs today, that snapshot might be replicated and extended regionally, nationally, and internationally. In another dated publication, the Association of Research Libraries (ARL) summarizes the services offered to users with disabilities in thirteen libraries. As noted in the introduction,

When the Americans with Disabilities Act [P.L. 101–336] became federal law in 1990, there was a flurry of publications on what the law meant for public spaces, including libraries. This issue [of *Transforming Libraries*] examines to what extent college and university libraries currently provide services to users with disabilities, how new and assistive technologies are being used in libraries, and how libraries are adapting their services to reflect and meet the needs of this community.[15]

Another publication, *Report of the Task Force on Access to Information for Print Disabled Canadians,* discusses resource-sharing services for persons with print disabilities.[16]

Rarely has research examined the value placed upon service to students with disabilities when compared to other library products and services. In the mid-1990s Rowena Cullen and Philip Calvert used the multiple constituencies model of organizational effectiveness to assess the perception of six different stakeholder groups about an *effective* university library.[17] They produced a list of 95 indicators, mainly taken from the existing literature or actual performance measures used in academic libraries, and then used the indicators in two surveys.

With the single instruction that respondents rate each indicator on a scale of 1 to 5, their survey was first sent to a population in all seven universities in New Zealand at that time. Six stakeholder groups were selected, the first being the resource allocators—the senior managers of the university who held the purse strings. The library staff was divided into senior library managers and others. Academic staff, graduate students, and undergraduate students were the only three groups surveyed. From the resulting data, a mean for each indicator was calculated according to responses from each stakeholder group. The ninety-five indicators were then sorted by the mean for each stakeholder group. One indicator referred to services to students with disabilities, and it is instructive to see where it was ranked by each of the six constituency groups. The resource allocators ranked the indicator "provision made for disabled users" seventeenth out of ninety-five indicators. The other (i.e., junior) library staff ranked it sixteenth. The graduate students ranked it eighteenth, and the undergraduates ranked it twelfth. What is rather surprising is that neither the senior library managers nor the academic staff ranked this indicator anywhere in their top twenty indicators. For the senior library managers, indicators such as "availability of library catalogs throughout the library" had greater significance as a measure of an effective library (they ranked it twentieth), and for academic staff, the twentieth-ranked indicator was "provision of multiple copies of items in high use." When each of the stakeholder groups was compared with the others, it was found that senior library staff and undergraduates had the lowest correlation of any pairing. Cullen and Calvert noted that senior library managers were not well in tune with expectations of several of the other stakeholder groups and noted that in the present competitive environment for students and resources, some expectations should be examined more closely. Knowledge of the expectations of each group provides better information on which to justify any shift of resources from one service area to another.[18]

In the second stage of their research, Cullen and Calvert gave the same list of ninety-five indicators to all staff working more than ten hours per week in a university library in New Zealand. This time the respondents were asked to rate their university library on its performance on each indicator. "Provision made for disabled students" was rated only fifty-fourth of the ninety-five indicators, demonstrating that library staff did not consider they were performing well on this aspect of service.[19]

ADAPTIVE TECHNOLOGIES

A number of books and articles discuss adaptive technologies that would enable students with disabilities to take full advantage of library services, whether the students are in the physical library or at remote locations.[20] In an article appearing in *The Chronicle of Higher Education*, Scott Carlson criticized many colleges for not having the technologies that could help students with disabilities complete distance education programs delivered over the Internet. As the reporter noted, students may experience problems in "accessing online course materials and keeping up with virtual class discussions." Moreover, "advocates for disabled students who have studied college Web sites say the accessibility of colleges' online resources is decreasing as college and course sites feature more video clips, animated menus, and pages that are most easily reached with a mouse."[21] Such incidents suggest that students with disabilities will question (and are doing so) the extent to which institutions of higher education provide adequate accommodations for individual courses. Apparently, those questions have resulted in charges being filed within institutions and before the Office for Civil Rights (see chapter 2).

ACCESSIBLE WEB PAGE DESIGN

The Americans with Disabilities Act and the Rehabilitation Act of 1998 mandate that organizations (e.g., libraries) extend accessibility to the digital environment. Eleanor Loiacono and Scott McCoy place Web site accessibility within an international context and observe that "Web designers design for the 'typical' user." They also identify validation software to measure the extent to which Web sites are accessible and show that a large number of Web sites are not fully accessible to people with disabilities.[22]

Paul Ryan Bohman randomly selected twenty universities in the United States and investigated their Web accessibility policies. He found that

the policies were inadequate on several levels, the most important of which being the fact that the majority of Web pages created at those universities had accessibility errors. In fact, 80% of the university home pages had at least one accessibility error when evaluated by WAVE 3.0, an online Web accessibility evaluation tool. Similarly, 77% of the sites had accessibility errors on pages other than the home page, based on a random sample of 6 pages per site. In some cases, the errors were minor.... In other cases, the pages contained more serious errors....[23]

His conclusion noted,

The Web sites of these universities often fail to meet minimum Web accessibility standards, and therefore present difficulties to students with disabilities. Part of the problem lies with the policies themselves. Many of them fail to delineate a specific technical standard, fail to indicate whether compliance with the policy is required, fail to indicate a timeline or deadline for compliance, fail to define a system for evaluating or monitoring compliance, and fail to enumerate any consequences for failure to comply. With all of these shortcomings, it should be no surprise that the policies are not as successful as they might otherwise be. These universities should seriously consider rewriting their policies to remedy these inadequacies.[24]

Tim Spindler notes, "numerous articles and books both within and outside of library literature ... discuss accessible Web page design."[25] He then identifies these writings and proceeds to study 190 library Web sites for their Bobby compliance. Bobby™ is a free service that enables the public "to test web pages and help expose and repair barriers to accessibility and encourage compliance with existing accessibility guidelines, such as Section 508 and the W3C's (World Wide Web Consortium) WCAG (Web Content Accessibility Guidelines)." Using this Web site, developers can "test web pages and generate summary reports highlighting critical accessibility issues before posting content to live servers."[26]

Spindler found that "a significant number of mid-sized colleges have problems with accessibility [to content] on their library Web sites." However, almost half of these sites "had five or fewer instances of accessibility error. In practicality, a site with five or fewer errors is quite simple to fix. It might be a matter of adding a one-word description in the alternate text of each of the given images."[27]

In an earlier study, Erica B. Lilly and Connie Van Fleet used the Bobby Web site to test the homepages of 100 academic libraries for their accessibility; these libraries represented Yahoo!'s 1998 list of "America's most wired colleges." They found that fewer than half of the libraries offered equitable access. Among the recommendations offered were "if possible, avoid using tables to format text documents in columns" and "client-side image maps contain a link not presented elsewhere on the page."[28]

Mark Yannie surveyed academic and public libraries in Minnesota about the accessibility of their Web sites. He found public academic libraries the most accessible and private ones the least successful. The public ones had better trained staff to assist students with disabilities and more equipment, whereas the private ones had no resources for such students.[29]

In a related study, Suzanne Byerley applied usability testing, "a methodology to determine how effectively a product can be used by a specific population to achieve certain goals with efficiency and satisfaction," to the library's homepage at the University of Colorado at Colorado Springs. The staff used the results to make changes on the homepage and thereby improve accessibility to its content.[30]

Michael Providenti, who surveyed the accessibility of academic library Web sites in one state, concluded, "Based on low levels of compliance with the basic principles of Web accessibility and the potential of legal threats, institutions need to take accessibility issues more seriously. While the impetus to do so should fall under the rubric of professional ethics rather than avoiding a legal threat, either reason will suffice."[31]

Jenny Craven, who also examined the extent to which Web sites adhered to the Bobby standards, stated, "raising awareness of creating accessible Web-pages is clearly of the utmost importance."[32] Based on the studies reported in this section, libraries need to pay greater attention to access issues on their Web sites—taking into account the different needs and capabilities of the community served.

Three other studies merit mention; they discuss the accessibility of types of Web-based products: e-journals, databases, and tables for library users with disabilities. Bryna Coonin of East Carolina University library, who examined "11 major electronic research journal services for basic accessibility," found that, with some exceptions, those service providers had little awareness of accessibility issues. The article also identifies ways for them to improve accessibility.[33] Suzanne L. Byerley and Mary Beth Chambers of the University of Colorado at Colorado Springs library encouraged the developers of commercial databases to conduct usability studies and to ensure that their products are accessible for visually impaired users.[34] However, they note that "accessibility does not necessarily equate with usability;" both are important.[35]

Dagmar Amtmann of the University of Washington Center for Technology and Disability Studies, Kurt Johnson of that university's Department of Rehabilitation Medicine, and Debbie Cook of the Washington Assistive

Technology Alliance remind readers that "reading and understanding information presented in tabular format have posed specific challenges for blind individuals who use screen readers to access computers.... [They identify] the types of problems blind individuals using screen readers experienced.[36] They also offer guidelines for improving the usability of Web-displayed tables.

GENERAL USER / USE STUDIES

In 1996, Charlene H. Loope conducted a small-scale study (sixteen students with disabilities) at the University of South Carolina. She discussed compliance with the ADA and noted "a need for easily accessible adaptive computer equipment, ... for readily available special library services, and better communication between the campus Office of Disability Services and the academic library staff."[37]

Clare Harris and Charles Oppenheim surveyed 230 librarians in education colleges in England, Scotland, and Wales about their awareness of, and adherence to, the Special Educational Needs and Disabilities Act (SENDA) of 2001. They found that, although there was great variation among the libraries regarding their current level of compliance, staff were exploring methods of best practices and trying to make library services accessible to visually disabled students.[38]

In a related study, Allison Jones and Lucy A. Tedd studied SENDA and the needs of the visually disabled community. They identified the disability statements of the institutions comprising the case studies and noted the challenges that distance education and e-learning present to this community. They concluded that the institutions are starting to meet the requirements specified in SENDA.[39]

Other authors focus more directly on distance education and access to library resources. They discuss how both instructors and librarians can address the needs of students with disabilities who engage in distance learning as well as reduce access barriers.[40]

In a report released in 2001, staff of the University of Arkansas Libraries cautioned that libraries, in effect, should listen to their customers and when they do so, it is important to inform them "how their suggestions are to be incorporated or not into library services and programs." Still, when librarians listen to their customers, they should realize that "survey fatigue is real; while it is important to develop ongoing mechanisms for collecting user opinions,... [they] should be very cautious about multiple surveys in a single year."[41] For clarification, we would add that they should be careful about how many different surveys are conducted each year and be aware that many surveys comprise self-reports—revealing what users want known. In *The Science of Shopping,* Paco Underhill points out that consumers may erroneously characterize their shopping behavior; in other words, observation reveals that self-reporting may not correspond to actual purchasing behavior.[42]

The Memorial Hall Library, in Andover, Massachusetts, developed a survey for people with disabilities who are library users and nonusers.[43] That general instrument could easily be revised to investigate the information needs and information-gathering behavior of faculty, students, and staff.

In *Wired for Well-being: Citizens' Response to E-government*,[44] Rowena Cullen and Peter Hernon conducted a series of focus group interviews in the Auckland, Hamilton, Taranaki, and Wellington areas of New Zealand. Although the study examined the citizen's perspective on e-government, it produced some findings relevant to this chapter, especially for improving library Web site architecture. One of the groups interviewed comprised disabled citizens, recruited from two local branches of the Disabled Persons Association. Those interviewed tended to be activists, who need information on assorted topics but who also think it is important to be informed citizens.

People with disabilities prefer to use standard sites that have been designed with disabled-enabled access in mind. Some complained about sites that were "too bland" and alternative sites for disabled users that are very plain. "Those with disabilities want to 'go in the front door' with everyone else. Why should we have to go through the back door?" They favor universal access—just as wheelchair users should be able to use the common entryway to a building, disabled Web users want to rely on the general Web page (with alternative text for graphics, and complying with W3C disability access guidelines (see http://www.w3.org/WAI/), not a separate plain site. As one interviewee explained, "'accessible' does not have to mean 'boring'. For disabled users, accessing information on Web sites still needs to be a pleasurable and useful experience."

Those with disabilities specifically associated six barriers with limited Web use—or with effective navigation of the Web. First, they identified inadequate compliance with the disability guidelines, especially the use of alternative text. A site might contain a lot of graphics, which would be difficult for sight-impaired people to navigate. Graphics and use of color contrast on the site might also present problems for people who are color-blind; careful attention to color contrasts and shading is necessary.

Second, there might be too many colors around words. People may be unable to see all of the colors on a page. It may be hard for them to discriminate among colors. (This is a separate issue from color blindness.) Third, some Web sites seemed to focus more on appearance than on functionality—there is a need to improve communication. Fourth, there might be insufficient explanation (in simple language) on the site about how to navigate it and find the information sought. The fifth point relates to information organization. It may be difficult to follow all of the information presented on a Web page and to sort out the relevant from the not so relevant (that part that meets their information need). And, sixth, the temptation might be to establish a mirror site for people with disabilities to use. Some of those interviewed rejected such a consideration.

People with disabilities find the Internet time-consuming to search, and, depending on their disability, it may be difficult for them to sit or concentrate for long periods of time. They find it hard to navigate some sites. They believed that "sites are competitive—each trying to look better than the others." Web sites might assume a sophisticated look whereas those with disabilities may need something simpler. They also noted that downloading material from the Web could pose problems. People with a visual disability may be unable to access and use pdf (portable document format) files. Furthermore, downloading and printing are time-consuming, and they may tie up the one telephone line in the home for a long time. Also, some files may be too large to e-mail from their computer.

One person with a disability wanted those constructing and maintaining Web sites to remember that use of homepages might be equated to "climbing Mt. Everest; the more difficult it is the more likely I'd try later" or find a different way to gather the information. "Disability," she explained, "means time limitations—someone with a disability may not have the same length of time in a day as someone without a disability."

For a number of the problems identified, the disability group participants suggested some general solutions, namely:

- Clear directions to show how to navigate the site;
- Use of plain language (avoid jargon and long words);
- Information presented in a straightforward manner;
- Avoid the placement of color on color;
- Focus on information provision (provide shortcuts);
- Avoid the use of a small font size; and
- Do not mix font sizes, do not use italics, and do not use small print with text underlined.

The Cullen and Hernon report complements other investigations such as Judy Brewer's "How People with Disabilities Use the Web," which was prepared for the W3C Web Accessibility Initiative (WAI). "WAI develops guidelines for accessibility of Web sites, browsers, and authoring tools, in order to make it easier for people with disabilities to use the Web. Given the Web's increasingly important role in society, access to the Web is vital for people with disabilities."[45]

SERVICE QUALITY

Quality is in the eyes of the beholder, and although it sound like a cliché, it is literally true. If customers say there is quality service, then there is. If they do not, then there is not. It does not matter what an organization believes about its level of service. Still, complexities lie behind surface-level glances at *quality*, including its linkage to *service*.

Service quality has been defined from at least four perspectives:

1. Excellence. The attributes associated with excellence may change dramatically and rapidly. Excellence is often externally defined.

2. Value. It incorporates multiple attributes, but quality and value are different constructs—one is the perception of meeting or exceeding expectations and the other stresses benefit to the recipient.

3. Conformance to specifications. It facilitates precise measurement, but users of a service may not know or care about internal specifications.

4. Meeting and/or exceeding expectations. This definition is all encompassing and applies across service industries, but expectations change and may be shaped by experiences with other service providers.[46]

Most marketing researchers have concentrated on the last perspective. The *gaps model of service quality* reflects that perspective and offers service organizations a framework to identify services in the form of the gaps that exceed (or fail to meet) customers' expectations. The model posits five gaps that reflect a discrepancy between:

1. Customers' expectations and management's perceptions of these expectations (Gap 1);

2. Management's perceptions of customers' expectations and service quality specifications (Gap 2);

3. Service quality specifications and actual service delivery (Gap 3);

4. Actual service delivery and what is communicated to customers about it (Gap 4); and

5. Customers' perceptions of expected services and of the service already delivered (Gap 5).[47]

Although all five gaps may hinder an organization in providing high quality service, the fifth gap is the basis of a customer-oriented definition of service quality that examines the discrepancy between customers' expectations for excellence and their perceptions of the actual service delivered. Expectations are *desired* wants—the extent to which customers believe a particular attribute is *essential* for an excellent service provider,[48] and perceptions are a judgment of service performance.

Jeffrey E. Disend correlates the gaps model with the concept of service quality. He maintains that poor service results if the gap, or difference, is large between what is expected and what is delivered. When what is delivered matches what is expected, customers find the service acceptable. If the service provided is better than what they expected, exceptional service materializes.[49]

Consequently, when expectations and perceptions are ranked on a scale, the gap is a number reflecting the difference between the two—expectations ranking minus perceptions ranking. If there is a poor service gap, a minus number occurs. If the number, by chance, is zero, service is acceptable (expectations match perceptions). If a positive value emerges (perceptions exceed expectations), the service organization has achieved exceptional service. In reality, this characterization is too simplistic; even a minus number may signify exceptional service.

The definition of service quality presented in the gaps model recognizes that expectations are subjective and are neither static nor predictable.[50] The model's designers were influenced by the confirmation/disconfirmation theory, which involves a comparison between expectations and performance. Before using a service, customers have certain expectations about it. These expectations become a basis against which to compare actual performance. After having some experience with a service, customers can compare any expectations with actual performance and their perceptions are confirmed (if they match), negatively disconfirmed (if expectations exceed perceptions), or positively disconfirmed (if perceptions exceed expectations).[51] Terry G. Vavra, in his discussion of satisfaction, regards such terms as "positive disconfirmation" as "confusing," and, instead, he prefers to use the words "confirmed," "affirmed," and "disconfirmed" to describe the three situations:

- Expectations are *confirmed* when perceived performance *meets* them;
- Expectations are *affirmed* (reinforced by positive disconfirmation) when perceived performance *exceeds* them); and
- Expectations are *disconfirmed* (failed by negative disconfirmation) when perceived performance *falls short* of them.[52]

His distinction definitely applies to service quality.

Dimensions

Valarie A. Zeithaml, A. Parasuraman, and Leonard L. Berry initially developed a 200-item survey instrument that ultimately became SERVQUAL. Through an iterative process of survey administration, factor analysis, and item elimination, they settled on their basic structure for investigating service quality. Through a series of revisions and refinements, they arrived at a set of twenty-two statements that encompasses five interrelated dimensions that customers highly value when they evaluate service quality provided by a service industry:

1. Tangibles, the appearance of physical facilities, equipment, personnel, and communication material;
2. Reliability, the ability to perform the promised service dependably and accurately;

3. Responsiveness, willingness to help customers and provide prompt service;

4. Assurance, knowledge, and courtesy of employees and their ability to inspire trust and confidence; and

5. Empathy—the caring, individualized attention that a company provides its customers.[53]

As part of this basic version of SERVQUAL—perhaps the most popular instrument in the broad field of service quality for measuring the fifth gap—respondents also rate the importance of achieving excellent service for each dimension by allocating 100 points among a set of descriptions of the five dimensions. These descriptions of the service quality dimensions and average point allocations among respondents in different service settings enable researchers to make comparisons among studies and service industries.

A more recent version of SERVQUAL asks respondents to comment on a series of statements from three contexts ("minimum service expectations," "desired service expectations," and "the perception of service performance"). Using a nine-point scale, Parasuraman, Zeithaml, and Berry regard the three-column format as preferable for its reconceptualization of expectations into desired and minimum expectations. Expectations, it has been argued, array on a continuum, with *desired* and *minimum* ones at either end; a *zone of tolerance* falls in between. That zone "represents the range of service performance a customer would consider satisfactory."[54]

As Benjamin Schneider and Susan S. White note, studies in different disciplines and with different groups have not always supported the importance of the five dimensions; in some instances, only one or two dimensions apply and, in other instances, more than the five do. "Of course, many of these differences might be due in part to changes that authors make to the survey (e.g., adding or rewording items, changing response scales) or the way they analyze the data (e.g., using different factor analysis methods). However, even the original authors of SERVQUAL have had some difficulty in replicating the five-factor structure that the survey was designed to reflect."[55] Consequently, "the problems in replicating SERVQUAL's five-factor structure have led some researchers to suggest that there is no universal set of factors that are relevant across service industries."[56]

Schneider and White conclude, "SERVQUAL does not appear to be universally applicable to all situations without modification.... The dimensions of Reliability, Tangibles, Responsiveness, Assurance, and Empathy may be too broad for some service industries, but too narrow for others."[57] Of direct value to subsequent chapters, they note:

A process similar to the one used to develop SERVQUAL in the first place can also be used to determine the appropriateness of SERVQUAL for a particular organization or industry and how it might need to be modified. That is, researchers could start their measurement process by using customer focus groups to identify service quality themes, developing new items or finding existing ones (e.g., SERVQUAL items) to measure the themes, and then refining the survey through statistical techniques such as factor analysis.[58]

The previously mentioned dimensions definitely do not address the uniqueness of libraries in comparison to other service industries, namely the provision of materials collections and related services. As a result, a revised set of the dimensions became

- Affect of service (a combined measure of the following dimensions)
  - º Empathy (caring, individualized attention the library provides to its customers);
  - º Responsiveness (willingness to help customers and provide prompt service); and
  - º Assurance (knowledge and courtesy of employees and their ability to inspire trust).
- Ubiquity and ease of access (timely, ready, and easy access to relevant material; convenient hours of operations; and improved remote access to collections);
- Reliability (ability to perform the promised service dependably and accurately);
- Library as a place (the physical building as a place of information gathering, study, and reflection and an affirming symbol of the life of the mind);
- Adequacy or comprehensiveness of collections (deep collections of relevant print and electronic resources to meet immediate needs); and
- Self-sufficiency or self-reliance (users can be self-reliant within the information-gathering process).[59]

Even the above-mentioned dimensions do not adequately cover the digital environment in which libraries function. Consequently, it becomes necessary to identify dimensions related to the provision of e-service quality. The following list represents a beginning pool of dimensions worthy of exploration:

- Ease of use (navigation, search, find, download, speed, and remote access);
- Web site aesthetics (e.g., colors, graphics, and size);
- Linkage (e.g., connectivity to relevant information, avoid broken links, and regularly update the accuracy of the links);
- Collections (quality, relevance, and deep collections of electronic material to meet immediate needs);
- Reliability (e.g., frequency of updating and proper technical functioning of Web site or electronic product);
- Support (e.g., help pages, section on frequently asked questions, and technical help if there is a problem or question);
- Security/privacy/ trust (e.g., belief the site is relatively safe from intrusion and personal information is protected);
- Ease of access (e.g., log on/off quickly);
- Flexibility (different search procedures: basic and advanced, and so forth); and

- Customization/personalization (e.g., receive e-mail announcements about the arrival of new books on topics of personal interest).[60]

None of the lists of dimensions has been applied to students with disabilities to ascertain what adjustments might be in order. The only exception is an Australian master's paper in which Elizabeth M. Forsyth aligned SERVQUAL's five dimensions with disability service standards set by the Disability Services Act (*1986*). One example is, "Staff should provide services in a way that protects my dignity and privacy." This statement was "specifically linked... to Standard Four, which reads 'Each consumer's right to privacy, dignity and confidentiality in all aspects of his or her life is recognized and respected.'" Forsyth administered the revised instrument to 150 carers/advocates working for open employment service providers in South Australia and New South Wales.[61]

SATISFACTION

Both service quality and satisfaction can be an end in themselves; each differs and is worthy of examination as a framework for evaluating customer service expectations. Service quality evaluates specific attributes, ones of some importance to the organization, and this judgment is cognitive. Satisfaction, on the other hand, focuses on a specific transaction or, in the case of overall satisfaction, it is a cumulate judgment based on collective encounters with a service provider over time. Satisfaction judgments are more affective and emotional reactions to an experience or a collection of experiences. "Simply put, satisfaction is a sense of contentment that arises from an actual experience in relation to an expected experience."[62]

Because service quality as a means of evaluation probes precise statements on which the organization seeks customer input, it serves as a planning tool. Judgments about satisfaction, on the other hand, tend to be global in the type of questions asked. Unlike service quality, satisfaction focuses less on specific statements and relies more on open-ended questions. In satisfaction studies, there can be a probing of how customers rate the organization or Web site in a few specific areas, although the list is much shorter and more general than found in a service quality questionnaire. The intention of satisfaction studies is to identify general areas that may require scrutiny, whereas service quality studies offer insights into specific problem areas.

Service quality as a strategic planning tool denotes the attributes of what a library should be, in the minds of its customers, and the expectations the library regards as essential to meet. In contrast, customer satisfaction is a measure of how the customer perceives service delivery and possible shortcomings at a particular time or over a prolonged period of time. The customer satisfaction measurement process includes an opportunity for customers to suggest areas that might require managerial intervention.

"In this sense, the customer satisfaction assessment is like taking the temperature and blood pressure of a patient, as distinct from conducting an extensive workup involving most, if not all, vital signs."[63]

If a service quality questionnaire asks, "Any other expectations that you consider important" and lets respondents insert whatever they want and to rate it on a seven-, nine- or ten-point scale,[64] then a study of service quality assumes a diagnostic function.

In summary, Schneider and White support the distinction between service quality and satisfaction but they also agree that they are "closely related constructs. They are both concerned with how consumers experience an organization, and ... it is useful to keep the two conceptually distinct... with satisfaction being more evaluative and emotionally laden, and quality being more descriptive and factually based."[65]

SOME SURVEY INSTRUMENTS AND THE RATIONALE FOR A LOCALIZED APPROACH

The fifth gap—the difference between customers' perceptions of what a service should deliver and how well that service meets idealized expectations—is the conceptual basis for SERVQUAL and its derivative LibQUAL+™. Libraries use the latter survey instrument "to solicit, track, understand, and act upon users' opinions of service quality."[66] An issue of the *Journal of Library Administration*™ addresses the use of LibQUAL+™ in different types of libraries. As the articles demonstrate, this data-collection instrument for gathering self-reports of perceived service quality is widely used; in fact, by mid-2003, there have been almost 250,000 respondents from four countries.[67]

LibQUAL+™ has mistakenly been labeled a satisfaction survey, one that produces an outcome metric. However, there are different types of outcomes, one of which, known as a student learning outcome, measures student learning over the duration of a course or a program of study. It answers questions such as

- How well do students transfer and apply concepts, principles, ways of knowing, and problem solving across their program of study?
- How well do they develop an understanding, behaviors, attitudes, values, dispositions, and ethics that the institution asserts it instills?

Service quality might produce a set of customer-related metrics, but the explanation of these metrics as outcomes has not been adequately advanced. At this time, we can only say that there are customer-related metrics related to service quality and satisfaction, and such measures might influence student learning and perhaps other outcomes.

Libraries applying the LibQUAL+™ process use a set of determined statements that probe perceived service quality. Using the data collected, libraries can make comparisons to other libraries, both domestically and internationally.

When particular statements have local relevance, libraries can use the data locally; if they continue to repeat survey administration over time, they can engage in local benchmarking and continuous quality improvement of perceived service quality.

In addition, libraries using this data-collection instrument can now pick another five statements that have local relevance from a pool of statements and add several questions related to satisfaction. Clearly, LibQUAL+™ is becoming a somewhat flexible instrument that represents one means by which librarians can listen to the user community.

As Vavra notes, "the very act of surveying customers conveys a very positive message: the organization is interested in its customers' well-being, needs, pleasures, and displeasures. While this is admittedly a 'marketing message', there is nothing wrong ... in allowing a survey to serve both ... *informational* and *communication* roles."[68] He defines the informational role as collecting information from customers about what "needs to be changed (in a product, service, or delivery system) or ... how well an organization is currently delivering on its understanding of these needs."[69] Communication focuses on messages and the image that the organization wants to portray.

Vavra argues that response rates for surveys of service quality "are declining" because they are often conducted with "a research mentality" and do not adequately address the informational role or re-involve customers in providing ongoing feedback to the organization about its services. The tendency is to downplay "the importance of reinforcing the customer's participation."[70] Clearly, customers must see that their input directly affects services and their delivery or, as Vavra explains, "the research mentality must be replaced with a customer-relationship mentality. In such a perspective, reinforcing the customer's participation is essential."[71]

If Vavra is correct, more studies initiated by library staff should use the data collected to improve their services over time, thus showing respondents that their views, perspectives, and comments were heard and valued. The communication aspect must be stressed more and linked to an informational role, while the research mentality must yield to the planning needs of an organization.

A Planning Tool

Believing that neither SERVQUAL nor subsequently LibQUAL+™ sufficiently addresses the local expectations and priorities of libraries, as well as the issues that Vavra raises, Hernon and his colleagues in the United States and New Zealand developed a generic set of expectations that individual libraries could use as a guide for deciding on those statements that they might treat as priorities.[72] Central to their approach is the belief that whatever expectations are probed should result from local review and the input of library staff and some customers. Their research focused on one library or service location—

listening to customers as Vavra recommends—and has not attempted to determine the relevancy of the statements across institutions or over time.

Nitecki and Hernon combined the local approach to identify service factors with the earlier version of the SERVQUAL questionnaire framework, trying to produce an instrument useful for local planning purposes. Their study took place at Yale University libraries, and the success of the project suggests that it could be replicated at other institutions. Central to this approach is that the statements require modification from setting to setting, as determined by the priorities for service improvement established by service providers and managers.[73]

Mention of Disabilities

Among the instructions that libraries participating in the LibQUAL+™ process receive are:

In order for the project to comply with the Americans with Disabilities Act, . . . [those conducting the study must] be prepared to make special arrangements for any respondents with disabilities. Print copies of the survey will be made available at the Survey Management Center. Participants will also want to address the need for the provision of special assistance at the local level, if necessary.[74]

When participating libraries report survey results, they might indicate that some students with disabilities responded and commented that the library perhaps lacks a sufficient print collection in their area (e.g., special education and rehabilitation and disability policy).[75]

CONCLUSION

As this chapter demonstrates, the literature tends to focus on adaptive technologies and legal compliance. In the area of service quality, there is a recognized need for an examination of the fifth gap using a data-collection instrument developed specifically to compare user perceptions of ideal service and the service they actually experience. As well, there is a need for research to address the other four gaps. Some researchers, for example, are beginning to explore the first gap (i.e., the gap between customers' expectations and management's perceptions of these expectations); however, none of the work addresses the expectations of students with disabilities.

Additional research might explore the

- Effectiveness of bibliographic instruction or information literacy, and the linkage of that instruction to *student learning outcomes*, which measures the learning that students with disabilities gained throughout a program of study; and
- Accessibility of the content (and use) of digital libraries by individuals with disabilities.

In addition, there is need to compile bibliographies that identify scarce and widely scattered resources available in accessible formats. In the United Kingdom, for instance, the Library and Information Commission recognizes that

visually impaired people have the same need for information and intellectual stimulation as the rest of the population but have difficulty in accessing the intellectual content in standard print. With only five per cent of the hundred thousand new British titles published each year converted into one or more of the accessible formats, a union catalogue is a key tool in identifying which titles have been converted into which formats, and where they are held.[76]

It is obvious that disabilities represent an area in which the library profession can develop new research studies and bibliographies intended to improve the quality of service that students and others with disabilities receive. We should all challenge each other—be we librarians or professors in schools of library and information studies—to raise service expectations, provide better service, create more conducive learning environments, and, to the best of our abilities, eliminate needless barriers. Remember, "It's not enough anymore to merely satisfy the customer; customers must be 'delighted'—surprised by having their needs not just met, but exceeded."[77]

People can have a wide range of functional impairments, affecting their vision, hearing, mobility, and cognitive abilities. Accessible Web design means designing our sites in a manner such that the information they contain is accessible regardless of a person's abilities or disabilities, software, or equipment.[78]

NOTES

1. Eli Edwards and William Fisher, "Trust, Teamwork, and Tokenism: Another Perspective on Diversity in Libraries," *Library Administration & Management* 17 (Winter 2003): 21.
2. See, for instance, Richard N. Tucker, "Access for All? It Depends Who You Are," *IFLA Journal* 29 (2003): 385–388.
3. See, for instance, Howard Kramer, "Meeting the Needs of Students at a Large University At CU Boulder," *Colorado Libraries* 28, no. 4 (Winter 2002): 31–34.
4. See, for instance, Rainer Ommerborn and Rudolf Schuemer, "Using Computers in Distance Study: Results of a Survey amongst Disabled Distance Students" (2001; available ERIC, ED456214); Katherine Read, "An Overview of Current Library Support for Readers with Special Needs," *Legal Information Management* 4 (Spring 2004): 54–55; Jenny Craven and Peter Brophy, *Non-Visual Access to the Digital Library (NoVA): The Use of the Digital Library Interfaces by Blind and Visually Impaired People* (Manchester, England: Manchester Metropolitan University, n.d.); Jenny Craven, "Understanding the Searching Process for Visually Impaired Users of the Web." Available at http://www.ariadne.ac.uk/issue26/craven/intro.html (accessed April 4, 2005).

5. Linda Lucas Walling, "Educating Students to Serve Information Seekers with Disabilities," *Journal of Education for Library and Information Science* 45 (Spring 2004): 137–148.

6. Margaret McCasland and Michael Golden, "Improving ADA Access: Critical Planning," *The Reference Librarian* 67/68 (1999): 257.

7. Mary Beth Applin, "Providing Quality Library Services for Students with Disabilities," *Mississippi Libraries* 67 (Spring 2003): 6.

8. Mary Beth Applin, "Instructional Services for Students with Disabilities," *The Journal of Academic Librarianship* 25 (March 1999): 139.

9. Vincent P. Tinerella and Marcia A. Dick, "Academic Reference Service for the Visually Impaired: A Guide for the Non-specialist," *College & Research Libraries* 66 (January 2005): 29.

10. Jennifer Church, Sharon Drouin, and Katherine Rankin, "Electronic Resources on Disabilities: A Wealth of Information on Topics from Jobs to Recreation," *College & Research Libraries News* 61, no. 2 (February 2000). Available at http://www.ala.org/ala/acrl/acrlpubs/crlnews/backissues2000/february3/electronicresources.htm (accessed November 5, 2004).

11. "Information Access for People with Disabilities," *Library Technology Reports* 40 (May–June 2004): 10–32.

12. Axel Schmetzke, "Web Accessibility Survey Homepage" (Stevens Point, WI: University of Wisconsin Library, 2004). Available at http://library.uwsp.edu/aschmetz/Accessible/websurveys.htm (accessed September 3, 2004).

13. Linda Lou Wiler and Eleanor Lomax, "The Americans with Disabilities Act Compliance and Academic Libraries in the Southeastern United States," *Journal of Southern Academic and Special Librarianship* 2, no. 1/2 (2000). Available at http://southernlibrarianship.icaap.org/content/v02n01/wiler_l01.html (accessed November 5, 2004).

14. Scott A. Carpenter, "Accommodation to Persons with Disabilities: A Census of Ohio College and University Libraries," *The Katherine Sharp Review* 3 (Summer 1996). Available at http://www.lis.uiuc.edu/review/summer1996/carpenter.html (accessed September 3, 2004).

15. Association of Research Libraries, "Service to Users with Disabilities," *Transforming Libraries: Issues and Innovation in...,* issue 8 (Washington, D.C.: Association of Research Libraries, April 1999). Available at http://www.arl.org/transform,/disabilities/ (accessed September 3, 2004).

16. See "Task Force on Access to Information for Print Disabled Canadians Formed." Available at http://www.nald.ca/WHATNEW/hnews/2000/cnib.htm (accessed September 4, 2004). For information about fulfilling the goals of that report, see Council on Access to Information for Print-Disabled Canadians (Ottawa). Its "Web site also seeks to be a clearinghouse of information for users and producers of multiple formats, and for organizations that provide services and information resources to Print-Disabled Canadians." See http://www.collectionscanada.ca/accessinfo/index-e.html (accessed September 4, 2004).

17. Rowena J. Cullen and Philip J. Calvert, "Stakeholder Perceptions of University Library Effectiveness," *Journal of Academic Librarianship* 21 (1995): 438–448.

18. Ibid. They drew on the work of Kim Cameron, for instance: Kim Cameron, "Measuring Organizational Effectiveness in Institutions of Higher Education," *Administrative Science Quarterly* 23 (1978): 604–629.

19. Rowena J. Cullen and Philip J. Calvert, "New Zealand University Libraries Effectiveness Project: Dimensions and Concepts of Organizational Effectiveness," *Library & Information Science Research* 18 (1996): 99–119.
20. See, for instance, Joseph Lazzaro, *Adaptive Technologies for Learning & Work Environments* (Chicago: American Library Association, 2001); "What Is the State of Adaptive Technology in Libraries Today?," *Library Technology Reports* 40 (May–June 2004): 81–92; Ravonne A. Green and Diane N. Gillespie, "Assistive Technologies in Academic Libraries: A Preliminary Study," *portal: Libraries and the Academy* 1 (2001): 329–337; the Assistive Technology Act of 1998 (P.L. 105–394).
21. Scott Carlson, "Left out Online," *The Chronicle of Higher Education* (June 11, 2004): A23.
22. Eleanor Loiacono and Scott McCoy, "Web Site Accessibility: An Online Sector Analysis," *Information Technology & People* 17 (2004): 90. See also Clare Harris and Charles Oppenheim, "The Provision of Library Services for Visually Impaired Students in UK Further Education Libraries in Response to the Special Educational Needs and Disability Act (SENDA), *Journal of Librarianship and Information Science* 35, no. 4 (December 2003): 243–257.
23. Paul Ryan Bohman, "University Web Accessibility Policies: A Bridge Not Quite Far Enough" (Logan, UT: WebAIM, 2004). Available at http://www.webaim.org/coordination/articles/policies-pilot (accessed November 5, 2004).
24. Ibid.
25. Tim Spindler, "The Accessibility of Web Pages for Mid-Sized College and University Libraries," *Reference & User Services Quarterly* 42 (Winter 2002): 150.
26. See Bobby™ Web site (Waltham, NA: The Watchfire Co.), available at http://bobby.watchfire.com/bobby/html/en/index.jsp (accessed August 27, 2004). See also http://bobby.watchfire.com/bobby/html/en/about.jsp (accessed August 27, 2004).
27. Spindler, "The Accessibility of Web Pages for Mid-Sized College and University Libraries," 152.
28. Erica B. Lilly and Connie Van Fleet, "Wired but Not Connected: Accessibility of Academic Library Home Pages," *The Reference Librarian*™ 67/68 (1999): 5–28.
29. Mark Yannie, "A Survey Can Measure the Accessibility of Your Institution's Library," *Disability Compliance for Higher Education* 87, no. 8 (March 2003): 9. See also Mark Yannie, "Extent of Service: Minnesota Libraries Disability Services and Quality of Websites: Assessing Public and Academic Libraries," *Christian Librarian* 47 (2004): 48–52.
30. Suzanne Byerley, "Usability Testing and Students with Visual Disabilities: Building Electronic Curb Cuts into a Library Web Site," *Colorado Libraries* 27, no 3 (Fall 2001): 22–24.
31. Michael Providenti, "Library Web Accessibility at Kentucky's 4-Year Degree Granting Colleges and Universities," *D-Lib Magazine* 10, no. 9 (September 2004): 12. Available at http://www.dlib.org/dlib/september04/providenti/09/providenti.html (accessed January 21, 2005).
32. Jenny Craven, "Good Design Principles for the Library Website: A Study of Accessibility Issues in UK University Libraries," *New Review of Information and Library Research* 6 (2000): 39.

33. Bryna Coonin, "Establishing Accessibility for E-journals: A Suggested Approach," *Library Hi Tech* 20 (2002): 207–220.
34. Suzanne L. Byerley and Mary Beth Chambers, "Accessibility and Usability of Web-based Library Databases for Non-visual Users," *Library Hi Tech* 20 (2002): 169–178.
35. Ibid., 177.
36. Dagmar Amtmann, Kurt Johnson, and Debbie Cook, "Making Web-based Tables Accessible for Users of Screen Readers," *Library Hi Tech* (2002): 221.
37. Charlene H. Loope, "Academic Library Services for Students with Disabilities: A Survey at the University of South Carolina" (Columbia, SC: University of South Carolina, 1996; ERIC ED396503).
38. Harris and Oppenheim, "The Provision of Library Services for Visually Impaired Students in UK."
39. Allison Jones and Lucy A. Tedd, "Provision of Electronic Information Services for the Visually Impaired: An Overview with Case Studies from Three Institutions within the University of Wales," *Journal of Librarianship and Information Science* 35 (June 2003): 105–113.
40. Sheryl Burgstahler, "Distance Learning: The Library's Role in Ensuring Access to Everyone," *Library Hi Tech* 20 (2002): 420–432; Sheryl Burgstahler, Bill Corrigan, and Joan McCarter, "Making Distance Learning Courses Accessible to Students and Instructors with Disabilities," *Internet and Higher Education* 7 (2004): 233–246; Steve Noble, "Delivering Accessible Library Services in a Distance Learning Environment," *Information Technology and Disabilities* 6, no. 1/2 (April 1999). Available at http://www.rit.edu/~easi/itd/itdv06n1/artricle5.html (accessed January 7, 2005).
41. University of Arkansas Libraries, "StaffWeb: Initiative Review Group I: Final Report, June 30, 2001" (Little Rock, AR: University of Arkansas Libraries, 2001), 5. Available at http://libinfo.uark.edu/Strategic Planning/irglfinal.asp (accessed August 24, 2004).
42. Paco Underhill, *The Science of Shopping* (New York: Simon and Schuster, 1999).
43. Memorial Hall Library, "User and Non-User Survey: Planning for Library Services for People with Disabilities" (Andover, MA: Memorial Hall Library, n.d.). No longer available at http://www.mhl.org/disabilities/ (however, it was available and accessed September 3, 2004).
44. Rowena Cullen and Peter Hernon, *Wired for Well-being: Citizens' Response to E-government.* A report presented to the E-government Unit, New Zealand State Services Commission (June 2004).
45. Judy Brewer, ed., "How People with Disabilities Use the Web: W3C Working Draft" (Cambridge, MA: World Wide Web Consortium, 2001. Available at http://www.w3.org/WAI/EO/Drafts/PWD-Use-Web/Overview.html (accessed August 27, 2004).
46. Adapted from C. A. Reeves and D. A. Bednar, "Defining Quality: Alternatives and Implications," *Academy of Management Review* 19 (1994): 419–445.
47. Valarie A. Zeithaml, A. Parasuraman, and Leonard L. Berry, *Delivering Quality Service: Balancing Customer Perceptions and Expectations* (New York: The Free Press, 1990).
48. A. Parasuraman, Leonard L. Berry, and Valarie A. Zeithaml, "Refinement and Reassessment of the SERVQUAL Scale," *Journal of Retailing* 67 (1991): 420–450.

49. Jeffrey E. Disend, *How to Provide Excellent Service in Any Organization* (Radnor, PA: Chilton Book Co., 1991), 108.

50. R. F. Blanchard and R. L. Galloway, "Quality in Retail Banking," *International Journal of Service Industry Management* 5, no. 4 (1994): 5–23.

51. See R. L. Oliver, *Satisfaction: A Behavioral Perspective on the Consumer* (New York: McGraw-Hill, 1997); R. L. Oliver and W. S. DeSarbo, "Response Determinants in Satisfaction Judgments," *Journal of Consumer Research* 14 (1998): 495–507.

52. Terry G. Vavra, *Improving Your Measurement of Customer Satisfaction: A Guide to Creating, Conducting, Analyzing, and Reporting Customer Satisfaction Measurement Programs* (Milwaukee, WI: ASQ Quality Press, 1997), 42.

53. Zeithaml, Parasuraman, and Berry, *Delivering Quality Service*, 26.

54. A. Parasuraman, Valarie A. Zeithaml, and Leonard L. Berry, "Alternative Scales for Measuring Service Quality: A Comparative Assessment Based on Psychometric and Diagnostic Criteria," *Journal of Retailing* 70 (1994): 201–230.

55. Benjamin Schneider and Susan S. White, *Service Quality: Research Perspectives* (Thousand Oaks, CA: Sage Publications, 2004), 32.

56. Ibid.

57. Ibid., 33.

58. Ibid.

59. Peter Hernon and Robert E. Dugan, *An Action Plan for Outcomes Assessment in Your Library* (Chicago: American Library Association, 2002), 123.

60. See Peter Hernon and Philip Calvert, "E-Service Quality in Libraries: Exploring Its Features and Dimensions," *Library & Information Science Research* 27 (2005): 377–404.

61. Elizabeth M. Forsyth, *Measuring and Delivering Quality in Open Employment Services for People with Disability: Is a System of Compliance to Performance Standards in Conflict with Furthering Quality in Service Delivery for Customers?* (Adelaide: South Australia: Adelaide University, Graduate School of Management, n.d.). Available at http://www.workable.org/au/archive/measuring_and_delivering_quality.htm (accessed August 31, 2004).

62. Peter Hernon and John R. Whitman, *Delivering Satisfaction and Service Quality: A Customer-based Approach for Libraries* (Chicago: American Library Association, 2001), 32.

63. Ibid., 32.

64. Danuta Nitecki and Peter Hernon, "Measuring Service Quality at Yale University's Libraries," *The Journal of Academic Librarianship* 26 (July 2000): 271.

65. Schneider and White, *Service Quality*, 53.

66. Association of Research Libraries, "LibQUAL+™ Survey Results" (Washington, D.C.: Association of Research Libraries, 2004). Available at http://www.arl.org/pubscat/libqualpubs.html (accessed August 29, 2004).

67. Fred M. Heath, Martha Kyrillidou, and Consuella A. Askew, eds., "Libraries Act on Their LibQUAL+™ Findings: From Data to Action," *Journal of Library Administration™* 40 (3/4) (2004): 1–240. See also http://www.libqual.org/Publications/index.cfm.

68. Vavra, *Improving Your Measurement of Customer Satisfaction*, 28.

69. Ibid.

70. Ibid., 83.

71. Ibid., 84.

72. Peter Hernon and Ellen Altman, *Assessing Service Quality: Satisfying the Expectations of Library Customers* (Chicago: American Library Association, 1998); Peter Hernon and Philip Calvert, "Methods for Measuring Service Quality in University Libraries in New Zealand," *Journal of Academic Librarianship* 22 (September 1996): 387–391; Philip Calvert and Peter Hernon, "Surveying Service Quality within University Libraries," *Journal of Academic Librarianship* 23 (September 1997): 408–415.

73. Nitecki and Hernon, "Measuring Service Quality at Yale University's Libraries," 259–273.

74. Association of Research Libraries, *LibQUAL+: Policies and Procedures Manual* (Draft) (Washington, D.C.: Association of Research Libraries, 2002), 11.

75. University of Massachusetts, Boston, Healey Library, "LibQUAL+™ Results: Library as Place (by Patron Group)." Available at http://www.lib.umb.edu/libqual/4a/cfm (accessed August 30, 2004).

76. Library and Information Commission, "REVEAL: The National Database of Resources in Accessible Formats" (London: Library and Information Commission, 2000). Available at http://www.ukoln.ac.uk/services/lic/sharethevision/ (accessed October 12, 2004).

77. Kristin Anderson and Ron Zemke, *Delivering Knock Your Socks off Service*, rev. ed. (New York: American Management Association, 1991), vii.

78. Cheryl H. Kirkpatrick, "Getting Two for the Price of One: Accessibility and Usability," *Computers in Libraries* 23 (January 2003): 27.

8

—◦•✦•◦—

DEVELOPING AND TESTING AN INSTRUMENT: NEW ZEALAND

Philip Calvert and Peter Hernon

> To understand the obstacles that people with disabilities encounter while navigating the Internet is to understand why developing accessible [Web] pages is necessary.[1]

The premise of this chapter and subsequent ones is that students with disabilities constitute a distinct and important group that, at times, has unique service expectations. Academic librarians need to understand (and proactively plan to address) the service expectations of the entire community of students, faculty, and staff. Those with disabilities constitute part of that community. Furthermore, existing survey instruments covering service quality are too general in the statements they contain to enable librarians to engage in continuous quality improvement to meet well (or fully) the service expectations of this group. Donna R. Euben, the legal counsel for the American Association of University Professors (AAUP), writes,

By engaging in good faith conversations about reasonable accommodations, the academic community can ensure the ongoing provision of quality teaching, research, and service while accommodating disabled colleagues in performing the essential functions of their [academic] appointments.[2]

She reminds the readership of *Academe,* the AAUP's monthly bulletin, that faculty might have disabilities (e.g., multiple sclerosis and chronic depression) and that the Americans with Disabilities Act prohibits discrimination in employment

"against a qualified individual with a disability because of the disability." The act defines a "qualified individual" "as one "who, with or without reasonable accommodation, can perform the essential functions of [the] position." Such discrimination includes the failure to make "reasonable accommodations" for qualified persons unless such accommodations impose an "undue hardship."[3]

Any discussion of service quality extends beyond legal accommodations and includes the service role of libraries in addressing the expectations of different members of the academic community. SERVQUAL and LibQUAL+™ identify dimensions that may be important to various segments of the academic community, but these instruments fail to address satisfactorily the expectations of all segments. Both this chapter and the next one describe the development of an instrument that any academic library (or for that matter, public library), regardless of country, might adapt to serve better communities that have disabilities. Libraries should not continue to treat SERVQUAL and LibQUAL+™ as instruments that produce insights relevant to the *entire* academic community.

By using the SERVQUAL model, which is based on gap analysis, it was our hope to identify areas in which customers with disabilities think that actual library service falls short of (or exceeds) their expectations. That instrument demonstrates sufficient flexibility so that library staff can select which statements might have local relevance and importance to faculty, students, and staff. The intention is to identify attributes of local importance that require attention from individual libraries, be they academic or public.

INSTRUMENT DEVELOPMENT

From February to June 2004, we held separate meetings with the librarians of four New Zealand universities who had responsibilities for serving the disability community within the institution. In addition, we met with the staff of the Disability Support Services (DSS) office at Victoria University of Wellington (VUW) to gain their perspective on statements and dimensions applicable to library services. With the assistance of both groups we began to compile a general list of statements related to service quality. We continued to review the literatures on disabilities, higher education, and library and information science (LIS), seeking the identification of additional statements. We also reviewed the statements contained in both SERVQUAL and LibQUAL+™ to ensure compilation of an extensive list of possible statements. Furthermore, we did not want to make any prejudgments about the appropriateness of specific statements. The disability staff at VUW and a staff member from the Royal New Zealand Foundation of the Blind ("New Zealand's primary service provider for blind, vision-impaired and deaf-blind people") with a postgraduate degree in LIS reviewed a draft instrument and the proposed dimensions. They thought that the ultimate list (see chapter appendix) was all-inclusive and that we could reduce the number of statements to a manageable set that would not tax respondents too much to evaluate.

Respondents were asked to rate each statement on a Likert scale of 1 to 10, for their expectations of ideal service, with 1 showing they "strongly disagree" that the statement has any importance for excellent libraries and 10 indicating their agreement that the statement has the highest importance. They also used the same scale to indicate the extent to which they thought the VUW library has that feature; 1 indicates they strongly disagree that the library does and 10 suggests they strongly agree that the library has the feature. They could select another number if they felt less strongly about the statement. They were also instructed to skip a statement if it did not relate to their particular experience, needs, or circumstance. Ultimately, we reduced the number of statements presented in the service quality survey form to eighty-four statements about library service.

Still, eighty-four statements are too many for any survey to probe; however, we did not want to reduce the number without input from library customers. Our intention was to continue to review the list, seeing what statements might be added or dropped, and which might be most essential for future studies to probe (see next chapter). We wanted therefore to develop a flexible instrument so that individual libraries could review their accommodations, auxiliary aids, and services; and settle on the particular statements most relevant to their services.

Instrument Testing

It is impossible to determine the precise size of the target population at VUW because not all students with disabilities register with the DSS, the academic disability support group. That unit estimated the population at 150, and 42 of them (28 percent) participated. Either individually or in groups they completed the survey. The percentage of participants might seem small; however, it merits comment that answering the complete list of statements (on an eight-page questionnaire) is a time-consuming and challenging task for students with disabilities. Yet, because the focus was on instrument development and refinement, neither the DSS nor library, nor we, wanted to insert our perspectives about which dimensions the students might find important. Furthermore, because this was the first round of a critical review of the instrument, we did not ask faculty or staff to participate.

An examination of completed survey forms indicated that respondents did not indiscriminately mark the same number for each statement. Rather, they appeared to have read and thought about each statement before answering. It merits mention that we retained the same format as the original version of SERVQUAL; we compared expectations and performance without distinguishing among minimum service expectations, desired service expectations, and the perception of service performance (see chapter 7). We concluded that such a distinction would unnecessarily complicate data collection.

In addition to refining the instrument, we wanted to see what types of results might be revealed through application of the survey instrument. Therefore, the remainder of this chapter focuses on the findings and a recasting of the survey form, setting the stage for chapter 9.

FINDINGS

The survey form that we tested contained three sections: (1) statements about service expectations and service delivery, (2) eleven dimensions related to library service, and (3) some descriptive information about the respondents. The mean for responses on expectations and performance was calculated and then the statements were ranked in order by mean. For each respondent, the score given for performance was subtracted from the score given for the expectation, and then we calculated the mean for the sum. This gives the *gap* between expectations and performance that shows how customers rate the service quality in the library.

Report on the First Section

Table 8.1 identifies the twenty-three biggest *gaps* between service expectations and actual service performance, as assessed by the respondents. These aspects of service had gaps of 4.00 or higher (although this is not a significant number it is still useful for analysis). It is the gap that measures service quality.

The primary objective of this survey was to test the instrument and subsequently to refine it. As already mentioned, the survey instrument included all eighty-four statements even though not all of them were relevant to the VUW Library because, at the time, that library did not offer the specific service or have the facility mentioned in some statements. Taking the statement "The library has directional signs that are in Braille" as an example, the mean for the expectation was 8.27 whereas the mean for performance was only 2.77 (the lowest of all scores), resulting in the gap of 5.50. The VUW Library does *not* have any directional signs in Braille (with the exception of floor numbers in the elevators), so the respondents were quite correct to give a low score for performance. Nor could it be argued that the expectations score was high enough to merit attention; even though a mean of 8.27 may sound high, it placed no higher than fifty-ninth out of eighty-four statements in the list of expectations sorted by the highest mean.

In practice, a library that does not have directional signs in Braille would omit this statement from the survey unless it was willing to meet expectations if the respondents considered it important (which the VUW students apparently do not). The other circumstance when this statement might be used would be a library serving a large number of students with major visual impairments, in which case the library might select all the statements relevant

Table 8.1
The Largest Gaps between Service Expectations and Service Performance

Aspect of Service	Gap (mean)
The library has directional signs that are in Braille	5.5500
The library embeds information about my specific needs into my student ID/library card	5.1765
The library supports students in getting texts put into Braille or onto audiotape	5.5100
The online catalog provides access to material with the aid of refreshable Braille	4.9500
The library Web site has either a TTY or TDD phone number for making contact with the library	4.9048
The library provides extended loan periods (e.g., for reserve material)	4.8125
The library has electronically adjustable foot rests	4.7857
The library has text phones	4.5455
The library offers guides in a range of accessible formats	4.5455
The library has portable and fixed induction loops at help desks	4.5200
The library has staff who have been trained (e.g., in communicating with someone who lip-reads)	4.4583
The library Web site provides library policies (e.g., regarding companion animals)	4.3793
The library has adaptive mice	4.2500
The online catalog provides access to material with the aid of speech synthesis	4.2500
The library has electronically adjustable tables/chairs	4.2143
The library sets aside books in advance for students who find it difficult to get to the library	4.2000
The library has ergonomic chairs	4.1944
The library provides networked computers with devices for connecting hearing aids to sound devices	4.1379
The library provides large print resources	4.1200
The library scans material into electronic text for me	4.1200
The library provides networked computers with drives for connecting hearing aids to sound devices	4.1000
The library has electronically adjustable monitors	4.0714
The library has wrist rests	4.0000

to visual impairments and test the level of expectations. However, this is only useful if the library managers want to move resources into those aspects of service identified by the customers as important and in need of remedial treatment.

The gap becomes much more significant when a statement has a high mean for expectations and a high gap score. Since the second statement on the gaps list also appears high in the expectations list (twelfth), VUW Library managers might consider addressing the statement "The library embeds information about my specific needs into my student ID/library card." However, that statement may require resource allocation and university approval. Furthermore, because the university does not require a single card, it may be more appropriate for the information to be embedded in the library card. What information do students want embedded in the card, and how would this information be used (presumably only by library staff or the library's automated systems)? The statement "The library provides networked computers with devices for connecting hearing aids to sound devices" was ranked eighteenth in the *gaps* list and much lower in the expectations list; the gap of 4.14 suggests that customers would like this service implemented.

No other items among the top twenty-three in the list of gaps appear highly rated in the expectations list. This should be good news for the VUW Library if either the library or the disability service already meets student expectations. In such a case, there is most likely no need to introduce significant changes. Still before dismissing the items, the staff might engage in a satisfaction study or focus group interview to verify student contentment with the present situation.

Table 8.2 identifies the ten lowest gaps for service expectations—a low gap means that the customers are reasonably satisfied with the service provided. Presumably, the library is doing well on these aspects of service, the respondents have other ways for addressing those expectations, or these expectations do not raise issues of importance to them. Note that many of the expectations relate to library staff, and perhaps the students rely on selected staff or they have their own channels for information gathering that do not involve interaction with library staff. Clearly, such a conclusion might be examined through the use of focus group interviews, which are outside the scope of this book.

Performance and Expectations

Respondents assessed the same elements of service discussed above but this time from the perspective of the performance of the VUW Library. Table 8.3, which reflects the statements with the fifteen highest mean scores, shows that the students gave good scores to library staff, thus modifying the impression suggested in the previous section. The students feel that they can navigate the library, go up and down the elevator without difficulty, and are comfortable with the library's Web site. The statements about a quiet study/rest area and an adequate number of workstations refer to the Sutherland Room, which is a special area set aside for students with disabilities, is located in the main library building, and is extensively used by students registered with the DSS.

The lowest rated statements about performance are:

- The library has portable and fixed induction loops at help desks (mean of 3.32);
- The library has staff who meet with me each year to discuss my needs (mean of 3.15);
- The library has electronically adjustable foot rests (mean of 3.07);
- The library has text phones (mean of 2.88); and
- The library has directional signs that are in Braille (mean of 2.77).

Although the library does not support these statements, this fact is not a concern of the students.

The statements for which students had the highest expectations (means greater than 9) include:

- The online catalog is an accurate source of information about all materials held by the library (mean of 9.43);
- The library has elevators in good working order (mean of 9.43);

Table 8.2
The Lowest Gaps between Service Expectations and Service Performance

Aspect of service	Gap (mean)
The library has staff who assist me willingly in photocopying material	2.4063
The library has electrical outlets for my laptop	2.3333
The library Web site has content that is easy to read and view	2.3243
The library has staff who are friendly and easy to talk to	2.2857
The library provides networked computers that have scanning and reading software to make printed and electronic texts more readable	2.1724
The library has staff who are approachable and welcoming	2.1538
The library has staff who treat my requests confidentially	1.9630
It is easy to enter and exit the building	1.9211
The library has staff who are courteous and polite	1.7895
The library provides a quiet study/rest area for students with disabilities	1.6923

Table 8.3
Highest Mean Scores for Service Performance by the Library

Performance	Mean
It is easy to enter and exit the building	7.45
The library provides a quiet study/rest area for students with disabilities	7.31
The library has staff who are courteous and polite	7.26
The library has staff who are friendly and easy to talk to	6.92
The library Web site has content that is easy to view and read	6.92
The library has staff who are approachable and welcoming	6.87
The library provides networked computers that have scanning and reading software to make printed and electronic texts more readable	6.69
It is easy to find my way around the library	6.66
The library has staff who assist me willingly in locating resources	6.67
The library has elevators in good working order	6.59
The library has good lighting	6.53
The library has staff who communicate clearly (allow me to see their mouths as they speak)	6.50
The library has staff who assist me willingly in using the online catalog	6.42
The library provides an adequate number of workstations in good working order	6.34
It is easy to move from floor to floor or about the book stacks	6.32

- It is easy to enter and exit the building (mean of 9.37);
- The library has good toilet facilities that are located near study space (mean of 9.34);
- The library has good lighting (mean of 9.34);
- The library has staff who communicate clearly (allow me to see their mouths as they speak) (mean of 9.33);
- The library Web site has content that is easy to view and read (mean of 9.30);
- The library has staff who are friendly and easy to talk to (mean of 9.28);
- The library has staff who are courteous and polite (mean of 9.28);
- The library has staff who are available when I need them (mean of 9.26);
- The library has staff who assist me willingly in using the online catalog (mean of 9.25);
- The library has comfortable seating (mean of 9.24);
- The library has good toilet facilities that are clearly signposted (mean of 9.23);

- The library embeds information about my specific needs into my student ID/library card (mean of 9.21).
- The online catalog displays information in a clear and understandable manner (mean of 9.20);
- The library provides an adequate number of workstations in good working order (mean of 9.13);
- The library has staff who assist me willingly in using equipment (mean of 9.13);
- It is easy to find my way around the library (mean of 9.13);
- The library has staff who assist me willingly in locating resources (mean of 9.10);
- The library has staff who fetch resources from inaccessible shelves (mean of 9.07);
- The library has directional signs that are clear, legible, and accurate, and have color contrast (mean of 9.06);
- The online catalog has easy-to-follow instructions (mean of 9.06);
- The library has staff who are approachable and welcoming (mean of 9.03); and
- It is easy to find staff to help me when I need assistance (mean of 9.03).

Given that the pool of statements probed is extensive (not comprehensive), respondents were asked if there were other expectations they considered important when they used library computers to gain access to information. Only a few points were mentioned more than once; these were:

- Getting physical access to library computers
  - The need for more computers
  - The distance from parking lots to the library
  - Need for orderly queues for the library computers;
- Instruction on using databases and software (e.g., EndNote);[4] and
- Reporting problems with computers.

It merits mention that, although not directly a matter of using computers, some respondents commented that they would benefit from longer loan periods. The results do not suggest a need to add more statements to the pool at this time. As well, any revision of the instrument should retain the question about the possible addition of statements.

Quadrant Analysis

The previous section shows that the initial instrument provides a large amount of information that might be difficult to interpret. Quadrant analysis, which is frequently used in marketing, is a graphic correlation technique that produces data easy to visualize.[5] The technique plots data about service attributes into four quadrants defined by two dimensions: one reflects the importance that customers give service attributes, while the other indicates the extent to which customers think a particular service has the attributes. Figure 8.1 illustrates the relative importance of attributes failing within the four quadrants, when the first dimension is plotted along the horizontal axis as the ideal expectation for excellent service quality, and the second dimension is plotted along the vertical axis as the library's performance.

Those attributes falling into Quadrant 1 are very important to library users and they perceive the library as possessing them or as performing well in their delivery. The library should retain these attributes in any reconfiguration of its services, and there should be no decline in its ability to meet them. Attributes failing into Quadrant 2 are also most important to the respondents but are not perceived as being prominent features of a library service. Within a library culture that strives to respond to user expectations, these service features merit improvement. Any attributes present in Quadrant 3 are relatively unimportant to the respondents, but they associate those attributes with library service. The staff might refocus the service so that its image matches the attributes shown in Quadrant 1. Alternatively, library staff might want to revisit resources allocated to providing the service attributes in Quadrant 3 and review the relative expense of providing a less valued activity. Quadrant 4 includes attributes that are neither valued by the customers nor performed well by the library. Those attributes might be ignored and resources reallocated.

Naturally, some statements were considered very important to the students and they thought the library performed them well (Quadrant 1). One example

Figure 8.1
Depiction of Quadrants (in Quadrant Analysis)

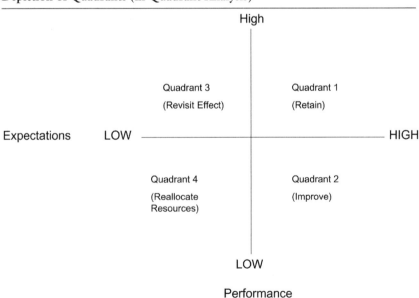

is "The online catalog displays information in a clear and understandable manner." An example of a statement appearing in Quadrant 2 (important for service excellence but respondents think these attributes are less evident in the library's delivery of service quality) is "The library Web site has lettering and colors that are distinguishable and easy to see." The respondents placed "The library has staff who meet with me each year to discuss my needs" as an example of a Quadrant 3 attribute—unimportant but within the library's perceived service strengths. Finally, Quadrant 4 applies to attributes (e.g., "The library has adaptive mice") that have low importance and low performance.

Report on Section B

SERVQUAL instruments tend to include this section in order to make comparisons across service industries. However, libraries have a unique dimension—their collections and related services. Unlike other studies in LIS and elsewhere, this one examines a set of dimensions applicable to libraries and a special community—students with disabilities.

The instructions stated,

Listed below are eleven features pertaining to libraries and the *services* they offer. We would like to know how important each of these is to you when you evaluate a library's quality of service. Please rank the list from the most to least important to you, with "1" being *most important* and "11" being *least important*.

As respondents ranked the most important feature with a 1 and the least important with 11, the lowest average and the lowest mode are the most important (see Table 8.4). Standard deviations were quite high for all the items in the list. The highest were for three features for which the standard deviation was over 3.00 in each case:

1. The appearance and functionality of the library's physical facilities and equipment;
2. A physical building that serves as a place of information-gathering, study, and reflection; and
3. Deep collections of relevant material—print and electronic—to meet my immediate needs.

This finding suggests a high degree of variation among respondents to at least three items on the list.

Some indication of consistency can be gained by looking at the mode for each dimension. The ranked list in Table 8.5 shows some variation for the list given in the previous table. Three dimensions appear in both tables 8.4 and 8.5 as highly rated. These focus on:

• Assurance that information essential for completing course assignments is readily available;

Table 8.4
Ranking of the Eleven Dimensions

Dimension	Rank	Average (%)
Timely, speedy, and easy access to material relevant to my course and research needs	1	3.29
Assurance that information essential for completing course assignments is readily available	2	3.62
The library's willingness to help users find and retrieve needed resources	3	5.12
The ability to be independent in my search for relevant information	4	5.41
Deep collections of relevant material—print and electronic—to meet my immediate needs	5	5.47
The knowledge, courtesy, and helpfulness of the library staff and the caring, individual attention the library provides its users	6	5.82
Ease of use (enlarged text, assistive technology)	7	6.12
A physical building that serves as a place of information-gathering, study, and reflection	8	6.62
The appearance and functionality of the library's physical facilities and equipment	9	7.56
Customization/personalization service	10	7.94
Web site aesthetics (appropriate colors, graphics, font types)	11	9.03

- Timely, speedy, and easy access to material relevant to my course and research needs; and
- The library's willingness to help users find and retrieve needed resources.

The dimension about Web site aesthetics ranked lowest by both calculations (average and mode). The dimension "A physical building that serves as a place of information-gathering, study, and reflection" had the joint lowest mode (eleven), but it ranked eighth by average. It had a high standard deviation; while most respondents ranked it low, a few gave it a much higher rating.

It seems that the dimensions developed for the instrument have relevance to the target audience and that the disability staff and member of the foundation for blind and deaf people were correct: the set of eleven dimensions merit close examination.

Table 8.5
Ranked List of Dimensions

Dimension	Rank	Mode
Assurance that information essential for completing course assignments is readily available	1	1
Timely, speedy, and easy access to material relevant to my course and research needs	1	1
The library's willingness to help users find and retrieve needed resources	3	3
Deep collections of relevant material—print and electronic—to meet my immediate needs	4	4
The knowledge, courtesy, and helpfulness of the library staff and the caring, individual attention the library provides its users	5	6
The ability to be independent in my search for relevant information	6	7
Customization/personalization service	7	8
Ease of use (enlarged text, assistive technology)	8	9
The appearance and functionality of the library's physical facilities and equipment	9	10
A physical building that serves as a place of information-gathering, study, and reflection	10	11
Web site aesthetics (appropriate colors, graphics, font types)	10	11

Factor Analysis

We used SPSS 12.00 to perform factor analysis (principal component analysis), with the rotation method being Varimax with Kaiser normalization. Possibly because there were only 42 responses the factor analysis did not present several clear *quality factors* (groupings of service statements). The best result provided five factors. The first (and obviously the largest) quality factor includes nearly all the highly rated statements from the expectations list. The statement with the highest central tendency in the first quality factor is:

• The library Web site identifies contact people who will provide me with assistance.

The next statements in this factor are:

• The library has staff who keep information about my disability confidential;
• The library Web site has content that is easy to view and read;

- It is easy to find staff to help me if I need assistance;
- The library has staff who have been trained (e.g., in communicating with someone who lip-reads);
- The library provides networked computers with ergonomic keyboards; and
- The library Web site identifies useful services.

The respondents seem to be saying, "We need assistance directly from staff and indirectly through the Web site. That assistance depends on good communication, and we need access to information resources through the use of suitable technology." Perhaps they also expect *empathy* (personal service, good communication, and understanding the special needs of these customers) from the library. This quality factor, though, was too large to be refined into one simple dimension, and aspects of *responsiveness* are also present.

The second quality factor concentrated on following statements:

- The library has staff who assist me willingly in photocopying material;
- The library provides networked computers that accept commands from my voice;
- The library has text phones;
- The library has electronically adjustable tables/chairs; and
- The library provides extended loan periods (e.g., for reserve material).

Most of the statements in this quality factor refer to accessing appropriate technology.

Respondents want assistive technology available to assist them, and they view it like any other service available to them (e.g., they want longer loan periods). This finding is worth comment, for no other service quality analysis has produced a *technology* dimension (see Section B), and it could be that the special needs of those with disabilities require managers to pay extra attention to technology access.

The third quality factor includes these statements:

- The online catalog is an accurate source of information about all materials held by the library;
- The library has elevators in good working order;
- The library provides networked computers that have scanning and reading software to make printed and electronic texts more readable; and
- The online catalog displays information in a clear and understandable manner.

Two of these statements pertain to the online public access catalog (OPAC), and it seems that respondents view the OPAC, in part, as equipment that needs to work for them. This quality factor has elements of the *reliability* dimension in it.

The fourth and fifth quality factors were small. The factor analysis would not spin out another factor. Looking at the five dimensions explored in the original SERVQUAL,[6] only *tangibles* and *assurance* dimensions are absent.

Report on Section C

Because only a small number of students participated in this phrase of questionnaire review, there is no need to provide descriptive data on them. Individual libraries would likely substitute their own questions in this section. They might consider the inclusion of the following questions:

- Please estimate how many times you have used library computers or online services during this school term (daily, several times a week, once a week, less than once a week, or other [please specify]);
- Which category best describes you? (undergraduate student, graduate student, faculty, general staff, or other [please specify]);
- What general category best describes your area of academic study? (Arts and humanities, behavioral sciences, business, engineering, law, medical sciences, physical sciences, social sciences, undecided, or other [please specify]).

One of the pretested questions asked:
What type of disability do you have? (Please tick all that apply):

a. __ Blind/vision impaired	f. __ Mobility impaired
b. __ Deaf/hearing impaired	g. __ Speech/communication
c. __ Head injury	h. __ Specific learning
d. __ Medical	i. __ Other (please specify):
e. __ Mental health	

The question was dropped from future inclusion for the following reasons. First, more than one-fourth of the students did not answer the question. Second, students might not want to disclose their disabilities for research that does not pertain to legal entitlements. Third, false responses might emerge when students have compensated for certain conditions that they no longer regard as disabilities. Consequently, the question does not elicit useful information. It would be most difficult to group the data by each disability and to report that for students who are deaf/hearing impaired the following attributes appear in Quadrant 1 and for students with mental health problems these attributes appear in Quadrant 1, and so on. Clearly, the number of respondents would have to be quite large and type of disability might have to be factored into the research design.

Table 8.6
The Revised Set of Statements (Section A)

The library Web site
- Has content that is easy to view and read
- Has helpful animations to help me focus on information content
- Identifies contact people who will provide me with assistance
- Identifies useful services
- Provides library policies (e.g., regarding companion animals)

It is easy to
- Enter and exit the building
- Find staff to help me if I need assistance

The library provides networked computers
- That accept commands from my voice
- That generate a "roaming profile" so I can customize the screen to meet my needs
- With ergonomic keyboards

The online catalog
- Displays information in a clear and understandable manner
- Is an accurate source of information about all materials held by the library
- Provides access to material with the aid of speech synthesis

The library
- Embeds information about my specific needs into my student ID/library card
- Has text phones
- Has comfortable seating
- Has good toilet facilities that are clearly signposted
- Has good lighting
- Has elevators in good working order
- Has staff who assist me willingly in using the online catalog
- Has staff who assist me willingly in photocopying material
- Has staff who are available when I need them
- Has staff who are friendly and easy to talk to
- Has staff who communicate clearly (allow me to see their mouths as they speak)
- Has staff who fetch resources from inaccessible shelves
- Has staff who have been trained, e.g., in communicating with someone who lip-reads
- Has staff who keep information about my disability confidential
- Provides a quite study/rest area for students with disabilities
- Provides computer workstations for wheelchair access
- Provides extended loan periods (e.g., for reserve material)

CONCLUSION

The factor analysis had greater clarity than the data reported in the tables. However, quadrant analysis still offers a visual clarification to the data depicted in those tables. Although the results did not define some of the factors in sufficient detail, it is clear that we are moving in the right direction in the development of an appropriate data collection instrument, one in which individuals with disabilities provide self-reports and the library demonstrates that it is listening to *all* of its customers—whether or not they have disabilities. The next chapter continues the refinement of the revised service quality instrument. Table 8.6 identifies statements from which libraries might develop Section A of the data collection instrument. The chapter appendix provides the shell for the insertion of those statements (and others) and includes Section B and Section C; the final sections provide the opportunity to gather descriptive information on study participants.

> Technology has only increased our ability to provide services to those with disabilities.[7]

APPENDIX: SERVICE QUALITY: POTENTIAL STATEMENTS AND DIMENSIONS

SECTION A

Ideal Library	**Library XXX**
Directions: Based on your experiences as a user of library services, please think about the ideal kind of library that would deliver excellent service quality. Please indicate the extent to which you think such a library should possess the feature described by each of the statements listed below.	*Directions:* The same set of statements relate to your feelings about services that Library __ offers. For each statement, please show the extent to which you believe the library has the feature described by the statement.
The scale is 1 2 3 4 5 6 7 8 9 10	The scale is 1 2 3 4 5 6 7 8 9 10
If you feel a feature is **"of no importance"** for excellent libraries, circle the number "1" for **"strongly disagree."** On the other hand, if you feel a feature is **"of highest importance"** for excellent libraries, write the number "10," for **"strongly agree."**	If you feel a feature is **"of no importance"** for Library __ , circle the number "1" for **"strongly disagree."** On the other hand, if you feel a feature is **"of highest importance"** for Library __ , write the number "10," for **"strongly agree."**

	Ideal Library		Library XXX	
	If your feelings are less strong, write a number between "2" and "9."		If your feelings are less strong, write a number between "2" and "9."	
	Please skip a statement if it does not relate to your needs or disability.		**Please skip a statement if it does not relate to your needs or disability.**	
	SD = strongly disagree		SA = strongly agree	
	IN IDEAL LIBRARY		IN LIBRARY _XXX	
	SD	SA	SD	SA
	↕	↕	↕	↕
[insert desired statements from below]	1 2 3 4 5 6 7 8 9 10		1 2 3 4 5 6 7 8 9 10	

Choice of Statements

The library Web site

- Has an adjustable font size
- Has content that is easy to view and read
- Has either a TTY (text telephone) or TDD (telephone device for the deaf) phone number for making contact with the library
- Has helpful animations to help me focus on information content
- Has lettering and colors that are distinguishable and easy to see
- Has visible text and image captions (to help understand sound on the Web)
- Identifies contact people who will provide me with assistance
- Identifies useful services
- Is validated by an accessibility tool/service (e.g., Bobby Watchfire)
- Provides library policies (e.g., regarding companion animals)
- Separates text and graphics well
- Uses a voice-activated Web browser

It is easy to

- Enter and exit the library building
- Find my way around the library
- Find staff to help me if I need assistance
- Move from floor to floor or around the book stacks

The library provides networked computers

- That accept commands from my voice
- That allow me to work (e.g., using voice recognition software) without others hearing what I am doing (privacy)
- That generate a "roaming profile" so I can customize the screen to meet my needs
- That have screen magnification
- That have scanning and reading software to make printed and electronic texts more readable
- That have text-help Wordsmith (e.g., speech feedback, spelling help, and word pronunciation)
- With adaptive technology to which students with disabilities have priority access
- With Braille keypads
- With devices for connecting hearing aids to sound sources
- With ergonomic keyboards
- With letters on the keypads that are easy to read
- With screen monitors of 17 or 21 inches
- With synthesized speech

The online catalog

- Displays information in a clear and understandable manner
- Has easy-to-follow instructions
- Is an accurate source of information about all materials held by the library
- Provides access to material with the aid of refreshable Braille
- Provides access to material with the aid of speech synthesis

The library

- Creates user profiles that enable me to have access to enlarged page display (magnification of content on page)
- Embeds information about my specific needs into my student ID/library card
- Has adaptive mice
- Has amplified phones
- Has portable and fixed induction loops at help desks
- Has text phones
- Has clearly marked fire and emergency procedures
- Has color contrast between library furniture and the floors
- Has comfortable seating

- Has directional signs that are clear, legible, and accurate, and have color contrast
- Has directional signs that are in Braille
- Has electrical outlets for my laptop computer
- Has electronically adjustable foot rests
- Has electronically adjustable monitors
- Has electronically adjustable tables/chairs
- Has ergonomic chairs
- Has wrist rests
- Has good toilet facilities that are clearly signposted
- Has good toilet facilities that are located near study space
- Has good lighting
- Has elevators in good working order
- Has elevators that give audible signals for each floor
- Has staff who
  - Assist me willingly in using the online catalog
  - Assist me willingly in locating resources
  - Assist me willingly in photocopying material
  - Assist me willingly in retrieving resources from the shelves
  - Assist me willingly in using equipment
  - Are approachable and welcoming
  - Are available when I need them
  - Are courteous and polite
  - Are friendly and easy to talk to
  - Communicate clearly (allow me to see their mouth as they speak)
  - Fetch resources from inaccessible shelves (e.g., too high or low)
  - Have been trained, for example, in communicating with someone who lip-reads, guiding someone with a visual impairment, or supporting someone having an epileptic seizure
  - Keep information about my disability confidential
  - Know how to respond if a disability is disclosed to them
  - Let me finish my thought before they speak
  - Let my personal assistant borrow material on my behalf
  - Meet with me each year to discuss my needs
  - Treat my requests confidentially

- Offers guides in a range of accessible formats (e.g., large print, audio, and Braille)
- Provides access to individual study rooms
- Provides an adequate number of workstations in good working order
- Provides a quiet study/rest area for students with disabilities

- Provides computer workstations for wheelchair access
- Provides extended loan periods (e.g., for reserve material)
- Provides large print resources
- Scans material into electronic text for me (if copyright is not an issue)
- Sets aside books in advance for students who find it difficult to get to the library
- Supports students in getting texts put into Braille or onto audio tape

SECTION B

Directions: Listed below are eleven features pertaining to libraries and the services they offer. We would like to know how important each of these features is to you when you evaluate a library's quality of service. Please rank the list from *most* to *least important* to you, with "1" being *most important* and "11" being *least important.*

Features	Ranking
The appearance and functionality of the library's physical facilities and equipment.	_____
The library's willingness to help users find and retrieve needed resources.	_____
The knowledge, courtesy, and helpfulness of the library staff and the caring, individual attention the library provides its users.	_____
The ability to be independent in my search for relevant information.	_____
Assurance that information essential for completing course assignments is readily available.	_____
Timely, speedy, and easy access to material relevant to my course and research needs.	_____
A physical building that serves as a place of information-gathering, study, and reflection.	_____
Deep collections of relevant material—print and electronic—to meet my immediate needs.	_____
Ease of use (enlarged text, assistive technology).	_____
Web site aesthetics (e.g., appropriate colors, graphics, and font types).	_____
Customization/personalization service (e.g., receive e-mail announcements about the arrival of new books on topics of personal interest).	_____

SECTION C

[insert whatever questions get at the demographic characteristics of most interest to your library]

Thank you very much for participating in this study.

NOTES

1. Kateri Abeyta and Mary Mouton, "Know Your Audience: Guidelines to Develop Accessible Web Sites," *Colorado Libraries* 28, no. 4 (Winter 2002): 47–48.
2. Donna R. Euben, "Disabilities and the Academic Workplace," *Academe* 90 (September–October 2004): 86.
3. Ibid.
4. EndNote, which ResearchSoft (Philadelphia, PA) produces, enables its users to format bibliographic citations according to a wide variety of style preferences.
5. James Lynch, Robert Carver, Jr., and John Michael Virgo, "Quadrant Analysis as a Strategic Planning Technique in Curriculum Development and Program Marketing," *Journal of Marketing for Higher Education* 7 (1996): 17–32. See also Terry G. Vavra, *Improving Your Measurement of Customer Satisfaction: A Guide to Creating, Conducting, Analyzing, and Reporting Customer Satisfaction Measurement Programs* (Milwaukee, WI: ASQ Quality Press, 1997), 311–315.
6. Danuta A. Nitecki and Peter Hernon, "Measuring Service Quality at Yale University's Libraries," *The Journal of Academic Librarianship* 26 (July 2000): 259–273.
7. Rachel Wadham, "Accessible Technology," *Library Mosaics* 14 (January/February 2003): 18.

9

REFINEMENT OF THE DATA COLLECTION INSTRUMENT

Peter Hernon and Jennifer Lann

The voice of the customer must guide service improvement.[1]

Chapter 6 introduced Landmark College, which "is one of the only accredited colleges in the United States designed exclusively for students with dyslexia, attention deficit hyperactivity disorder [ADHD], or other specific learning disabilities." Since its entire student body has some form of documented learning disability and/or ADHD, the college does not have a special disability service department.[2] Its library is "committed to ensuring that . . . students can acquire the skills necessary to find, evaluate, and utilize all information, regardless of format. . . . The Library's service philosophy is one of teamwork, open-mindedness, confidentiality, and respect."[3] This library is probably not as different from other academic libraries as one might expect. Even though the library staff know that all of the students have some learning difference, they usually do not know a student's particular learning profile ahead of time. A student with dyslexia, for example, has some different challenges than a student with ADHD, and, just like at other academic libraries, most students do not announce their learning difficulties at the reference desk. As a result, the library relies on a universal design or best-instructional-practices approach to working with students. In other words, the instructional practices that work optimally for all students are particularly important for students who learn differently.

The college's faculty, staff, and students served as the population for an additional examination of the instrument highlighted in the previous chapter. The purpose of this pretest was to continue the development of a flexible instrument that provides libraries with meaningful information—relevant to the planning process and involving the entire institution in that process—and to review the features (section A) and dimensions (section B) of the emerging survey instrument. This chapter also shares basic information gathered from use of the instrument, and, like the previous chapter, it shows librarians ways to analyze and interpret evidence gathered from the application of the instrument. The chapter also sets up the next one on how to conduct the study and, it is hoped, to produce an acceptable response rate.

REVIEW OF THE DATA COLLECTION INSTRUMENT

The library director and two members of the reference staff conducted an in-depth review of the instrument tested in the previous chapter. They found that this instrument too heavily focused on physical disabilities and asked if they could expand its relevance and utility. Given that the instrument is intended to address local circumstances and needs, permission was granted. They then made substantial changes to the statements or features included in section A. Their intent was to include statements relevant to the community that the library served—in this case, primarily students with language-based learning disabilities and/or ADHD; a minority of students has nonverbal learning disabilities, Asperger's Syndrome, or traumatic brain injury. Clearly, the student population differs dramatically from the population found at the other test site—Victoria University in Wellington, New Zealand (see chapter 8).

While the Landmark College librarians eliminated questions that were exclusively applicable to persons with physical disabilities, they kept or modified those questions that apply to persons with LD and/or ADHD. For example, the question "The library has directional signs that are clear, legible, and accurate, and have color contrast" might be relevant not only for persons with visual impairments, but also for persons with dyslexia. Other statements were modified to be more familiar to the target group (e.g., replacing the term "adaptive technology" with "assistive technology") or to be more relevant to their needs (e.g., replacing "The library supports students in getting texts put into Braille or onto audiotape" with "The library supports students in getting texts put onto audiotape or into digital text format"). They reworded one statement to reflect a value that they have heard students with learning disabilities and/or ADHD express; they replaced "The library has staff who are courteous and polite" with "The library has staff who are courteous and respectful." They also added a few statements, listed below:

- The library Web site:
  - Is easy to navigate
- It is easy to:
  - Find where materials are located

- The online catalog:
  - º Is readable by text readable software
- The library:
  - º Has enough directional signs
  - º Offers materials with a variety of reading levels

The librarians also reformatted the survey for readability and clarity, listing the items in a table and including the rating scale at the top of each page of section A. Because students with dysgraphia might find writing numbers cumbersome due to difficulties with handwriting, they included the numbers one through ten for both the *Ideal Library* and the *Landmark College Library* columns, so that respondents needed only to circle the appropriate number.

Noting that the introductory explanation of the instrument was quite brief, Peter Hernon encouraged the librarians to develop a cover letter that explained the project, the value of the library listening to its community, and use of the information gathered to continue to improve services that the library provides the academic community. They decided to keep the cover letter brief for readability; instead providing the additional information in a campus-wide e-mail message about the project, as well as adding the following statement to the cover letter:

This survey considers the potential preferences of people with a wide variety of disabilities, and therefore not all of the questions may be relevant to your disability. The term "disability" is used in an Americans with Disabilities Act context and is not meant to imply judgment about your abilities or differences.

Such an acknowledgement may be important to many of the students at Landmark College who may prefer to think of their learning disability and/ or ADHD as a learning difference.

Because the survey involved members of the broad student population, the college's institutional review board required a confidentiality statement and release form, and accepted both the instrument and the data collection process. The board granted approval but inserted a reminder, the reliability of the instrument would require additional examination. Continued local review and testing of the instrument increase reliability.

THE PRETEST

For five days of one week (February 28 to March 4, 2005) and two days of the following week, the Landmark College Library distributed the survey to its students, as well as to faculty and staff members, some of whom have a diagnosed learning disability and/or ADHD. Table 9.1 lists the various means the library used to promote the study. As an incentive, participants were entered in a drawing for gift certificates to Amazon.com (three certificates of $75, $50, and $25 value for the purchase of books, music, DVDs, electronic games, clothing, and so on).

From a student population of 380, there were only thirty-five completed surveys, and five of these were from faculty and staff with a diagnosed learning disablility and/or ADHD. The response rate of 7.9 percent was notably low. The library director suspected that the low response rate was in part due to the fact that participation was voluntary. She discussed the survey turnout with some faculty and staff, who confirmed that voluntary survey completion at Landmark College tends not to produce a high response rate. She also

Table 9.1
Promotion of the Survey

Monday	Announced the survey on the Student Digest (a collection of the day's e-mail messages) with an attachment of the survey in Word and Kurzweil (text-to-speech software). The message advertised the Amazon.com drawing the library offered, briefly explained the purpose of the survey, and indicated three locations for receiving a copy of the survey (their mailboxes, electronic attachment to the e-mail message, and the front desk of the library).
Wednesday, Thursday, and Friday	The students received an e-mail reminder with the Word and Kurzweil files attached. Library staff varied the message in each e-mail, but retained the themes of helping the library and participating in the Amazon.com drawing.
The next Monday	Friday had been announced as the due date, but, this morning, the library e-mailed the students to extend the deadline to midnight that day. The library also resent the electronic copies of the survey.
Every day of data collection	The library posted image-rich color fliers about the survey and drawing throughout campus and updated those fliers with a piece of paper announcing the new deadline in bold-type face.
Every day of data collection	Library staff at the front desk invited people who came to the desk to fill out a survey, and the evening library assistant approached regular students when he saw them. He emphasized that as regular library users, their opinion was particularly important.
Every day of data collection	The survey was also advertised and attached to the Faculty and Staff Digests, and extra paper copies of the survey were available in the faculty mailroom.
The weekend	The shuttle bus driver asked students to complete a survey during their trip to local and distant towns.

reviewed the literature on survey research for additional insights and reinforced two critical issues identified in Table 9.2:

- Reduce the number of statements included (only ask those of greatest interest or value to library services); and
- Gain faculty buy-in to supporting the library with its data collection. Perhaps the faculty might be asked to have students complete the survey at the end of class. However, a complication is that there is so much to accomplish during class time, especially when severe weather conditions result in the cancellation of some classes. For this reason, Landmark College might consider survey completion in the fall, perhaps as part of a broader assessment day.

The response rate might also have been improved if the survey was also available online. Response rates for online versus paper surveys vary by institutional context,[4] but a recent study suggests that offering both format options is ideal.[5] Survey-participation rates at Landmark College are high whenever the surveys are administered to a captive audience, such as a class. Perhaps survey distribution might be linked to some type of information literacy instruction or, as mentioned above, an assessment day.

Also worth noting is that the Amazon.com gift certificate drawing may have been an inadequate incentive. Interestingly, a review of the survey-research literature indicates that incentives only positively affect response rates when they accompany the survey, thereby invoking the "norm of reciprocity."[6] Compensation contingent upon survey completion appears to have no effect on response rates, and a study of the effect of a lottery incentive on response rates among high school students yielded at best a mere increase in response rate of 2.3 percent. This study also used the incentive of an Amazon.com gift certificate drawing (this one for either $50, $100, $150, or $200, while the control group had no gift certificate incentive), and surprisingly, it was the $100 gift certificate incentive group that produced the highest response rate.[7]

According to the review of survey research, some of the library's survey promotion techniques that may have been effective include sending out the survey multiple times in multiple formats (albeit not online), and with a request to help the library, including some personal requests from library staff to regular patrons of the library.[8] In retrospect, the cover letter and e-mail messages could have emphasized this notion of help more, and a prenotification letter might also have increased response by previewing the survey and further underscoring the survey's relevance and the library's need for student input.[9] The survey cover letter might be further revised to include an explicit request for help.

Institutional context can also impact response rate,[10] and the characteristics of Landmark College's students may be unique due to their learning differences. Adults and college students with ADHD typically experience difficulty on focusing on low-interest activities.[11,12] For those students with ADHD

Table 9.2
Possible Reasons for Low Response

1. It probably would have helped to have the survey online. The email Digest message could directly link to the survey for students to complete and return the survey immediately.

2. The hurdles of printing the survey, going to the printer to pick it up, filling it out, and returning it to the library may have deterred some students from starting or completing the survey.

3. When they picked up the survey from their mailbox, they may have seen no urgency in its completion. Subsequently, they may have forgotten about it or decided not to participate.

4. Survey length can moderately decrease response rates (see Stephen R. Porter, "Survey Response Rates: What Works?" *Overcoming Survey Research Problems,* in *New Directions for Institutional Research* 121 (Spring 2004), 12). This negative impact on response rate may have been amplified by the disabilities of this particular student body. The form may have been appeared too long and complex for students with dyslexia to want to complete, and procrastination tendencies could have played a role for some students with ADHD. Some students who chose not to participate in the survey informed library staff that the survey was too long. A few students who were offered the survey on the weekend campus shuttle bus indicated that the survey was "work" that was not worth doing on their time off.

5. The page-long confidentiality statement/release form required by the institutional review board could have added to the perceived cumbersomeness and length of the survey. Confidentiality statements can lower response rates in surveys with non-sensitive information, perhaps because they might falsely imply that the survey will ask sensitive questions. (See Stephen R. Porter, "Survey Response Rates: What Works?," 15.)

6. The Amazon.com incentive may have been insufficient.

7. Student stress levels increase as they approach midterm examinations, and the survey might have seemed like one more to-do item on an overwhelming list of obligations.

8. Because many students only come to the library when their instructors send classes there, they might not feel like spending the time to give the library feedback. Survey salience can significantly affect response rate. (See Stephen R. Porter, "Survey Response Rates: What Works?," 14). Perhaps a survey about the library lacks relevance for many students. The majority of respondents (76.5 percent) indicated that they use the library at least once a week, and thus the library may be more important to them than a majority of their peers who may use the library less frequently.

9. Some members of the faculty and staff have stated that students are typically unresponsive to surveys unless they are asked to complete them during class time. Class-time distribution of surveys also allows students to receive immediate help with any confusion or questions they may have about a survey.

who were interested in the survey, their potential for distractibility, disorganization, and a difficulty with completing tasks[13,14] may have derailed their efforts to complete and return the survey. They may have a low tolerance for stress,[15] and therefore, distributing the survey just before mid-term examinations may have been poorly timed. It seems logical to assume that students with reading-based learning disabilities are likely to view a survey as more work than a student without any reading difficulty, be it language-based or attention-based. Adolescent students with learning disabilities "are viewed as poor or inefficient information processors" who have difficulty using the learning strategies necessary to plan and complete tasks effectively.[16] In a review of the learning disabilities literature, B. Keith Lenz and Donald D. Deshler indicate that learning-strategy instruction is recommended for these students,[17] and Landmark College takes such an approach. However, because Landmark College students may struggle with learning strategies and task completion due to their learning disabilities and/or ADHD, and because they work to learn and use these strategies as a key part of their academic work, a survey that requires them to harness their learning strategies may seem like too much work to be worth the extracurricular effort—particularly for those students who do not already view the library as an important part of their Landmark College experience.

FINDINGS

The low response rate eliminated the value of engaging in gap analysis and factor analysis to assess survey responses. Quadrant analysis, however, could still provide helpful information, even though the low response rate should still be recalled when using the results to inform service planning.

Quadrant Analysis of Statements

Because respondents were asked to skip any statement that did not relate to their information "needs or learning difference, or if [they did] not know how to respond," the number of responses for each of the thirty-seven statements in section A varied from twenty to thirty-five—the actual number of respondents. Furthermore, the placement of a statement in one of the four quadrants associated with quadrant analysis might have shifted if more students, faculty, and staff had participated in the study.

Given these caveats, eleven statements appeared in the first quadrant and seem to merit retention. These include:

- The online catalog
  - Has easy-to-follow instructions
  - Is an accurate source of information about all materials held by the library
  - Is readable by text readable software

- The library has good lighting
- The library provides adequate quiet study areas
- The library has staff who help me for a sufficient amount of time in
  - ○ Locating and retrieving material
  - ○ Photocopying material
- The library has staff who are available when I need them
- The library has staff who communicate clearly (allow me to see their mouths as they speak)
- The library has staff who keep information about my disability confidential
- The library has staff who know how to respond if a disability is disclosed to them
- The library supports students in getting texts put onto audiotape or into digital text format.

The library might improve on its delivery of the three statements in quadrant two:

1. It is easy to find where materials are located;
2. The library has ergonomic chairs and tables; and
3. The library has good toilet facilities that are clearly signposted.

The five statements in quadrant 3—perceived strengths that, because they are less valued, they might be revisited—include:

1. The library has comfortable seating;
2. The library has staff who help me for a sufficient amount of time in using the online public access catalog;
3. The library has staff who are courteous and respectful;
4. The library has staff who are approachable, friendly, and easy to talk to; and
5. The library offers materials in a range of accessible formats.

Despite the location of these items in quadrant 3—a quadrant that can suggest that resources might be more effectively allocated elsewhere—the Landmark College Library might choose to continue to maintain these attributes since most of them are low-cost, and the staff attributes are a part of basic public service. The library's Digital Text Services (scanning all required course texts into Kurzweil text-to-speech software format and providing access to online versions of text) is a high-cost service; however, the library also needs to consider the low response rate and the probability that the students who need digital text the most may not have participated in the survey, despite its availability in Kurzweil format, because of the work involved. In future administrations of the survey, a question could be added to section C (respondent characteristics) to inquire about Kurzweil and Digital Text Services use, and the library could make an effort to target those students who have requested digital versions of their course texts.

The remaining eighteen statements belong in quadrant 4 and merit review to see if the library should reallocate resources or improve on their delivery. For example, two questions about directional signs fell into this quadrant. Does the library have "enough" signs that are "clear, legible, and accurate, and have color content?" The library plans to facilitate student focus groups to explore some of the survey's questions from quadrants 2 and 4 in greater depth. For example, although signs are not rated as important, finding materials easily is rated as important but lacking. Would signs offset this lack, and if not, what else might? On the other hand, at this time, the library may not need to create user profiles that enable students and others to have access to an enlarged page display.

Section A concludes with the question "Are there any other expectations that you consider important when evaluating the quality of library service you receive?" If a respondent checked "Yes," the survey requested, "Please specify and assign a number between 1 and 10," and then a one-to-ten scale was listed twice; each time it was followed by a line for respondents to write an expectation. Most respondents checked "No," but among those who added expectations, some indicated a need to clarify whether they were rating the expectation as important, or rating how well the Landmark College Library met that expectation. This ambiguity could have been easily avoided by formatting question 6 as a table that mirrored the table preceding it, in which the respondent would write the expectation in the first column, circle the rating for the "ideal library" in the second column, and then circle the rating for the Landmark College Library in the final column. The survey instrument presented in the chapter appendix is revised accordingly.

Dimensions

Section B of the questionnaire identified eleven dimensions pertaining to libraries and the services they offer and asked the respondents to rank their importance from one to eleven (one as most important and eleven as least important). Of the thirty-three respondents who completed the section, thirteen (39.4%) did not follow instruments properly, but instead appeared to use the one-to-eleven scale as a rating scale rather than a ranking scale. For example, many assigned the number 1 to a majority of the dimensions. Some respondents limited themselves to the numbers 1 and 11, presumably because those were the only numbers explicitly listed.

The librarians hoped to avoid confusion by bolding the word "rank" in the suggestions, but in retrospect this revision may have been insufficient. Adding the bolded explanation, "(Please use each number only once in your ranking. This section uses a different scale from the previous section.)" may have helped to clarify the directions. An article from the *Journal of Learning Disabilities* recommends that changes in directions for tests given to mainstreamed students with learning disabilities should be highlighted by a change in format (such as bolding the word "rank"), as well as making it clearer by offering an example of an appropriate way to follow the directions.[18] This latter suggestion has its disadvantages: it could take up too much space if it were an example that illustrated ranking of non-library-service items, or it could unintentionally influence responses if it took the form of an added column labeled "Example of potential responses."

Turning to the twenty respondents who correctly followed the instructions, we calculated the mean for each of the eleven dimensions, added mean scores, and divided the total by eleven, giving a figure (5.5) useful for general comparative purposes. The means for four dimensions were less than the 5.5:

1. The library's willingness to help users find and retrieve needed resources (4.1);
2. The knowledge, courtesy, and helpfulness of the library staff and the caring, individual attention the library provides its users (4.4);
3. Timely, speedy, and easy access to material relevant to my course and research needs (4.4); and
4. Assurance that information essential for completing course assignments is readily available (5.4).

The other seven dimensions exceeded the 5.5:

1. Deep collections of relevant material—print, audiovisual, and electronic—to meet my immediate needs (5.7);
2. A physical building that serves as a place of information-gathering, study, and reflection (6.2);
3. The ability to be independent in my search for relevant information (6.3);
4. Ease of use (enlarged text, adaptive technology) (7.3);
5. The appearance and functionality of the library's physical facilities and equipment (7.9);
6. Customization/personalization service (e.g., receive e-mail announcements about the arrival of new books or topics of personal interest) (8.3.); and
7. Web site aesthetics (e.g., appropriate colors, graphics, and font types) (8.7).

Although more than one-third of the questionnaires had to be disregarded, three observations emerge. First, turning to the four dimensions that were less than the 5.5 figure, two of them deal with staff; these might be combined into a new dimension:

The knowledge, courtesy, and helpfulness of the library staff, including their willingness to help users find and retrieve needed resources; and the caring, individual attention they provide.

The other two dimensions relate to access to appropriate resources in the collections; these become a new dimension:

Timely, speedy, and easy access to material relevant for completing course assignments and meeting my research needs.

Second, "deep collections of relevant material" exceeded the 5.5 figure. It should not be regarded as unimportant because when asked if there were other expectations—ones not identified in the list of features in section A, respondents were most likely to mention collections being inadequate or outdated (e.g., in the sciences). These comments target the same areas in the collection that the librarians are already targeting as areas in need of focused collection development. The comments affirm the need for these collection development efforts and suggest that at least some of the Landmark College community would appreciate it if the librarians promoted these efforts and increased their solicitations for acquisitions requests.

Third, the customized/personalized service and Web site aesthetics ranked at the bottom of the list. Further research might suggest their removal from section B or their reconfiguration. We have reduced the number of dimensions from eleven to nine, and perhaps further investigations can refine the list even more. While the elimination of two dimensions might not prevent future confusion about how to rank dimensions (although we hope the addition of clarifying directions will), shortening section B may reduce the potential cognitive burden for students with learning disabilities and/or ADHD who may struggle with working-memory deficits.[19,20]

Respondent Characteristics

Of the respondents to this section of the questionnaire, twenty-six (76.5%) estimated their use of the library computers or online services during the school term as at least once a week; the mode (twelve) was several times a week. Four estimated their use at less than once a week, and another four explained that they either used library computers only when their laptop computers did not work or consulted library resources only when they had to work on research assignments.

When asked to explain the purpose of their visit to the library, the major reasons given were to either study (twenty-five responses) or work on a research assignment outside of class time (twenty-four responses). The next most frequently mentioned reason was for leisure activities (nineteen responses); however, everyone marking this category checked at least one of the other choices. Class visits were mentioned thirteen times, and a campus tour was indicated six times.

The respondents were predominately undergraduate students (twenty-nine); two were faculty members and three were members of the staff. The areas of study or work were given as business (nine respondents), arts (seven), communications (seven), and education (six); six people failed to identify a category.

CONCLUSION

Although the pretest encountered problems (e.g., the low response rate and the failure to follow the instructions), it still produced useful information and enabled the investigators to make further modifications in the questionnaire (see chapter appendix). These problems actually yielded insights, inspired from reflection and a review of the relevant survey research and learning disabilities literature that could potentially inform and improve other libraries' survey-promotion efforts. To highlight key insights about the response rate: it is likely to be increased by sending the survey multiple times and in multiple formats (print, Microsoft Word document, and Kurzweil text-to-speech file), but making it also available online may have increased response rates; distributing the survey to a captive audience in research instruction classes may have increased the response rate; and the use of Amazon.com gift-certificates as incentives—or any incentive contingent on survey completion—should be reconsidered. Confusion about the survey directions might be avoided in the future by elaborating on the directions in Section B.

In their added comments, it appears that some respondents want to be positive and not to be perceived as critical of the library and its services. Another observation is that this institution (like many others) lacks an ongoing culture of comprehensive community feedback to the library for the improvement of services. While many students have the opportunity to assess library research instruction during class visits, they are not regularly asked to assess other aspects of the library. Developing such a culture of feedback places the library in regular contact with the community served and makes it possible for the library to incorporate user opinion into service planning.

The disability-focused service quality questionnaire is directed at students, be they undergraduate or graduate, regardless of the country in which they receive their education. The instrument might also be aimed at faculty and staff who have declared their disabilities; it would be impossible to identify the population that has refused to declare a disability or that has a hidden disability. The instrument is flexible and can be adopted to meet local needs and priorities. Over time, if libraries want to benchmark the service expectations of students with disabilities across institutions, they might do so; however, such an effort would require that all libraries retain certain statements and that benchmarking only focuses on those statements (features) and perhaps dimensions, once the number and characterization of the nine dimensions have been the subject of further scrutiny.

Great service is not a pipe dream.[21]

APPENDIX: SERVICE QUALITY: LIBRARY COLLECTIONS AND SERVICES FOR THOSE WITH DISABILITIES

This survey considers the potential preferences of people with a wide variety of disabilities and therefore not all of the questions may be relevant to your disability. The term "disability" is used in an Americans with Disabilities Act context and is not meant to imply judgment about your abilities or differences.

There are no right or wrong answers. All we are interested in is a number that truly conveys your feelings regarding excellent service quality in libraries. Your individual response will be kept confidential but will help us to understand your expectations for library services and to help inform our planning processes.

Please help the Landmark College Library to understand your library preferences better so that we can better ensure that the Library serves you optimally.

SECTION A

Ideal Library	Landmark College Library
Directions: Based on your experiences as a user of library services, please think about the ideal kind of library that would deliver excellent service quality. Please indicate the extent to which you think such a library should possess the feature described by each of the statements listed below.	*Directions*: The same set of statements relate to your feelings about the services offered by the Landmark College Library. For each statement, please show the extent to which you believe the Library has the feature described by the statement.
The scale is 1 2 3 4 5 6 7 8 9 10 Strongly Disagree/ Strongly Agree/of No Importance Highest Importance	The scale is 1 2 3 4 5 6 7 8 9 10 **Strongly Disagree** **Strongly Agree**
If you feel a feature is **"of no importance"** for excellent libraries, circle the number **"1"** for **"strongly disagree."**	Circling a **"1"** means that you **"strongly disagree"** that the library has that feature.
If you feel a feature is **"of highest importance"** for excellent libraries, circle the number **"10"** for **"strongly agree."**	Circling a **"10"** means that you **"strongly agree"** that the library has that feature.

Ideal Library	Landmark College Library
If your feelings are less strong, write a number between 2 and 9.	If your feelings are less strong, write a number between 2 and 9.
Please skip a statement if it does not relate to your needs or learning difference, or if you don't know how to respond.	*Please skip a statement if it does not relate to your needs or learning difference, or if you don't know how to respond.*

	Ideal Library	Landmark College Library
1. The library Web site		
a. Can be easily read aloud by text reader software	1 2 3 4 5 6 7 8 9 10	1 2 3 4 5 6 7 8 9 10
b. Has content that is easy to view and read	1 2 3 4 5 6 7 8 9 10	1 2 3 4 5 6 7 8 9 10
c. Has lettering and colors that are distinguishable and easy to see	1 2 3 4 5 6 7 8 9 10	1 2 3 4 5 6 7 8 9 10
d. Identifies useful services	1 2 3 4 5 6 7 8 9 10	1 2 3 4 5 6 7 8 9 10
e. Is easy to navigate	1 2 3 4 5 6 7 8 9 10	1 2 3 4 5 6 7 8 9 10
2. It is easy to		
a. Find staff to help me if I need assistance	1 2 3 4 5 6 7 8 9 10	1 2 3 4 5 6 7 8 9 10
b. Find where materials are located	1 2 3 4 5 6 7 8 9 10	1 2 3 4 5 6 7 8 9 10
3. The library provides networked computers		
a. That allow me to work privately	1 2 3 4 5 6 7 8 9 10	1 2 3 4 5 6 7 8 9 10
b. With assitive technology for students with disabilities	1 2 3 4 5 6 7 8 9 10	1 2 3 4 5 6 7 8 9 10
c. With ergonomic keyboards and mice	1 2 3 4 5 6 7 8 9 10	1 2 3 4 5 6 7 8 9 10
4. The online catalog		
a. Displays information in a clear and understandable manner	1 2 3 4 5 6 7 8 9 10	1 2 3 4 5 6 7 8 9 10
b. Has easy-to-follow instructions	1 2 3 4 5 6 7 8 9 10	1 2 3 4 5 6 7 8 9 10

	Ideal Library	Landmark College Library
c. Is an accurate source of information about all materials held by the library	1 2 3 4 5 6 7 8 9 10	1 2 3 4 5 6 7 8 9 10
d. Is readable by text readable software	1 2 3 4 5 6 7 8 9 10	1 2 3 4 5 6 7 8 9 10

5. The Library

	Ideal Library	Landmark College Library
a. Creates user profiles that enable me to have access to enlarged page display	1 2 3 4 5 6 7 8 9 10	1 2 3 4 5 6 7 8 9 10
b. Embeds information about my specific needs into my student ID/library card	1 2 3 4 5 6 7 8 9 10	1 2 3 4 5 6 7 8 9 10
c. Has comfortable seating	1 2 3 4 5 6 7 8 9 10	1 2 3 4 5 6 7 8 9 10
d. Has enough directional signs	1 2 3 4 5 6 7 8 9 10	1 2 3 4 5 6 7 8 9 10
e. Has directional signs that are clear, legible, and accurate, and have color contrast	1 2 3 4 5 6 7 8 9 10	1 2 3 4 5 6 7 8 9 10
f. Has ergonomic chairs and tables	1 2 3 4 5 6 7 8 9 10	1 2 3 4 5 6 7 8 9 10
g. Has good toilet facilities that are clearly signposted	1 2 3 4 5 6 7 8 9 10	1 2 3 4 5 6 7 8 9 10
h. Has good lighting	1 2 3 4 5 6 7 8 9 10	1 2 3 4 5 6 7 8 9 10
i. Has library has staff who help me for a sufficient amount of time in	1 2 3 4 5 6 7 8 9 10	1 2 3 4 5 6 7 8 9 10
• Locating and retrieving material	1 2 3 4 5 6 7 8 9 10	1 2 3 4 5 6 7 8 9 10
• Photocopying material	1 2 3 4 5 6 7 8 9 10	1 2 3 4 5 6 7 8 9 10
• Using equipment	1 2 3 4 5 6 7 8 9 10	1 2 3 4 5 6 7 8 9 10
• Using the online public access catalog	1 2 3 4 5 6 7 8 9 10	1 2 3 4 5 6 7 8 9 10
j. Has staff who are available when I need them	1 2 3 4 5 6 7 8 9 10	1 2 3 4 5 6 7 8 9 10
k. Has staff who are courteous and respectful	1 2 3 4 5 6 7 8 9 10	1 2 3 4 5 6 7 8 9 10
l. Has staff who are approachable, friendly and easy to talk to	1 2 3 4 5 6 7 8 9 10	1 2 3 4 5 6 7 8 9 10
m. Has staff who communicate clearly (allow me to see their mouths as they speak)	1 2 3 4 5 6 7 8 9 10	1 2 3 4 5 6 7 8 9 10

	Ideal Library	Landmark College Library
5. The Library		
n. Has staff who keep information about my disability confidential	1 2 3 4 5 6 7 8 9 10	1 2 3 4 5 6 7 8 9 10
o. Has staff who know how to respond if a disability is disclosed to them	1 2 3 4 5 6 7 8 9 10	1 2 3 4 5 6 7 8 9 10
p. Offers materials in a range of accessible formats	1 2 3 4 5 6 7 8 9 10	1 2 3 4 5 6 7 8 9 10
q. Offers materials with a variety of reading levels	1 2 3 4 5 6 7 8 9 10	1 2 3 4 5 6 7 8 9 10
r. Provides an adequate number of assistive technology work-stations in good working order	1 2 3 4 5 6 7 8 9 10	1 2 3 4 5 6 7 8 9 10
s. Provides adequate quiet study areas	1 2 3 4 5 6 7 8 9 10	1 2 3 4 5 6 7 8 9 10
t. Supports students in getting texts put onto audio tape or into digital text format	1 2 3 4 5 6 7 8 9 10	1 2 3 4 5 6 7 8 9 10

6. **Are there any other expectations that you consider important to you when evaluating the quality of library service you receive?**

___ No

___ Yes (Please specify) and assign a number between 1 and 10.

Expectation	Ideal Library	Landmark College Library
	1 2 3 4 5 6 7 8 9 10	1 2 3 4 5 6 7 8 9 10
	1 2 3 4 5 6 7 8 9 10	1 2 3 4 5 6 7 8 9 10

SECTION B

Directions: Listed below are nine features pertaining to libraries and the *services* they offer. We would like to know how important each of these features is to you when you evaluate a library's quality of service.

Please **rank** the list from most to least important to you.

1 = most important to you   9 = least important to you

(Please use each number only once in your ranking. This section uses a different scale from the previous section.)

Features	Ranking
The appearance and functionality of the library's physical facilities and equipment	_____
The knowledge, courtesy, and helpfulness of the library staff in helping users find and retrieve needed resources; and the caring, individual attention the library provides its users	_____
The ability to be independent in my search for relevant information	_____
Timely, speedy, and easy access to material relevant for completing course assignments and meeting my research needs	_____
A physical building that serves as a place of information-gathering, study, and reflection	_____
Deep collections of relevant material—print, audiovisual, and electronic—to meet my immediate needs	_____
Ease of use (enlarged text, adaptive technology)	_____
Web site aesthetics (e.g., appropriate colors, graphics, and font types).	_____
Customization/personalization service (e.g., receive e-mail announcements about the arrival of new books on topics of personal interest)	_____

SECTION C

1. Please estimate how many times you have used library computers or online services during this school term.

   a. ___ Daily

   b. ___ Several times a week

   c. ___ Once a week

   d. ___ Less than once a week

   e. ___ Other (please specify):

2. Please indicate the purpose of your library visit (please check all that apply)

   a. ___ Campus tour

   b. ___ Class visit

c. ___ Research assignment (outside of class time)

d. ___ Study/Non-research

e. ___ Leisure

3. Which category best describes you?

a. ___ Undergraduate student

b. ___ Graduate student

c. ___ Faculty

d. ___ General Staff

e. ___ Other (please specify):

4. What general category best describes your area of academic study?

a. ___ Arts

b. ___ Business

c. ___ Communications

d. ___ Education

e. ___ Humanities

f. ___ Life sciences

g. ___ Medical sciences

h. ___ Social sciences

i. ___ Undecided

j. ___ Other (please specify):

Thank you very much for participating in this study.

NOTES

1. Leonard L. Berry, *On Great Service: A Framework for Action* (New York: The Free Press, 1995), 59.
2. Landmark College, "About Landmark" (Putney, VT: Landmark College, 2005). Available at http://www.landmark.edu/about/index.html (accessed March 11, 2005).
3. Landmark College Library, "Welcome to the Library" (Putney, VT: Landmark College, 2005). Available at http://www.landmark.edu/Library/index.html (accessed March 11, 2005).
4. Stephen R. Porter, "Survey Response Rates: What Works?" *New Directions for Institutional Research* (special issue, *Overcoming Survey Research Problems*) 121 (Spring 2004), 10.
5. Linda J. Sax, Shannon K. Gilmartin, and Alyssa N. Bryant, "Assessing Response Rates and Nonresponse Bias in Web and Paper Surveys," *Research in Higher Education* 44 (August 2003), 423.

6. Porter, "Survey Response Rates: What Works?," 13.
7. Stephen R. Porter and Michael E. Whitcomb, "Understanding the Effect of Prizes on Response Rates," *New Directions for Institutional Research* (special issue, *Overcoming Survey Research Problems*) 121 (Spring 2004): 51–62.
8. Porter, "Survey Response Rates: What Works?"
9. Ibid., 10.
10. Ibid., 16.
11. Paul H. Wender, *ADHD: Attention-Deficit Hyperactivity Disorder in Children and Adults* (Oxford: Oxford University Press, 2000), 161.
12. Lynda J. Katz, "Students with ADHD in Higher Education" in *Learning Disabilities in Higher Education and Beyond: International Perspectives,* edited by Susan A. Vogel, Gila Vogel, Varda Sharoni, and Orit Dahan (Baltimore: York Press, 2003), 159.
13. Wender, *ADHD,* 162, 166.
14. Katz , "Students with ADHD in Higher Education," 159.
15. Wender, *ADHD,* 168.
16. B. Keith Lenz and Donald D. Deshler, "Adolescents with Learning Disabilities: Revisiting *The Educator's Enigma,*" in *Learning about Learning Disabilities,* third edition, edited by Bernice Wong (San Diego, CA: Elsevier Academic Press, 2004), 542.
17. Ibid., 542.
18. Suzanne Salend and Spencer J. Salend, "Adapting Teacher-Made Tests for Mainstreamed Students," *Journal of Learning Disabilities* 18 (June/July 1985): 373–375.
19. Virginia W. Berninger, "The Reading Brain in Children and Youth: A Systems Approach," in *Learning about Learning Disabilities,* 222.
20. Russell Barkley, *ADHD and the Nature of Self-control* (New York: Guilford Press, 1997).
21. Berry, *On Great Service,* 7.

10

———•••••———

CONDUCTING YOUR OWN STUDY

Philip Calvert

If a survey is worth doing at all, it is worth doing well.[1]

The purpose of this chapter is to assist those librarians and disability office staff who want to apply the service quality instrument as presented in chapters 8 and 9, and who want to include some of the statements identified in chapter 12. Peter Hernon and Ellen Altman identify the steps in conducting a survey. The seventeen steps they identify collapse into five general groupings: plan, identify the customers or population to study, construct and ask the questions, edit and archive the data, and analyze and present the results.[2] To their list, we would add, "apply the results to continuous quality improvement." Nonetheless, we encourage readers to review some basic texts and to discuss data collection with researchers who deal with students and other disability groups before they undertake a study.[3] They should also seek to develop an ongoing relationship with the population they serve in order to get the community to accept the imposition of completing the survey and to share perceptions that are relevant to planning library services. Finally, it merits mention that surveys provide self-reports about what respondents want to say or believe to be true. There are other means of gathering self-reports and to provide direct evidence about how individuals gather information. This chapter, however, focuses on self-reports as reflected in surveys.

THE FIRST STEP

Before conducting a survey the essential question that must be asked is, "What do we need to know?" Useful surveys are tightly focused on a set target, and service quality assessment is no exception. A general service quality survey might ask two questions:

1. Where are the most significant weaknesses in our overall provision of service quality?
2. On what matters do we value customer input?

There might be a narrower investigation that addresses one aspect of the total service, such as service quality in the audiovisual suite or service quality as perceived by the science or business faculty or students. Even when the aim is to determine the quality of library service provided to students with disabilities, there is still an opportunity to narrow the focus, for instance, to students with a visual disability or those with learning differences. The choice belongs to those conducting the survey and the areas which they want to address as part of continuous quality improvement.

As with any survey project, planning must precede other activities. Surveys not only require the design of the instrument, which is unfortunately the only concern of some inexperienced librarian researchers, but also address matters such as getting ethical approval, seeking funding, and setting a timeline for conducting the survey and reporting the results. Most colleges and universities have one or more ethics committees that must approve, or at the least, give advice on, applications to conduct research. It may be considered that a library survey need not fall under the auspices of an ethics committee, but all surveys use human subjects and if those subjects are members of a disadvantaged group then ethical issues are sure to arise. If no member of the ethics committee wants to comment then there will be groups that can be approached for advice (e.g., an advocacy association).

Initially, this chapter will discuss printed questionnaires for data collection. Elizabeth M. Forsyth wanted to examine service quality dimensions for disability services provided by the Australian government and chose to use a questionnaire rather than interviews for the following reasons: time availability, transport and communication problems for the people being questioned, and her need to ensure "distance" from the process of data collection (she worked in the organization she was surveying).[4] The budget will have to cover the printing of the survey forms, plus envelopes and postage if the survey is to be posted out. A. N. Oppenheim notes that the inclusion of a stamped addressed envelope will increase the response rate because no potential respondent wants to pay for the postage on someone else's survey.[5] Most likely there will be labor costs even if library staff conduct the whole survey. Perhaps one or more research or student assistants will be needed to assist with printing forms and the stuffing of envelopes, and the more demanding tasks of data entry and data analysis. If the intention is to conduct some moderately detailed data analysis then it will be necessary to ensure that a member of staff has the skills to use a statistical software package such as SPSS, or else it will be necessary to hire someone for the project.

The timeline has to consider the best time to conduct a survey in an academic institution. It is widely accepted that the best time lies in the middle of an academic term, not too close to the start when new students do not know much about the library, and not too close to the end when the pressures of examinations and paper and project completion absorb almost all of a student's attention. The timeline needs to consider matters such as staff review (perhaps conducted by means of a focus group interview), ethics approval, and the design and piloting of the survey instrument. Careful attention should be given to the cover letter and how the survey will be promoted and how the staff will phrase the imposition and report back to the community on the results—including the actions they took. All of these matters need to be completed before the full survey gets underway.

TARGET POPULATION AND DISTRIBUTING THE SURVEY

If this chapter were designed as a flowchart, the first bifurcation in the diagram would occur with a question about privacy. A key question is, "What is permitted and forbidden in a country's privacy legislation, and does it affect a library's ability to conduct a survey of students with disabilities?" In New Zealand the Privacy Act of 1993 places severe constraints on accessing data held in institutional databases.[6] Because personal information, such as contact details for students with disabilities (e.g., postal addresses and e-mail addresses), may be covered by the legislation, when a person provides an organization with personal information, he or she may need to sign a declaration that offers some protection of the data and assurance that the data will not be used unethically. Typically, the declaration describes the purposes to which the data will be used, and, in some countries, in the case of a library, the declaration may be written in a relatively general way to cover use of the data in the library's circulation system, but often no more than that. The legislation forbids the organization to use the data for purposes other than those agreed to when the person signs the consent form. Many New Zealand libraries have not included adequate wording in the form to allow personal information to be used in more general management activities, such as sending evaluation or promotional material to customers. Even if this had been included in the consent form, it is unlikely it could be interpreted to mean using the data for research conducted for academic purposes, even if by one of the organization's own staff—although this is the sort of grey area often left open to interpretation.

Organizations cannot simply write sweeping statements of purpose that allow them to use the personal information in multiple ways at the discretion of the library management. So, if the intention is to conduct a service quality survey, is it possible to use the library's database for that purpose? This is the first question. Even so, will the library have details of which people consider themselves to have disabilities? If they do, and this is coded into the database, then it might be possible to use this information, but in New Zealand no libraries have such data. That information will be held, as much as any organization holds it, by the university's disability support service, a separate part of the university's organizational structure that is likely to be part of a students' services group (the names will vary). This group would almost certainly not release any personal information to another agency (this is forbidden by the Privacy Act of 1993 unless the person agrees to such divulgence when signing the consent form). Even so, students are not obliged to register with a disability service, so even that database will be incomplete, should it be possible to access it. The New Zealand case suggests that no complete list of students with disabilities exists simply because registration is voluntary and the evidence given by staff of disability services suggests that students sometimes choose not to register. The only conclusion to draw from this is that if the survey is not conducted by a part of the organization that already holds the necessary personal information and the right to use it for a survey, then some other way of finding respondents must be found. This will be the situation in many countries with privacy legislation similar to that of New Zealand, such as the United Kingdom, and the countries of the European Union.[7]

In the case of the United States, it is best that the library planning the study meet with the institution's disability office, the human subjects committee, and perhaps the college or university attorney to review the steps to take to comply with federal and state laws. Similar to the situation in New Zealand, there will be no listing of everyone on campus with a disability; there is only a list of those students who have declared their disability to the office of disability services. Library staff, however, will not have access to that list. They will need to meet with staff at the disability office to discuss how to identify a relevant study population, knowing that the number does not include those students who do not want to register with the office of disability services. The lack of such a list, and having no means of recording those who have responded, presents problems for conducting a survey, because there is no easy means to follow-up nonresponse. Those conducting a survey will need to be aware of this and allow for lower than hoped for response rates.

INCENTIVES

It may seem inappropriate to discuss incentives even before the instrument itself is ready, but the planning process should include preparations to ensure the best response rate possible, which is why researchers must make an early decision on whether or not to use incentives. If the researchers seek funding, it is likely that the incentives will be part of the financial support that is requested. If the researchers comprise library staff, it is possible that library funds might cover a modest incentive. A small amount of money, perhaps given as a voucher, is suitable as an incentive and will likely increase the response rate. Research conducted at the University of Otago, New Zealand, into student drinking patterns, sent a prenotice letter with a token gift (a 40-cent pen) and an invitation to complete an e-mail survey. They reported, "The pen and the pre-notice were positively remarked upon by several participants."[8]

There has been no conclusive evidence that incentives increase the response rate for library surveys, but intuitively it makes sense, and those researchers who have offered incentives know from casual comments that even a small amount of money makes a difference. Phil Edwards and his colleagues conducted a meta-review of 292 trials with the intention of identifying methods reported as increasing response rates to postal questionnaires. They found that offering an incentive (usually money) increased the odds of a response, though perhaps curiously, the incentive did not have to be conditional upon a response.[9] There are no ethical issues resulting from offering a small incentive. Should the researchers intend offering a large incentive then they should consult with an ethics committee as to its appropriateness.

THE SURVEY INSTRUMENT

Chapters 8 and 9 described the development of an instrument that can be used with students (as well as faculty and staff) with disabilities. After a lengthy process of scanning the literature and consultation with experts, we arrived at the list of eighty-four statements for the New Zealand study, with each statement describing library service quality as the individual customer will experience it. The list (as well as the one contained in chapter 9) included statements describing the library's service from the point of view of someone with a disability. However, the list of statements contained in chapter 12 recognizes that students (as well as faculty and others) may have hidden disabilities and want to be treated like everyone else; they do not want to receive special treatment. Thus, library staff can review the statements in the three chapters as they decide which ones are most relevant to their situation. They might even substitute other statements or focus on a particular group, such as students (and faculty) with a visual disability. Altogether, twenty-six statements in chapter 8 deal with some aspect of service to students with some visual impairment or full blindness. Examples include:

- The library Web site separates text and graphics well; and
- The library has directional signs in Braille.

To these can be added other statements that deal with disabilities in a general way or that describe service quality as all the library's customers experience it. Because library users often have to consult the online public access catalog, a useful statement might be "The online catalog has easy-to-follow instructions."

The testing of the instrument at Victoria University of Wellington (New Zealand) did not reveal any particular problems with the terminology used in the statements. Nonetheless, all statements should be reviewed with staff at the office of disability service to prevent the use of unnecessary jargon and of terms unfamiliar to the intended respondents. A 1991 survey sent to people in New Zealand with a disability discovered that some of the terms used lacked an explanation, and this lack of clarification was confusing for recipients. As a consequence, the value of the results was compromised. Some terms might be familiar to anyone concerned about disability issues, but others (e.g., "independent living," "mobility," and "travel") might be confusing.[10]

DETAILED FORM DESIGN

Instead of inserting the numbers from "1" to "10" in the printed survey instrument and then asking the respondents to circle the number that best matched their expectations or perception of performance for a statement, we suggest that two open boxes be used instead and the respondents asked to write in a number between "1" and "10" that matched their expectations or perceptions of performance. There are two reasons for this approach. First, if the numbers were included in the printed instrument, they would have to be in small font size (perhaps ten-point) and would therefore be difficult for someone with a visual disability to see. Second, the form looks much cleaner with the numbers removed and perhaps more likely to encourage a response. On the other hand, chapter 9 offers a counterargument and favors the inclusion of the numbers. Clearly, the psychology of response is difficult to assess, but, as has already been stated, disability means time limitations and what appears to be a long survey will easily discourage those with a disability and hence lower response rates. Intuitively, this makes sense. Consequently, the instrument should be short.

In the original SERVQUAL, Valarie A. Zeithaml, A. Parasuraman, and Leonard L. Berry included two types of questions on the dimensions of service quality.[11] First, all available dimensions are listed and the respondent is asked to give each one a score, with the total given across all dimensions expected to add up to 100 (see Section B of the instrument). Second, all available dimensions are listed and the respondents are asked to indicate which one is most important to them and which one is least important to them. Those disability advocates and staff within national disability organizations and university offices of disability services we consulted informed us that some people in the target population, such as those with learning differences, would find such questions too difficult and time-consuming to complete. As a result, we compressed Section B of the service quality questionnaire to one question in which we listed all the available dimensions and asked the respondents to rank them in order of importance, from most important to least important. Independently, Elizabeth M. Forysth asked the same style of question in her study of employment services for the disabled in Australia. She used this question to verify comprehension of the other questions, and

"While this alone would not allow the same level of sophistication in analysis, it ensured that consideration was given to the importance of one variable against another."[12]

Oppenheim pointed out that a person's perception of whether or not a questionnaire is too long is influenced by factors such as how interested he or she is in the topic and whether a prepaid envelope is provided.[13] Consequently, the library director and head of the office of disability services might co-sign the cover letter assuring potential respondents of the importance they attach to the survey and the possibilities for improving services that will follow from the results. That letter should emphasize the organizational value attached to completion of the survey.

PRINTED FORM

Printed survey forms should be legible. There are some simple suggestions for the design of printed materials for people with sight disabilities:

- Use at least a twelve-point font in a sans-serif font (e.g., Helvetica);
- Make the structure of the text apparent by the use of heading, spaces, numbering, bullets, and other devices;
- Use directive clues such as bold type, underlining, and italics; and
- Maintain a high contrast between the text and its background.

The survey instrument that we used in chapter 8 included light shading of every second statement to make each line clearly separate from the ones either side of it. Again, this gave the form a clean appearance that was intuitively beneficial. The only difficulty discovered was that the shading did not photocopy well; in fact, the type in the shaded areas becomes illegible after photocopying. This is not a significant obstacle if laser printing, rather than simple photocopying, is used because the results from a laser are sharp and legible.

However useful this advice is for the design of a survey instrument for the sight disabled, many students with disabilities have no problems reading standard printed materials. Clearly, there is a balancing act to follow. Part of that balancing act is recognition that a general survey may have to make allowances for students with different types of disabilities. Thus, one version of the instrument may not satisfy everyone.

The survey instrument must be delivered to the intended respondents, or deposited at a chosen location, together with all other necessary information, including a covering information sheet explaining the purpose of the research and its benefits, the respondent's rights, an assurance of anonymity, any information about incentives, how to return the completed form (e.g., put into the stamped addressed envelope and place in a mail box, or deposit it at certain locations in the library and around campus), a note on how feedback will be supplied or can be obtained, and finally how to contact someone in the survey team for further information. If the matter of informed consent is raised prior to the conduct of the survey, a sentence should be included in the information sheet along the lines of "By completing and returning this questionnaire you have given your informed consent to participation in this survey."

WEB-BASED AND E-MAIL SURVEYS

Those institutions using LibQUAL+™ might want to develop a Web-based equivalent to the instrument intended for those with disabilities. However, a number of issues would have to be resolved prior to its adoption. Examples of these issues include the extent to which font size is adjustable for those needing large print (e.g., a font size of twenty-point), and the amount of time it would take them to complete the form digitally. Clearly, before using a Web version, the researchers should scrutinize the literature and discuss the issues with knowledgeable personnel. It might be necessary to have different versions of the same instrument, each of which is available in a different font size.

There is fairly widespread availability of screen reading software that can interpret and read text. Unfortunately, in some versions of PDF (portable document format) there are still problems for the software to handle, and the professional advice we received was to avoid this format, at least until there is a degree of certainty that *all* screen reading software will be able to cope with *all* PDF versions.

Jennifer Horwath reports on a research project that demonstrates how a survey can be distributed by e-mail to people who are blind or visually impaired.[14] The initial call for respondents was sent out on an e-mail distribution list of the Canadian National Institute for the Blind, Library for the Blind. The survey population became: (1) those who were comfortable with using the Internet, and (2) those who were willing to participate. Thus, the researchers did not have the names and addresses of people in the target population; however, it is fair to point out that only eleven respondents took part in the survey and that data collection was not used for improving the service of a particular library. The survey, sent out by e-mail, with respondents completing it online and returning it, was long (124 questions)—longer than the instrument we used to preview service quality in libraries. Respondents were asked to give ratings as their answers, similar to entering a number in response to statements listed in the service quality survey. Horwath's study provides supporting evidence for the belief that libraries could conduct the service quality survey with the use of e-mail, but they may have to make allowance for respondents with different disabilities. Again, one form may not meet all user needs for effective and efficient completion.

The use of Web-based surveys has increased since their first appearance in the late 1990s. Some Web surveys involve nonprobability sampling in which respondents are completely self-selected or comprise volunteer respondents. If the library only seeks general indications of service quality leading to a more thorough analysis, then a nonprobability survey is sufficient. For purposes of strongly supporting a point, perhaps to the institution's administration, a probability survey might be more desirable (though conducting a probability survey does not guarantee representativeness because nonresponse can threaten the inferential value of these surveys).[15] Using the Web, a probability survey can be:

- An intercept survey. Such surveys are often conducted on the street (street intercepts), in shopping malls (mall intercepts), or in retail outlets themselves, or in any space where there is a good representation of target consumers. They are carried out by trained interviewers who deliver a short (five- to twenty-minute) questionnaire concerning the consumer's behavior, habits, preference, or perceptions. On the Web, this kind of survey could be random, and simply "pop up" on the user's screen.
- A survey that obtains respondents from an e-mail request. This kind of survey is very useful for a subset of the population with very high coverage, and this would include students with disabilities. Access must be controlled to prevent multiple completions by the same respondents, or passing the survey along to others (e.g., friends) to complete.
- A mixed-mode survey in which the Web is one option.
- A survey using a prerecruited panel of the target population as a probability sample.[16]

The intercept survey might poll every nth visitor to a Web site (a systematic sample). Should there be a specific service for students with disabilities that has its own Web site, this could be a suitable method, for it is unlikely that many uninterested people will visit that site. The use of the mixed-mode survey has considerable merit when librarians survey people with disabilities. As the range of disabilities is so great, it is almost impossible to find a single method that meets all needs equally well. Because a well-designed Web survey form can be read aloud by suitable software, this method will be good for those with significant visual disabilities. If there is at least one other mode that caters to other disabilities, this should work well, bearing in mind that the use of two different methods must be allowed for in the data analysis. Finally, gaining respondents from an e-mail request generally gets a low response and that is a problem if the target population is already small.

Chapters 2 and 7 cite additional works that offer other suggestions for the design and development of Web sites suitable for people with disabilities. Some, but not all, of the principles identified in these works apply to Web-based survey design for the same population. The purpose of a survey is to elicit responses, and that is best done using forms that are easy to read and comprehend, so the emphasis is on a clean design that is easy to read by people with visual disabilities, or that can be read by common screen-reading software packages. A decent-sized type font is an obvious place to start, and making it possible to increase the size of the text on screen if the reader chooses to do so is advisable. The survey might be available in html rather than PDF unless the researcher is positive that all potential respondents have access to software that can read the PDF. Other advice includes the avoidance of unnecessary graphics, frames on the screen, and forms that are difficult to read. As discussed in chapter 7, it is possible to check a Web site for accessibility compliance simply by using the Bobby™ Web site.[17]

The issue of privacy must be addressed when using a Web-based survey because it is possible to collect information about the respondents without their knowledge. Because some potential respondents will know this they might be unwilling to provide a response. A statement in the covering information sheet covering the survey guaranteeing that no personal information will be collected is therefore essential.

The use of Web-based surveys may appeal to researchers, but there are some points to remember. It is impossible to add personal touches to a Web-based survey (e.g., personalized signatures and letterheads) that can increase responses to mail surveys. Interviews allow for the explanation of unclear terms, reassurance of confidentiality, and the maintenance of motivation, none of which can be done as effectively over the Web. The effective use of stimulus materials on the Web (e.g., amusing video and sound bytes) are limited by the kinds of disabilities found among the target population, and what will work well for one disability group may not work for another. Technical difficulties with Web-based surveys include the large number of different browsers and operating systems, especially when in different combinations; the consequence may be unpredictable results. In other words, the use of Web-based surveys needs to be considered carefully in the context of the research questions and the intended population, and only when there is a good match will a survey on the Web be better than printed surveys or interviews. It is worth noting that the University of Otago study mentioned previously used a mixed-mode survey (Web and pen-and-paper completion) and found no modality effects.[18]

PILOTING AND TESTING

As with all survey research, piloting the instrument is essential. Ideally the instrument should be tested on members of the target population, but these same people then should not complete the real survey when it is ready; this is especially true when the population is small. Alternative surrogates, such as staff of the university's disability service, might be shown the instrument for comment. The surrogates might be the ones to walk through the instrument with members of the target population. Sometimes the researcher will deliver the draft instrument and come back later to gather comments, as was the case in chapter 8; participants were told that the researcher would return to collect the questionnaires and to answer any questions about problems they experienced. Some researchers, though, want to be present while the testers read through the draft instrument and complete it. They want to hear the comments made and watch participants for their reactions. However, they need to guard against biasing the results by trying to influence what respondents say.

SUPPLEMENTARY DATA COLLECTION

Sometimes it is desirable to follow up a survey with a different form of data collection. Focus group interviews offer a significant contrast because they garner detailed data from a small number of respondents. Because the typical survey lacks an opportunity to probe responses in depth and to let different respondents react to the comments that others make, library staff might consider the use of focus groups. The staff might even ask the students in those groups to meet them periodically throughout their program of study so that their responses might be gathered and compared over time.

CONCLUSION

There is no single way to conduct a study of students (and/or faculty) with disabilities. A review of the relevant research literature and conversations with knowledgeable people who work with the disability community are essential. Some of the tentative conclusions we drew are:

- On a printed survey form, use half tones to make the form clearer for those with poor eyesight. It can make the form easier to read, but does not photocopy adequately. If halftones are used, then the form must be laser printed, not photocopied, with obvious implications for cost.

- Lists must all be printed on the same page. Responses show that some respondents do not check all statements if a list continues onto the next page, and they only rank or rate the items immediately visible on the first page.

- Consider offering a voucher as an incentive. For chapter 8 we had a prize drawing and awarded the winner a $50 voucher. We left the choice of where the voucher could be redeemed to the eventual winner. (Chapter 9 also addresses incentives.)

- Recognize that the researchers probably will not have access to the names and addresses of the students registered with the office of disability services. Laws protect their identities. Depending on how the survey is administered, the researchers may have to pack the forms in envelopes, together with a stamped, self-addressed return envelope, and place them where the target population is likely to find them. The office of disability services is one obvious place. In the case of chapter 8, the forms so deposited were taken quickly. If the library sets aside a room for use by those with disabilities, here is another obvious location.

- Provide a covering information sheet that assures the respondent of confidentiality, and explains how to complete and return the survey. Also, emphasize the value of the survey and how the results will be used to improve library service to students with disabilities.

- Make as many contacts with potential respondents as possible; introductory letters and e-mail messages, follow-up letters or phone calls all help to increase response rates.

There remains an undocumented portion of the target population who might not visit the survey distribution locations. For them, forms were left at the main reference or circulation desk. It is also possible to deposit the form on the library's homepage. These choices raise the question of whether or not all the forms were taken by people in the target population or (1) were some taken in error by people who did not read the sign properly, though once they read the survey form properly they presumably did not complete the form and return it; and (2) whether students who do not match the target population see a voucher prize and decide to enter on the chance of winning. If the latter occurs, there are implications for the integrity of the data collected, as people not in the target population might have completed survey forms.

Although data collection is a complex process, that complexity should not keep the library from listening to students, faculty, and staff with disabilities and factoring their expectations into the ongoing delivery of library services. The challenges may be formidable but they are worth the effort. Library staff might even create an advisory group to make recommendations for dealing with the types of issues discussed in this chapter.

> A simple survey well executed is of much more use than a sophisticated or complex one poorly executed.[19]

NOTES

1. Maurice B. Line, *Library Surveys: An Introduction to the Use, Planning, Procedure and Presentation of Surveys* (London: Clive Bingley, 1982), 143.
2. Peter Hernon and Ellen Altman, *Assessing Service Quality: Satisfying the Expectations of Library Customers* (Chicago: American Library Association, 1998), 128.
3. Examples of relevant textbooks include Minnesota Office of the Legislative Auditor, *State Agency Use of Customer Satisfaction Surveys: A Program Evaluation Report* (St. Paul, MI: Minnesota Office of the Legislative Auditor, 1995); Terry G. Vavra, *Improving Your Measurement of Customer Satisfaction: A Guide to Creating, Conducting, Analyzing, and Reporting Customer Satisfaction Measurement Programs* (Milwaukee, WI: ASQ Quality Press, 1997); Ronald R. Powell and Lynn Silipigni Connaway, *Basic Research Methods for Librarians*, 4th ed. (Westport, CT: Libraries Unlimited, 2004). Also see the many books that Sage Publications (Thousand Oaks, CA) has produced on conducting survey research.
4. Elizabeth M. Forsyth, "Measuring and Delivering Quality in Open Employment Services for People with Disability: Is a System of Compliance to Performance Standards in Conflict with Furthering Quality in Service Delivery for

Customers?" Available at http://www.workable.org.au/archive/measuring_and_delivering_quality.htm (accessed August 31, 2004).

5. A. N. Oppenheim, *Questionnaire Design, Interviewing, and Attitude Measurement* (New York: Pinter Publishers; distributed exclusively in the United States and Canada by St. Martin's Press, 1992).

6. "The Privacy Act sets out 12 information privacy principles dealing with the collection, holding, use and disclosure of personal information, and the assigning of unique identifiers;" see New Zealand, Office of the Privacy Commissioner, Fact Sheet No. 3: "Information Privacy Principles" (Wellington, New Zealand: Office of the Privacy Commissioner, 2004). Available at http://www.privacy.org.nz/people/peotop.html (accessed November 28, 2004). For coverage of privacy within the United States, see Peter Hernon, Harold C. Relyea, Robert E. Dugan, and Joan F. Cheverie, *United States Government Information: Policies and Sources* (Westport, CT: Libraries Unlimited, 2002), 199–221.

7. European Union, *Data Protection in the European Union* (Brussels: European Union, n.d.). Available at http://europa.eu.int/comm/internal_market/privacy/docs/guide/guide-ukingdom_en.pdf (accessed November 28, 2004). See also Office of the Information Commissioner, homepage (London: Office of the Information Commissioner International, 2004). Available at http://www.informationcommissioner.gov.uk/ (accessed November 28, 2004).

8. Kypros Kypri, Stephen J. Gallagher, and Martine L. Cashell-Smith, "An Internet-based Survey Method for College Student Drinking Research," *Drug and Alcohol Dependence* 76 (2004): 45–53.

9. Phil Edwards, Ian Roberts, Mike Clarke, Carolyn DiGuiseppi, Sarah Pratap, Reinhard Wentz, and Irene Kwan, "Increasing Response Rates to Postal Questionnaires: Systematic Review," *British Medical Journal* 324, no. 7347 (2002): 1183–1187.

10. New Zealand Disabilities Resource Centre, *Survey of Information Needs of People with Disabilities* (Wellington, New Zealand: New Zealand Disabilities Resource Centre, 1991), 11.

11. Valarie A. Zeithaml, A. Parasuraman, and Leonard L. Berry, *Delivering Quality Service: Balancing Customer Perceptions and Expectations* (New York: The Free Press, 1990).

12. Forsyth, "Measuring and Delivering Quality in Open Employment Services for People with Disability."

13. Oppenheim, *Questionnaire Design, Interviewing, and Attitude Measurement.*

14. Jennifer Horwath, "Evaluating Opportunities for Expanded Information Access: A Study of the Accessibility of Four Online Databases," *Library Hi Tech* 20 (2002): 199–206.

15. Mick B. Couper, "Web Surveys: A Review of Issues and Approaches," *Public Opinion Quarterly* 64 (2000): 464–494.

16. Ibid.

17. See chapter 7, note 26.

18. Kypri, Gallagher, and Cashell-Smith, "An Internet-based Survey Method for College Student Drinking Research."

19. Line, *Library Surveys,* 143.

11

REPORTING AND USING
THE RESULTS

Philip Calvert

It is vital that libraries act on or are responsive to the needs and concerns of their users as highlighted in surveys or other information seeking instruments.[1]

Many novice researchers and evaluators make an elementary mistake by assuming that the hardest part of conducting a survey is the actual administration of the instrument. In practice, that can sometimes appear to be a relatively trivial matter when compared to the issues that can arise in the conceptualization of the study and the entry, analysis, and presentation of the resulting data. Although this is sounded as a warning to the uninitiated, it is not intended to warn off potential researchers, for with some advance thought and planning the postcollection phases of a survey can run quite smoothly. Thus, the emphasis needs to be on thinking ahead to what might happen and how to react to any eventuality if it does. Prior preparation for contingencies is greatly aided by conducting a pilot survey that tests the instrument before the main survey is actually conducted. A pilot survey will collect a small number of responses, and with the resulting data, the surveyors will work through the cycle of data entry, analysis, and presentation to see what problems might occur. Do several respondents omit one question and, as a result, make analysis of that question difficult or meaningless? Do they give unexpected responses to open questions that are hard to code? Once the data are entered, can they be verified? Do the researchers know in advance what statistical test(s) they intend to use, and if so, do the data need to be entered in any particular fashion to the spreadsheet, or perhaps a spreadsheet is not adequate for the tests that the researchers have planned? With these points in mind, this chapter serves as a guide to the newcomer to service quality surveys who wishes to make decisions about software, data entry and analysis, presentation, and reporting.

THE SOFTWARE

For libraries that do not have much money to spend on new software and hence must make do with what they already have or what is licensed by the parent institution, a mix-and-match approach is about all that can be hoped for. Nevertheless, assembling different pieces of software will work well provided the investigators are comfortable with moving data from one software package to another. This approach also has the benefit of using specialized software for each part of the operation. The initial stage of questionnaire design can be done in a word-processing program. As this will allow for the relatively easy creation of tables, it is well suited to a service quality survey instrument such as the ones described in this book. Should it be possible to gather names and addresses of potential respondents (e.g., by sending e-mail messages asking for expressions of interest), then a database package is the obvious application for storing the contact data. It is usually quite easy to generate mailing labels from this sort of database software, which should reduce the time taken on sending out the surveys. For data entry and analysis, the choice is between a standard spreadsheet and more complex, specialized statistical software. As will be explained later in this chapter, the typical spreadsheet cannot be used for some of the necessary calculations needed in gap analysis—at least, it will not perform them without the use of fairly complicated formulae. Finally, data from the data analysis will have to be presented in a report or reports, and word processing software is again the easiest vehicle for that. Some software vendors (e.g., Corel, Lotus, and Microsoft) offer integrated suites of software in which word processing, spreadsheet, and database applications are all available, the attraction being that importing and exporting data between applications ought to run smoothly. It is equally likely that presentation software is also available in the suite, so quotations from reports and tables from the data analysis can be copied across ready for visual presentations. In order for this approach to be effective, the investigators must be proficient with the software themselves or be able to hire research assistants who can use the software—and ideally without constant supervision.

The alternative is the use of completely integrated survey software. This combines all the operations of a survey into one package, providing a one-stop-shop. An example of an integrated package is Snap Survey (http://www.mercator corp.com/), which claims to offer on-screen questionnaire design, data collection, and analysis for all types of surveys. The software can be used to create a paper survey, a Web site survey, a Web "pop-up" survey, and even a mobile PDA survey. Another suitable package is SurveyPro (http://www.apian.com/), which includes a database function. The integrated package should contain templates for questionnaires, but ought to allow the user complete control over the look and expression of the questions. The user should be able to select the survey delivery method (e.g., whether it is completed in paper or through e-mail or the Web). The software should then provide an easy-to-use data entry facility, data checking, strong data analysis, and a report writing function. There are two points to remember if considering the use of a particular integrated survey software package. First, does the institution have a license for it, or can the library afford to purchase one? Second, can it do all the various tasks needed, with the data analysis being something that needs to be examined very carefully? If the integrated software cannot perform the necessary data analysis and something as powerful as SPSS or SAS must be used instead, is it worth using an integrated package at all? This question has to be asked.

DATA ENTRY AND ANALYSIS

Surveys of service quality typically focus on the extent of the gap between customer expectations and the services actually provided by the library. Each returned copy of the survey should therefore have two responses to each statement, one for expectations and one for performance. In the case of a respondent who thinks the statement is of importance, but the library is not delivering that service well, the difference could be something such as an "8" for expectation and a "5" for performance. That gives a gap of 3. For data entry it will be necessary to record two different responses to each statement, plus one more item of data that will be the calculation of the gap score. The gap score must be calculated for every statement rated by each individual respondent.

Before attempting to analyze the data, the investigators think about what they will do before entering the data into a spreadsheet or similar software. Sometimes the data analysis calls for solutions that are not easy to calculate in a typical spreadsheet. Commonly, a spreadsheet (and more powerful packages such as SPSS) will use a *cell* as the basic unit of data entry, with a column for each question and a row for each respondent (spreadsheets may allow the axes to be set up the other way around, but SPSS only permits one structure). One way to enter the data, then, will be to have a row for each respondent, and three columns, one for the expectation score, one for performance, and one for the gap. All these data will be integers. It will be easier to analyze the data if the columns for expectations are kept together, and similarly the performance and gap scores. This will result in the scores for each respondent being spread out across the row, but this does not cause much confusion.

Nonresponses create a problem. It may not appear that way initially, which is why some forward thinking is essential. Logically, a nonresponse should have no data entered in the spreadsheet, so the cell is left blank. This looks fine. Now try to subtract one score from another (which is what has to be done to calculate the gap score) and wherever a cell has been left blank the spreadsheet is likely to produce a zero as the answer. This would be the same return as if the rating given for performance was the same as that given for the expectations (e.g., $8 - 8 = 0$), and that is not the same as a nonresponse. If all the gap scores for one statement were then included in an average (mean) for that statement, the zeros that had resulted from the nonresponses would count as the same as a real zero, and this would *flatten* the average for that statement. A high number of nonresponses to a statement would produce a low gap score, which could be very misleading. There are ways of circumventing this problem, even if the investigators use a spreadsheet (because they do not feel comfortable in using more powerful statistics packages), to avoid a complicated correction procedure. Thus, it is important to ask someone familiar with the use of a spreadsheet or other software for guidance in dealing with this matter.

The most common form of data entry is simply manual. For the number of responses that can be expected to the kind of survey described in chapter 8, this is almost certainly adequate. In Tables 11.1 and 11.2, the data for expectations and for performance have been entered for ten respondents and ten statements. Note that the mean for responses to each statement has also been calculated, with the null cells ignored.

Verify the Data

Several specialized survey packages have a facility for checking the data that requires all data to be entered twice, and any discrepancies are brought to the user's attention. This might not be justified for a relatively small survey such as is anticipated here. Visual checking will spot some errors, but asking the software to produce a list of *frequencies* is another method. It will not help the user spot small errors, such as a 9 entered instead of an 8, but with this output the user ought to notice the use of a 99 rather than a 9, and as this is the sort of error that really distorts the results it is worth the effort needed to catch it. A scatter plot does much the same thing, for it presents a graphical report that makes it quite easy to spot outliers.

Analyze the Data

If the method for calculating the gap between expectations and performance is followed precisely as prescribed in theory, the rating given by each respondent for expectation would be subtracted from the rating given by that same respondent for performance $(P - E)$, and this would be done on each statement in the questionnaire. The reader will see intuitively that this will result in a negative score far more often than not, simply because most respondents give a higher rating for expectations than they do for performance. As a digression, respondents can and do rate performance higher than

Table 11.1
Hypothetical Expectations Data

	EXP1	EXP2	EXP3	EXP4	EXP5	EXP6	EXP7	EXP8	EXP9	EXP10	Mean
Statement 1	8	10	7	8	8	10	6	9	9	10	8.50
Statement 2	7	5	6	5.	—	6	7	5	8	8	6.33
Statement 3	8	4	8	9	10	10	8	8	9	10	8.40
Statement 4	9	6	8	8	8	10	8	9	10	9	8.50
Statement 5	—	10	9	8	8	9	10.	—	9	9	9.00
Statement 6	9	9	9	9	10	10	9	9	10	9	9.30
Statement 7	5	2	8	9	7	4	5	7	7	8	6.20
Statement 8	9	10	10	7	8	9	9	8	9	10	8.90
Statement 9	10	8	9	7.		8	10	10	9	10	9.00
Statement 10	9	10	8	9	9	10	10	10	9	9	9.30

Table 11.2
Hypothetical Performance Data

	PER1	PER2	PER3	PER4	PER5	PER6	PER7	PER8	PER9	PER10	Mean
Statement 1	6	6	6	7	6	6	5	6	5	6	5.90
Statement 2	4	4	2	4	5	4	2	3	7	7	4.20
Statement 3	5	4	3	6	7	3	8	5	9	7	5.70
Statement 4	7	6	8	5	4	8	8	3	4.	—	5.89
Statement 5	6	4	7	5	6	6	6	5	6	6	5.70
Statement 6	8	6	9	4	9	5	6	3	10	9	6.90
Statement 7	4	3	2.	—	—	4	7.	—	7	8	5.00
Statement 8	8	2	6	1	8	9	2	2	10	7	5.50
Statement 9	7	1	8	1	7	4	4	5	9	7	5.30
Statement 10	8	3	4	3	8	10	10	5	9	6	6.60

expectation on some statements when they think that the library is doing a good job, but often on some aspect of service that they consider to be relatively unimportant. It is quite common to discover that students think the library does a very good job with orientation programs and library skills classes, but in practice perhaps they do not really care all that much about them.

Using the expectations and performance data from Tables 11.1 and 11.2, the resulting gap score is given in Table 11.3. This is a typical spread of gap scores. There are some large gaps, many small ones, and quite a few zeros. There are also a few negative scores. It should be obvious why there are more empty cells in the gap scores than in either of the two previous tables (because if either the expectation or the performance score was omitted by the respondents, there can be no gap score).

What to Look for in the Means

The most obvious thing to do with the mean scores is rearrange the table so that the statements are ranked by their means (usually from highest to lowest). Much of what now becomes apparent is useful management information.

The highest mean scores for expectations are exactly what this says they are; these are the statements that customers regard as highly important to service quality. In Table 11.1 there are two statements with means of 9.30 so both must be considered as important for further analysis. At the other end of scale, does a statement that only attracts a mean of 6.20 merit much attention? This is a matter for judgment; there are no absolutes. Both the statements with the highest expectations score of 9.30 also have gap scores that point to problems (2.40 and 2.70), and though these are not the largest gap scores, the combination of a high expectations score and a significant gap score suggests that customers are concerned about this aspect of service.

Looking at the performance data it is clear that the surveyed library is not doing well on statement 2, which has a mean of 4.20. Is this a cause for alarm? It all depends upon a number of other circumstances. Does the library claim to offer the service described in the statement, or is the statement there to discover if there are hidden wants? Is the expectations score for the same statement high or low? In this case the expectations score for statement 2 is only 6.33, which is the second lowest mean in the expectations table (Table 11.1). This does not suggest that customers are overly concerned with this service, hence low performance is not necessarily a problem for the library management.

Much of the same applies when analyzing the gap scores. A large gap score could be a sign of a significant problem in the library's service quality. In Table 11.3 the largest gap score is 3.89 for statement 9. Checking the other tables, the expectations score is 9.00 and the performance score is 5.30. This points to this aspect of service being a problem that ought to concern the management, for the expectations score is tied as third highest. Yet, a high

Table 11.3
Gaps Scores (Calculated from the Previous Tables)

	GAP1	GAP2	GAP3	GAP4	GAP5	GAP6	GAP7	GAP8	GAP9	GAP10	Mean
Statement 1	2	4	1	1	2	4	1	3	4	4	2.60
Statement 2	3	1	4	1.	—	2	5	2	1	1	2.22
Statement 3	3	0	5	3	3	7	0	3	0	3	2.70
Statement 4	2	0	0	3	4	2	0	6	6.	—	2.56
Statement 5	—	6	2	3	2	3	4.	—	3	3	3.25
Statement 6	1	3	0	5	1	5	3	6	0	0	2.40
Statement 7	1	−1	6.	—	—	0	−2.	—	0	0	0.57
Statement 8	1	8	4	6	0	0	7	6	−1	3	3.40
Statement 9	3	7	1	6.	—	4	6	5	0	3	3.89
Statement 10	1	7	4	6	1	0	0	5	0	3	2.70

gap score does not always mean there is a problem that must be addressed with new resources, staff training, and so on. The gap score for statement 2 is 2.22, which is not a large gap, but one that must be investigated. This statement only achieved an expectations score of 6.33, the second lowest mean in the table. It could well be that this is not something that unduly bothers the customers.

Management has to assess the figures critically rather than simply accepting them all at face value. Suppose the managers saw the mean scores for statement 7 and decided that a gap score of 0.57 suggested that this service was meeting all customer expectations, and then when the expectations score of 6.20, the lowest of all the means in Table 11.1 is taken into account, managers could think that this is a service that might be de-emphasized in terms of staffing and other resources. That might be a valid choice, if it is made by management. There is an alternative to this view, however, for it could be that statement 2 describes a valuable service that the library *must* offer, and the problem lies in the low expectations that customers have for this service. Suppose this statement described the information literacy classes; in effect, the survey is saying, "The library does a good job with these classes, but we do not really care about them." Is this a sufficient cause for cutting resources for those classes, or should management decide to increase efforts to promote these classes as something the students should not do without—in other words, to raise customer expectations? This is a choice that management must make. The survey data can provide very useful information for management decisions, but the data should not determine operational decision making.

PRESENTING THE DATA

Report generation is the activity that makes survey results respond directly and meaningfully to the information needs of interested parties. Typically, that means arranging the results of a survey to make them easy to understand by those needing the information, such as funding agents or senior managers. Before dealing with reports to specific stakeholders, here are some graphical presentation techniques.

Graphs

Graphic presentation is an attempt to make a large mass of data more readily comprehendible to the reader. Aspects of the data, such as proportions or annual trends, become instantly visible in even a simple graph because a graph uses size and space, plus juxtaposition, to display relationships.

A simple bar chart or column chart illustrates all the means of data from one table, such as the mean of all expectations. Two or more sets of data can be compared with a split bar chart or split column chart, but though this would show high and low performers very clearly, the reader is asked to draw conclusions about its value compared to a simple list of figures. Figure 11.1 shows a simple graph for performance scores. It can help investigators and interested readers alike to see if some statements score much higher or lower than others—sometimes people see this better in graphic form.

A variation suitable for gaps data is the mean comparative score bar chart. Its advantage over other bar charts is simply that it can show negative scores as well as positive.

Quadrant Analysis

Quadrant analysis is a graphic correlation technique that produces data easy to visualize. Those statements falling into quadrant 1 are very important to the users and these individuals perceive the library as possessing them or as performing well in their delivery. The library should *retain* these statements in its services. Statements falling into the second quadrant are also most important to the respondents, but they are not perceived as prominent features of a library's service. The library should *improve* on these service features. Statements in quadrant 3 are relatively unimportant for achieving excellent to customers, although they associate those features with library service. These statements merit *revisiting*. Finally, quadrant 4 includes statements that customers neither value nor perceive the library as performing well. Statements in quadrant four might see a reallocation of resources.[2]

Figure 8.1 offered a generic depiction of the four quadrants. The first step in constructing those quadrants for the data gathered in an actual survey is to calculate the mean score for both the *expected* and *actual* service and to report

Figure 11.1
Graphical Representation of Data (taken from Table 11.2)

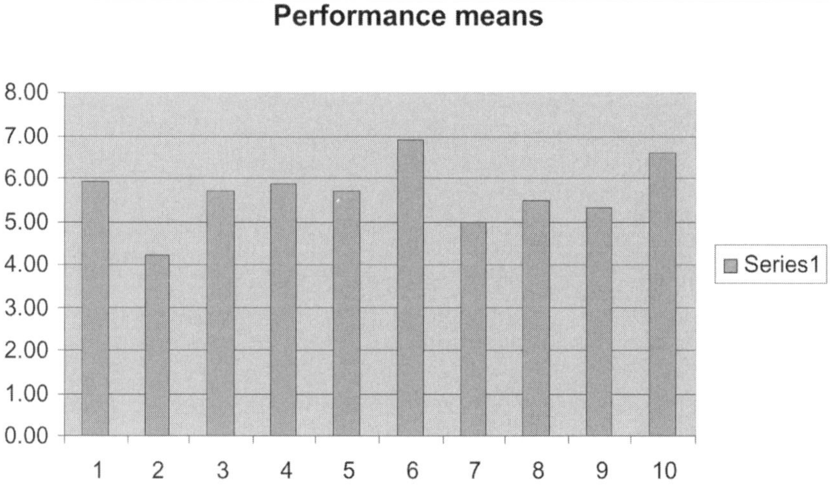

Performance means

the gap between the two means. The mean scores for the expected services are positioned along the vertical axis and the gaps between these scores and the perception of the actual service are positioned along the horizontal axis. The midpoint of the 10-point scale is 5 and is represented by solid lines. This represents an idealized situation.

Second, we add the mean *expected* scores (e.g., if one score was 6.68, the next 6.65, and so on, we add 6.68 + 6.65, etc.) and divide the total by the number of statements in Section A. The resulting number is represented on the chart's vertical axis with a dashed line.

Third, we take the mean *actual* scores, add them together, and divide by the total number of statements in Section A. The resulting number is represented on the chart's horizontal axis with a dashed line.

The quadrant chart now has dashed lines that divide the chart into four quadrants that reflect the dataset. Let us say that, by adding the mean *expected* scores and dividing that number by the total number of statements, we got the number 8.302. Turning to the mean *actual* scores, we add the various means and divide the total by the number of statements, getting 6.418. As a result,

- Quadrant 1 includes statements that rated higher than both 8.302 and 6.418;
- Quadrant 2 contains statements that exceeded 8.302 but fell under 6.418;
- Quadrant 3 has statements that fell under 8.302 but exceeded 6.418; and
- Quadrant 4 includes statements that fell under both 8.302 and 6.418.

To summarize, statements in quadrant 1 merit retention, those in quadrant 2 need improvement, those in quadrant 3 require a revisit, and those in the final quadrant might be dropped and resources reallocated.[3]

Comparison with the Grand Mean

Because respondents often give scores above the midway point (i.e., 6 and over) the mean for each statement will often be more than half the possible mean of 10.00. The result is that many statements appear in the upper half of the quadrant (high expectations) or on the right hand side of the quadrant (high performance). This can be adjusted to present a more balanced view, though it has to be said that this is by no means essential. To do this, simply set the dividing lines between quadrants at the mean of all means, or the *grand mean*. This will certainly split the points more evenly between the four quadrants. As an illustration of this, the following are ten expectations means for statements 1 to 10, with the grand mean in the final box.

St 1	2	3	4	5	6	7	8	9	10	Grand Mean
8.50	6.33	8.40	8.50	9.00	9.30	6.20	8.90	9.00	9.30	8.343

A manager needing or wishing to know if any statement has received *significant* scores can use a one-tailed T-test on the statement mean compared with the grand mean.[4]

REPORTING THE RESULTS

Reporting is not simply something that is done after the completion of the project. In good projects, dissemination of information will begin as soon as possible, when information about the project is sent to those who will be the audience of the results. The flow of information should be maintained throughout the project, with a continuous flow of reports going to the funding agents, colleagues who might be working on similar projects, and perhaps even the community being researched, provided this does not color any survey responses that still might be due. "The process of creating an awareness of the project is extremely important, but often overlooked."[5]

It ought to be axiomatic that after a survey has been completed, the results should be communicated as clearly and as quickly as possible to all relevant groups and individuals, yet often in practice the reporting is done slowly and sporadically, with the net result that the survey achieves much less than it could have done if the reporting had been more efficiently organized.

Participants in the Survey

Earlier, the chapter noted that ethical behavior required feedback to participants in the survey who willingly give their time. They do not wish to see a long report, so a summary of the results and some basic conclusions will be sufficient. The means of getting the feedback to the participants is not always obvious, and one significant problem is that the names and addresses of the participants will, most likely, not be known to the researchers. That is why it is necessary to plan the feedback even before data collection has started and to inform all participants how the feedback will be provided once the results have been calculated. In many cases it will be sufficient to say that a summary of the results will be given to a student newspaper, or put on the disability service Web site.

Survey Partners

A much fuller report must be written and sent to any partners, such as the university library director and the head of the student disability services. They will want to see the full set of results and a detailed analysis. They do not, though, wish to see the equivalent of a research report as might be written for journal publication. There is no need to include a full literature review, or the various extras that would be normal in a scholarly piece, such as assumptions or the pros and cons of various methodologies. Yet, the knowledge that these people will have about surveys should not be underestimated, as they may have some experience in conducting research, marketing, or scholarship that includes awareness of various statistical methods and what the data mean. As an example, do not remove the standard deviation— a descriptive statistic that measures the dispersion of scores around the mean—from the report on the assumption that these readers would not understand what it means. Even if they do not know they could easily ask a colleague to interpret the data for them, and the absence of the data might lower their perception of a high quality report.

This kind of audience is usually composed of busy people who do not want to read lengthy reports and sometimes do not get beyond the first page of a document if it looks uninteresting or irrelevant. So, make this like a business report, and start with an executive summary. Include only the key highlights from the survey, with the objective that the whole executive summary takes no more than five minutes to read as an absolute maximum. The report itself should focus on the results of the survey and key recommendations that have resulted from the analysis. The report must stimulate interest, create curiosity, and demand a response. Use simple, direct sentences and avoid the passive tense; the curse of much academic writing (e.g., "it was decided that ..."). Use bullet points where appropriate, add many headings, and highlight key phrases. Finally, give considerable attention to the look of the finished product. The appearance of the report *does* matter. As a final point, it does not matter if the body of the report repeats what was said in the executive summary. Repetition might enhance the effect.

Another method of reporting is the face-to-face presentation, and this is entirely appropriate for survey partners, though the investigators have to convince them it is worth their time to attend. Presentations are good for immediacy, but they are not so good for detail. Do not try to use the presentation as a substitute for a written report because interested parties will always want to see the extra detail that can only be provided in detailed data tables. It is unwise to put survey data on the screen for it probably will not be read by those at the back of the room. What the presentation *is* good for is putting forward conclusions and recommendations. A good presentation should not take longer than twenty minutes, and it can have a simple structure: this is the situation we have at the moment, this is the complicating factor (e.g., higher customer expectations or a declining budget), and this is what we can do about it. Before the presentation make it clear what benefits the audience will receive from the presentation, and give them the *rules of the road* (e.g., questions at the end). During the body of the presentation, be sure to *signpost* digressions or links to earlier/later topics. Wrap up on an optimistic note, but avoid humor unless the investigators are absolutely sure about its impact.

The Wider Public

Some surveys will be of interest to a wider public even if the results do not immediately affect them. Chapter 7 reported that graduate and undergraduate students in a New Zealand university library survey had shown considerable interest in the statement "provision made for disabled students," although most of the respondents would not have had any disability. Students will be interested in improving service for students with disabilities, and so a short report should be sent to a campus newspaper, assuming there is one, and radio and television stations in those universities that have them. It could be that a student journalist will see the report and ask one of the survey team for an interview, which will give more publicity to the results.

CONCLUSION

There is an extensive monographic and periodical literature that investigators can consult for data entry and analysis and report writing. Graphics become an excellent way for the community to see trends without having to read a report. One reason for spending so much time in informing different communities about any service quality survey is to demonstrate that the library is listening to what they have to say. Any service quality or satisfaction survey should be a regular occurrence—perhaps once or twice a year. Furthermore, it is critical to demonstrate that no segment of the community is left behind—ignored or their perspectives assumed.

> The value of any completed report is latent. It exists, but it requires dissemination to make it active.[6]

NOTES

1. Helen Hayden, Terry O'Brien, and Maoiliosa O Rathaille, "User Survey at Waterford Institute of Technology Libraries: How a Traditional Approach to Surveys Can Inform Library Service Delivery," *New Library World* 106, no. 1208/1209 (2005): 49.
2. For application of quadrant analysis and other ways to analyze the data, see Danuta A. Nitecki and Peter Hernon, "Measuring Service Quality at Yale University's Libraries," *The Journal of Academic Librarianship* 26 (July 2000): 259–273.
3. For an actual example, with a depiction of the different charts, see Peter Hernon and Ellen Altman, *Assessing Service Quality: Satisfying the Expectations of Library Customers* (Chicago: American Library Association, 1998), 198–202.
4. See Ugur Yavas and Dogan Eroglu, "Assessing Competitive Edge: Exposition and Illustration of a Diagnostic Tool," *Journal of Consumer Marketing* 12, no. 2 (1995): 47–59.
5. Nick Moore, *How to Do Research* (London: Library Association, 1983), 123.
6. Ibid., 122.

12

CONTINUING TO IMPROVE SERVICE QUALITY FOR STUDENTS

Peter Hernon and Philip Calvert

> We cannot fulfill our mission as librarians until we do our best to ensure that the tools and resources we offer are equally available to people with disabilities.[1]

For more than fifteen years, government policies, especially those shaped through legislation, have guided the approach that institutions of higher education have taken to provide services for students with disabilities. That approach has tended to focus on making facilities more accessible to the community that has physical disabilities. In some instances, it seems that institutional administrators have believed that in making such accommodation they have fully complied with the legal requirements, and of course they have not. Physical disabilities constitute only one type of disability; some others might be hidden or not apparent because there is no obvious physical disability. It also necessary to ask if simple compliance is sufficient. Should not the organization be seeking to provide excellent service for the entire community specified in the institutional mission?

Classroom teachers, in conjunction with the institution's office of disability service, often see that students with disabilities receive the academic support they need to complete courses and programs of study successfully. That support, for instance, might include the provision of an ergonomic chair, letting students tape classroom lectures, finding a note taker, and providing students with copies of PowerPoint slides for the topics discussed in each class session, or providing an extension on the due dates for the submission of papers or on the length of time needed for completing a written test, even allowing students to dictate examination answers. The critical issue is that the students and their instructors enter into a dialogue and the office of disability services assists and even encourages that dialogue, with the ultimate aim being the achievement of the student's full potential.

Against this background, the purpose of this chapter is to suggest that meeting or exceeding the service expectations of students with disabilities, or any special population for that matter, is more than a service quality or satisfaction issue. It also impacts other services and the accomplishment of the institutional mission statement. In a way, working with every group making up the student body places the library in the broader context of meeting educational and institutional outcomes and answering question such as:

- What should students learn?
- How well are they learning it?
- How do the institution and its educational programs use information gathered to improve student learning?

Exploring the reasons why students do not fully achieve program and institutional expectations means examining the connection between academic programs and relevant support services for the entire student population. Contrary to the claim of some stakeholders, the purpose of higher education should be to educate students and not merely train them for their first professional position. Critical thinking, problem solving, excellent communication skills, and a well-read student are all goals of a general undergraduate program. Each of these traits becomes important in setting student learning outcomes and measuring the extent of their achievement.

INFORMATION LITERACY

Information literacy, which encourages critical thinking and reflection, has been defined as

an intellectual framework for identifying, finding, understanding, evaluating and using information. It includes determining the nature and extent of needed information; accessing information effectively and efficiently; evaluating critically information and its sources; incorporating selected information in the learner's knowledge base and value system; using information effectively to accomplish a specific purpose; understanding the economic, legal and social issues surrounding the use of information and information technology; and observing laws, regulations, and institutional policies related to the access and use of information.[2]

Such a definition highlights the fact that both the teaching faculty and librarians have a role to play in making students information literate and lifelong learners able to engage in critical reading, the evaluation of information, "and the use of information to produce understanding and new knowledge."[3]

In 1998, the Wisconsin Association of Academic Librarians (WAAL) adopted standards for information literacy and competencies for statewide implementation that outline specific information competency skills.[4] In 2001, the Association of College and Research Libraries (ACRL), American Library Association, approved *Objectives for Information Literacy Instruction: A Model Statement for Academic Librarians,* which provides standards, related performance indicators, and outcomes.[5] For example, ACRL's Competency Standard One, "The information literate student determines the extent of the information needed," has performance indicator four, which states "The information literate student reevaluates the nature and extent of the information need." The outcomes include the following:

- Reviews the initial information need to clarify, revise, or refine the question
  - Identifies a research topic that may require revision, based on the amount of information found (or not found);
  - Identifies a topic that may need to be modified, based on the content of information found; and
  - Decides when it is and is not necessary to abandon a topic depending on the success (or failure) of an initial search for information.
- Describes criteria used to make information decisions and choices
  - Demonstrates how the intended audience influences information choices;
  - Demonstrates how the desired end product influences information choices (e.g., that visual aids or audio/visual material may be needed for an oral presentation); and
  - Lists various criteria, such as currency, which influence information choices....[6]

Information literacy, as reflected in the above-mentioned definition, standards, related performance indicators, and outcomes, is an ambitious and ever-evolving concept. Student subpopulations such as those for whom English is a second language and with disabilities require accommodation to help them achieve such ambitious outcomes; after all, those outcomes do not state that they exclude the portion of the student population that has disabilities or for whom English is a second language.

As a consequence, when librarians conduct an information literacy program in the library or in the classroom do they use software (e.g., PowerPoint) and Internet sites to highlight key points and to offer illustrations of the content? Do they expect students to follow along at a workstation and to answer questions and complete basic tasks? Furthermore, do the students fill out a pretest and posttest that demonstrates what they have learned? Perhaps, at the end of the instruction, the students are asked to complete a task such as:

You've been selected to lead a group of students on a four-week trip to another country. In preparation you need to find background information of the country's history, current events, language, local customs, art and music. How would you locate the information? What type of information would you expect to find?[7]

This task relates to the location and retrieval of "relevant information, in all its various formats, using, when appropriate, technological tools." Let us assume that the paper is due in one week. Do any of the students need special accommodation? This does not mean that they turn in a paper of lesser quality.

At the same time, is the library's Web site compliant with the requirements specified in Title II of the Americans with Disability Act and Section 508 of the Rehabilitation Act? This means, for instance, the inclusion of more enhancements such as the presence of more style sheets and less reliance on tables and large blocks of dense text. Clearly, librarians need to subject their homepages to usability testing as they pursue universal access issues.

Still, enhancing the learning process is not confined merely to making the Web site and digital resources more accessible. It must be remembered, and factored into the teaching and learning process, for instance, that learning differences may involve any of the following:

- Spoken language: Delays, disorders, or discrepancies in listening and speaking;
- Written language: Difficulties with reading, writing, and spelling;
- Arithmetic computations: Difficulty in performing arithmetic functions or in comprehending basic concepts;
- Reasoning: Difficulty in organizing and integrating thoughts; and
- Organization skills: Difficulty in organizing all facets of learning.[8]

Some students might process information slowly, be unable to accelerate their rate of thinking, and require more time to move through tasks successfully. They might ask questions about information the instructor just finished explaining or they might need to ask the same question repeatedly. As a result, they should be allowed an extension on turning in assignments and be given extended time for the completion of tests. They might even want to make tape recordings of the instructions so that they can hear them again but at their own pace.

It is clear that information literacy involves a partnership between the classroom faculty and librarians. Together, both groups must create a culture of intellectual curiosity and advance learning, which educator Peggy L. Maki sees as encompassing "not only knowledge leading to understanding but also abilities, habits of mind, ways of knowing, attitudes, values, and other dispositions that an institution and its programs and services assert they develop."[9] As a result, she encourages academics to give greater attention to such matters as "pedagogy," "instructional design," "curricular and co-curricular design," and "institutional programs and services that support, complement, and advance student learning."[10]

If the literature is any indication, we know almost nothing about the effectiveness of information literacy programs given to students with disabilities. Later in the chapter the point is made that more research exploring information literacy for subpopulations is required. For example, freshman students with disabilities might find the standard information literacy program useful, but what is *not* included in the content that they really need to know? Instead of joining a typical library orientation library tour, do they require individual attention? As has been mentioned earlier, students may have impairments, but it is the environment that turns an impairment into a disability, so what barriers will they encounter in the library building, in its equipment, and in the use of collections and services that will need to be explained to them? They need to be shown any special accommodation provided in the library building and special equipment, as well as given instruction in the use of adaptive technology, and shown how to get the best (most appropriate) information from the Web site and the library online public access catalog. They must be told how to request help whenever they engage in photocopying material, retrieving items from difficult locations, and scanning texts into electronic format. This is still scarcely scratching the surface of what they will need to know. Later, they will want to hear how to make their needs and expectations heard via suggestions boxes and disability committees.

Sheryl Burgstahler, Bill Corrigan, and Joan McCarter of the University of Washington discuss that university's distance learning program and its partnership with the access technology laboratory and DO-IT (Disabilities, Opportunities, Internetworking, and Technology). Commenting on the experiences of that partnership in providing distance education programs, they note that "some potential students and instructors who have access to these technologies [a computer and the Internet] cannot fully participate because of the inaccessible design of courses."[11] For instance,

Online courses can inadvertently erect barriers for students and instructors with disabilities. Web pages with complicated navigation can be difficult for people with mobility impairments to use. Content within graphics images may be meaningless to someone who is blind. Words spoken in an audio clip are potentially unavailable to someone who is deaf.[12]

Furthermore,

Real-time chat communication, in which students communicate synchronously, is difficult or impossible to use by someone whose input method is slow, perhaps because of limited hand function or a learning disability, and some chat systems are not accessible to those who are blind. Therefore, it is important that an instructor who typically uses a synchronous tool such as chat is prepared to provide an accessible alternative, such as electronic mail, if a student who cannot use chat enrolls in a course.[13]

Burgstahler, Corrigan, and McCarter reinforce the need for instructors engaged in online instruction to be fully aware of their students' needs and to create the necessary learning environment—one that does not disadvantage students with disabilities if they enroll in the course or otherwise receive online instruction. Librarians, as well, need to realize that some students they instruct might have disabilities—apparent or hidden—and that the same methods of instruction and of delivering information literacy inhibit learning. The instruction might also be in conflict with existing laws, standards, and guidelines.[14]

OUR VARIATION OF A DATA COLLECTION INSTRUMENT FOR GAUGING SERVICE QUALITY

Chapters 8 and 9 of this book report on two pretests of the disability service quality instrument that we developed. The initial version, developed and tested in New Zealand, focused on students with physical disabilities, whereas the modified version (see chapter 9) applies to students with learning differences. In developing both instruments, numerous individuals in libraries and disability service positions provided critical comments to assist in guiding the development of an instrument that libraries can modify to meet their local needs.

Some students need special accommodation in the library such as a special room where they can work at their own pace, rest, and have special equipment handy. As John Redmayne of Massey University explained (chapter 6), it is worth considering if students should be *mainstreamed* but usually students with impairments will hope that a separate, specially designed and equipped accommodation is provided for their needs. Other students might have hidden disabilities and prefer to be seen as no different from other students. Consequently, one set of statements cannot apply to every library, its resources, and the community it serves. Chapters 8 and 9 identify a pool of questions from which libraries can select; more importantly, the staff might discuss those questions with staff in the office of disability services and select a subset for placement in a questionnaire. Those statements selected should be ones that are locally important; if users find them important, the library should be prepared to act on them.

The statements depicted in both chapters are suggestive and library staff should feel that they can substitute other statements or modify existing ones. Figure 12.1 identifies even more statements from which the staff might select. Whatever statements they settle on should not be placed in a lengthy questionnaire that the students will find time-consuming to complete. In other words, library staff should keep the questionnaire short—no more than three pages with all of its parts. Section A of SERVQUAL contains twenty-two statements, and this number might serve as the upper limit in determining the number of statements to include in the future.

Instead of (or in addition to) conducting a mailed, hand distributed, or other type of survey, librarians might benefit from a meeting in which they get together and discuss various statements and the effectiveness of the services provided. They might also invite staff from the office of disability

Figure 12.1
Supplementary Set of Statements

Part I [1]

1. The online catalog:
   a. Displays information that is clear and easy to understand
   b. Has easy-to-follow instructions
   c. Indicates the number of copies available
   d. Is an accurate source of information about *all* material sheld by the library
   e. Is easily accessible from outside the library building

2. The library Web site:
   a. Is attractive
   b. Is easy to navigate
   c. Enables me to:
      i. Access a variety of electronic resources
      ii. Interact with library staff
      iii. Log on easily
      iv. Log on whenever I want
   d. Includes online request forms (reference and interlibrary loan)

3. Equipment in good working order is available when I need it:
   a. Computer dedicated only for online catalog use
   b. Computer printers
   c. Computer research workstations (e.g., for access to the Web, and electronic texts and journals)
   d. Microform/fiche readers
   e. Microform/fiche readers/printers
   f. Photocopiers

4. The staff are:
   a. Approachable and welcoming

[1] Reprinted from *The Journal of Academic Librarianship*, 26, Danuta A. Nitecki and Peter Hernon, "Measuring Service Quality at Yale University's Libraries," 270-271, 2000, with permission from Elsevier.

Figure 12.1
Supplementary Set of Statements (continued)

  b. Available when I need them

  c. Courteous and polite

  d. Expert in:

   i. Finding general information

   ii. The literature of my discipline

  e. Friendly and easy to talk to

5. The staff provide assistance to help me:

  a. Identify resources I need

  b. Retrieve resources I need

  c. Evaluate information I need

  d. Learn how to find information

6. Library materials:

  a. Encompass curriculum-supporting videos and films

  b. Meet my course/research needs

7. There is a paging service for retrieving material

8. Materials I requested to be paged come within the time frame quoted by the library staff

9. When I request materials, I am told how long they will take to arrive:

  a. From restricted collections

  b. Through interlibrary loan

10. Materials are:

  a. In their proper places on the shelves

  b. Re-shelved promptly

11. It is easy to:

  a. Browse print collections

  b. Find where materials are located in the building

Figure 12.1
Supplementary Set of Statements (continued)

12. Directional signs are clear and helpful

13. It is easy to find out, in advance, when the library is open

Part II [2]

1. The library Web site:

   a. Allows me to:

      i. Find names and contact details of key library staff

      ii. Find out about library hours, locations, services, and policies

      iii. Find out about forthcoming library tutorials and programs (e.g., library instruction classes and online guides to my course interests)

   b. Arranges library databases by general subject/discipline

   c. Arranges links to Web sites by general subject disciplines

   d. Contains services for which I do not mind providing personal information

   e. Enables me to:

      i. Determine which electronic resources are most relevant to my course needs/research interests

      ii. Download material:

         • Onto computer screen quickly

         • Onto removable media (e.g., floppy disk or USB drive)

      iii. Have access to:

         • Online guides to information about my subject interests

         • Online library tutorials

   f. Has links that function (no dead links or re-directed links that do not work)

   g. Includes online request forms (e.g., for reference/interlibrary loan)

   h. Informs and assists me in personalizing the use of online databases

   i. Informs me about regular updating of content/resources

   j. Is easy to navigate

   k. Is easy to return to the library Web site after using other Web sites/online resources

[2] Reprinted from *Library & Information Science Research*, 27, Peter Hernon and Philip Calvert, "E-Service Quality in Libraries: Exploring Its Features and Dimensions," 377–404, 2005, with permission from Elsevier.

Figure 12.1
Supplementary Set of Statements (continued)

l. Is kept current by regular updating of content

m. Is well structured with:

    i. Consistent headings and labels on every page

    ii. Links that provide access to relevant information, allowing the serendipitous discovery of sources

    iii. A navigation means (e.g., breadcrumbs)

    iv. An option to search the library Web site

    v. The presence of a site map

    vi. Menus that help me understand how information/content is organized

n. Utilizes colors, background, fonts, icons, images, text size, and layout that are:

    i. Attractive

    ii. Easy to view

2. The online catalog:

a. Allows me to:

    i. Check the status of items I borrow and find out about overdue notices, and holds on items I borrow, renew material, place a hold on material, and view fines

    ii. Pay fines

    iii. Save my search results to a disk, USB drive, my e-mail, or bibliographic software (e.g., EndNote)

    iv. Save my search strategies (queries) and use them again

b. Can be trusted with my personal information

c. Displays information that is clear and easy to understand

d. Explains how to place a hold on items found while searching

e. Has easy-to-follow instructions

f. Has links that:

    i. Function (no dead links or re-directed links that do not work)

    ii. Provide access to relevant information

g. Is a comprehensive source of information about all materials in the library's electronic collections

h. Is easy to search

Figure 12.1
Supplementary Set of Statements (continued)

i. Indicates the number of copies available

j. Is easily accessible from outside the library building

k. Keeps an accurate record of:

  i. Any monies I owe

  ii. My library transactions

l. Provides access to e-reserves (course material available electronically)

m. Provides the option of a *simple* or *advanced* search

n. Provides Web links:

  i. That are distinguishable from other information on the screen

  ii. To all e-resources identified in the online catalog

3. The library provides:

a. An adequate number of computer workstations in good working order

b. Access to laptop ports

c. Computers dedicated only for online catalog use

d. Computer printing:

  i. At a reasonable cost

  ii. From equipment in good working order

e. Computer workstations (e.g., for access to the Web, electronic texts, and journals)

f. Computer workstations for group work

g. Computers with:

  i. Access for USB memory devices

  ii. All the software I need to access curriculum material

  iii. Campus e-mail

  iv. CD ands/or DVD buring

  v. Document/photo scanning

  vi. Productivity processing software (e.g., word processing and spreadsheets)

  vii. Web e-mail

  viii. Wireless networks

h. Laptop computers available for loan

i. Technical help and support

Figure 12.1
Supplementary Set of Statements (continued)

4. When I use the university's computer network, I can:

   a. Log on easily/quickly

   b. Log off easily/quickly

   c. Log on whenever I want from any off-campus location

   d. Pay online for Internet/printing/library charges

5. Course materials available from the library are:

   a. Accessible through

      i. Campus-based course managment software (e.g., Blackboard)

      ii. The online catalog/library Web site

   b. Easy to find on the library's online catalog

   c. Easy to download:

      i. To paper copy

      ii. And save as a file

   d. Easy to read/view once downloaded

6. The library provides access to a wide range of electronic resources in my subject area, in particular:

   a. E-books

   b. Full-text e-journals

   c. Online databases

   d. Online indexes

   e. Other electronic files (e.g., music files and art slides)

7. The library communicates with me effectively through:

   a. Internet chat

   b. E-mail

   c. The online catalog

   d. Text messaging

8. The library provides electronic document delivery (full text to customer's desktop) services for material that the library does not subscribe to

Figure 12.1
Supplementary Set of Statements (continued)

9. For the electronic desktop delivery services mentioned in the previous question, the library:

   a. Advises me how long to expect to wait for the item to be received

   b. Enables me to make a fully electronic request (i.e., search a database and download bibliographic information to a library request form)

   c. Enables me to ascertain online the progress of fulfilling my request

   d. Has no hidden printing costs for the service

10. The library:

    a. Alerts me about newly published material based on a personalized user profile the staff help me create

    b. Gives me personalized support if I have problems in using library resources

11. The library provides online information services that:

    a. Are easy to contact at any time by:

       i. E-mail

       ii. Online inquiry form

    b. Are easy to locate on the library's Web site

    c. Acknowledge my question within 24 hours

    d. Answer my question within five days

    e. Encourage me to provide feedback on my satisfaction with the service received

    f. Enable me to interact with library staff 24/7/365

    g. Give me pointers and paths to useful resources that will enable me to help myself better in the future

    h. Have staff who provide expert assistance when I need it

    i. Interact with me in a:

       i. Courteous manner

       ii. Respectful manner (e.g., maintaining privacy)

    j. Offer real time audio/video so that I can interact with someone

    k. Provide a statement on the scope and the procedure for asking questions

services to join in those discussions. They might even meet with some students in formal focus group interviews and raise some of the statements and library policies for student comment.

Finally, evidence upon which to base continuous quality improvement should be collected longitudinally, with perhaps a subset of the service quality statements appearing in each iteration of the survey. Other statements could be unique to each data-collecting activity.

MANAGEMENT'S KNOWLEDGE OF STUDENT EXPECTATIONS

Service quality can be defined in different ways, but the method most commonly used is the analysis of the *gap* between customer expectations of the organization and their simultaneous perceptions of performance by the same organization. Gap analysis, or disconfirmation, has been discussed for over twenty years,[15] but the most frequently cited approach is the SERVQUAL instrument and method that Valarie A. Zeithaml, A. Parasuraman, and Leonard L. Berry devised.[16] Essentially, gap analysis argues that an organization, whether it is in the private or public sector, must know what its customers perceive as excellent service, for unless it does there is no chance that managers can allocate resources, train staff, and establish procedures that will result in the organization's performance approaching its customers' expectations.

Zeithaml, Parasuraman, and Berry stated there was not simply one gap that needed analysis, but five. Gap 5 was defined as the gap between customer's expectations and their perceptions of actual performance, and almost all research into service quality has examined that gap. For this book the authors developed an instrument that examines the gap for a specific group of university library customers. The justification for this focus is that gap 5 is the *real* measure of service quality and hence it must be dealt with, but the other gaps "are the major causes of the service-quality gap customers may perceive."[17] As noted in chapter 7, the other gaps include:

- Gap 1: Customers' expectation (management-perceptions gap);
- Gap 2: Management's perceptions (service-quality specifications gap);
- Gap 3: Service-quality specifications (service-delivery gap); and
- Gap 4: Service delivery (external communications gap).

Zeithaml, Parasuraman, and Berry predicted that there would be three main factors contributing to gap 1: a lack of marketing orientation; inadequate upward communication; and too many levels of management.[18] In one of the few studies of gap 1 in a library setting, Rowena Cullen and Philip Calvert confirmed that these factors all played a major part in causing gap 1.[19] Those university libraries doing better on gap 1 conducted regular customer surveys (including full gap 5 surveys) and made extensive use of focus groups to elicit information about what the customers wanted. Moreover, managers

paid close attention to the survey findings and used them in resource allocation decisions. Management examined and replied to all comments and complaints made by customers and incorporated this information into future
planning. The successful libraries sought upward communication from front-
line staff who dealt with customers for most of the day. They sought more
direct dialogue between customers and management by sitting on library
committees and, in some cases, using liaison librarians. Importantly, the communication flow was not only inwards, but also the management announced
news about library services via newsletters and contributions to student magazines.

If library management sincerely wishes to get a better understanding of the
expectations of students with disabilities, then it can use a variety of means to
get the necessary information. One obvious means is to survey the target
population with the instrument developed for this book, or a variation of it.
Similarly, the management can meet with students in focus groups, with the
possibility of having different groups: one for those with physical impairments
and another for those with learning impairments.

Does library management encourage dialogue with relevant students by
meeting with them formally and informally whenever possible? If the university has a special committee to deal with general issues related to students with disabilities (e.g., the committee at Massey University,
New Zealand, described in chapter 6), does the library have a representa-
tive on that committee, and what feedback from its meetings goes to the
library management? Managers should not assume that if they do not hear
anything then nothing significant has happened. If the library has a suggestions box and/or a complaints procedure then this must extend to students
with disabilities, some of whom may be reluctant to complain through a
formal process. Individual staff who interact with students on public desks
(and even the shelving assistants) are an excellent source of information
about customer satisfaction and dissatisfaction. They should be used as a
source of information that can help close gap 1, and in this context those
who deal with students with disabilities should be encouraged to offer
information directly to senior library management. Too many layers of
management will weaken the process because, too often, compliant middle
managers only send good news up to the senior managers. The single most
important point is that a library director who sincerely wishes to gather better information about service quality for students with disabilities will have
to ensure that the necessary information is being gathered and that it
reaches the senior managers intact and in a short space of time. Only then
will gap 1 close and managers be able to convert what they know into better
service quality that should eventually close gap 5, which is the real measure
of service quality.

The campus office of disability service may publish a regular newsletter in
print or electronic form and will almost certainly welcome news from the
library about new materials and services that are of interest to the students

with disabilities. Other relevant stories can be placed in general student publications to catch those students who do not register with the disability service and to raise the profile of the library's services to a niche group of customers.

RESEARCH AGENDA

Self-reports reflect what students choose to relate or what they believe to be true. In other words, there might be discrepancies between what they say and actually do. Nonetheless, self-reports provide useful information upon which to base continuous quality improvement; however, they do not provide a complete (or necessarily totally accurate) picture.

It is important that librarians review the tool chest of methodological choices—both quantitative and qualitative—and select those best relevant to what they want to know and have the resources (time and money) to investigate. The instruments presented in chapters 8 and 9 could be delivered in various ways, such as in focus group or one-to-one interviews, Web-based surveys, or mailed questionnaires. Complementary insights might be gained from usability studies of Web sites and databases, observation of search behavior, and other methods. Those instruments should continue to be reviewed, refined, and adopted locally to provide insights useful for enhancing the quality of services provided.

Any research agenda should continue to examine customer expectations (service quality and satisfaction) from different perspectives and apply more of that methodological tool chest. Studies have investigated what libraries "are doing to provide access to their programs and services for persons with disabilities."[20] Future survey research should go beyond addressing the extent to which institutions and libraries have eliminated or reduced physical barriers. These studies should examine issues related to reference service (e.g., conducting the reference interview from the librarian and user perspective) and information literacy programs for students with hidden disabilities, and link the findings to outcomes assessment at the course, program, and institutional levels. It needs to be remembered, "staff members may have preconceptions and misconceptions about persons with certain disabilities and may be unaware that some disabilities are invisible or not readily apparent to others. Without training they may feel self-conscious or uncomfortable serving patrons with disabilities and this may lead to a different level of service from what is offered to other patrons."[21] Research needs to examine the effectiveness of:

- Instruction given to classes consisting solely of students with disabilities;[22]
- Instruction delivered to classes in which some students have hidden disabilities; and
- Staff training programs and the extent to which the staff demonstrate sensitivity to the needs and expectations of persons with disabilities.

Research has employed case studies to examine how well individual libraries meet the information needs of students with disabilities.[23] That research might be expanded to include more libraries and to base the comparison on a stratified random sample taken from a source such as *The Carnegie Classification of Institutions of Higher Education*.[24] At the same time, research might adopt an international perspective and make comparisons and observations across countries. Needless to say, the legal framework differs across countries but the desire to make services relevant and to advance learning may not differ.[25] Clearly, the instruments advanced in chapters 8 and 9 can be applied in different countries, with minor modification.

Because students with disabilities may prefer to use the same services as other students and not to call attention to their disabilities, research might examine the application of universal design principles so that everyone can use particular products and environments. Universal design advances the following principles:

- Equitable use: The design is useful and marketable to people with diverse abilities [and neither disadvantages nor stigmatizes them];
- Flexibility in use: The design accommodates individual preferences and abilities;
- Simple and intuitive use: Use of the design does not require special experience, knowledge, language skills, or current concentration level;
- Perceptible information: The design communicates critical information effectively to the user, regardless of ambient conditions or his or her sensory abilities;
- Tolerance for error: The design minimizes adverse consequences of accidental or unintended actions;
- Low physical effort: The design can be used efficiently and comfortably and with minimum fatigue.
- Size and space for approach and use: The user's body size, posture, or mobility does not inhibit information searching, navigation, and manipulation.[26]

Once the design principles have been fully translated into a set of standards or guidelines, research can study library Web sites and the extent to which they meet those principles for students with and without disabilities.

Research might also examine faculty members with disabilities and how library collections and services meet their information needs and service expectations related to teaching and research. Another area for research would be to examine the online documentation in which libraries announce their services to students with disabilities, and then to conduct case study research in which the adequacy and utility of that documentation are investigated (a gap 4 study). Somewhat related would be a determination of best practices and which academic libraries provide exemplary service for faculty, staff, and students with disabilities. What makes those services so outstanding? For example, the University of Wisconsin–Stout (UW-Stout) Library Learning Center, like many other academic libraries, has designated a librarian to assist library users with disabilities who need special services. The library, however, offers different

Web pages to detail those services and encourage "patrons with disabilities . . . to attend library orientation programs."[27] How many students with disabilities are aware of those services? How effective are those orientation programs in getting the students to recognize and work with the designated librarian? "As the first university to receive the Malcolm Baldrige National Quality Award, UW-Stout is playing a national leadership role in higher education through the services provided through . . . [its] Center for Assessment and Continuous Improvement."[28] Does that center impact faculty and student expectations for the services they receive? On the surface, the Learning Center might serve as a model that others could emulate. However, before making the final determination, this library might serve as one of those case studies.

Because a number of libraries have pages on their Web sites devoted to individuals with disabilities, it would be relevant to examine those pages and perform a content analysis of the information presentation. Do the pages cover the identical points? Furthermore, do students consult those pages and how satisfied are they with the contents? How do staff in offices serving students with disabilities view those pages? To what extent are library staff aware of these pages? As well, research should continue to examine homepages and their compliance with legal requirements. Paul T. Jaeger of the School of Information Studies, Florida State University, examines the Web sites of U.S. government agencies and observes that Section 508 "is hardly the only law establishing accessibility requirements."[29] He then identifies the other laws. It might be relevant to extend his comparison to the Web sites of libraries, especially those serving public institutions.

CONCLUSION

Even when libraries assign one person to coordinate services for students with disabilities and to interact with the campus office of disability services, others may be involved in any interaction, especially when students need assistance in retrieving a book or journal issue or volume; when they interact with reference staff during a reference interview intended to identify their specific information need; when students participate in information literacy programs, especially those linked to outcomes assessment; and so on. Now that a number of libraries are engaged in service quality assessment through the application of LibQUAL+™, which does not specifically target or address the expectations of students with disabilities, the timing is appropriate to expand the analysis of service quality to other segments of the student population. It is important for the library to be perceived as listening to all segments of the population—student and other—that they serve. Whatever information is collected provides evidence that the staff can factor into their planning process and ensure continuous quality improvement in the services they provide to *all* students, faculty, and other communities they serve.

> . . . [L]ibraries generally enjoy a reputation for emphasizing good user
> services. To maintain this image, libraries should develop and implement

plans to improve access to library programs and services for persons with disabilities.[30]

NOTES

1. Suzanne Byerley, "Usability Testing and Students with Visual Disabilities: Building Electronic Curb Cuts into a Library Web Site," *Colorado Libraries* 27, no 3 (Fall 2001): 24.

2. Middle States Commission on Higher Education, *Characteristics of Excellence in Higher Education: Eligibility Requirements and Standards for Accreditation* (Philadelphia, PA: Middle States Commission on Higher Education, 2002), 32.

3. Middle States Commission on Higher Education, *Developing Research and Communication Skills: Guidelines for Information Literacy in the Curriculum* (Philadelphia, PA: Middle States Commission on Higher Education, 2003), 5.

4. Wisconsin Association of Academic Librarians, Information Library Committee, "Information Literacy Competencies and Criteria for Academic Libraries in Wisconsin" (October 1998). Available at http://www.wla.lib.wi.us/waal/infolit/ilcc.html (accessed November 10, 2004).

5. American Library Association, Association of College and Research Libraries, *Objectives for Information Literacy Instruction: A Model Statement for Academic Librarians* (Chicago: Association of College and Research Libraries, 2001). Available at http://www.ala.org/ala/acrl/acrlstandards/objectives information.htm (accessed November 10, 2004).

6. Ibid.

7. Kathleen Dunn, "Assessing Information Literacy Skills in the California State University: A Progress Report," *The Journal of Academic Librarianship* 28, no. 1/2 (January/February 2002), 28.

8. See Santa Monica College Library, "Learning Disabilities" (Santa Monica, CA: Santa Monica College, n.d.). Available at http://library.smc.edu/research/topics/learning_disabilities.htm (accessed November 27, 2004); LD Online, "Types of LD" (n.d.). Available at http://www.ldonline.org/abcs_info/ld_types.html (accessed November 27, 2004); University of Maryland Medicine, "Learning Disabilities—Types" (A partnership of the University of Maryland Medical Center and the University of Maryland School of Medicine) (Baltimore, MD: University of Maryland Medicine, n.d.). Available at http://www.umm.edu/mcadd/ld_types.html (accessed November 27, 2004).

9. Peggy L. Maki, *Assessing for Learning: Building a Sustainable Commitment across the Institution* (Sterling, VA: Stylus Publishing, 2004), 3.

10. Ibid.

11. Sheryl Burgstahler, Bill Corrigan, and Joan McCarter, "Making Distance Learning Courses Accessible to Students and Instructors with Disabilities: A Case Study," *The Internet and Higher Education* 7 (2004), 233.

12. Ibid., 234.

13. Ibid., 235.

14. See ibid., 235–238, for an identification of the legislation, standards, and guidelines.

15. See Philip Calvert, "Service Quality in Libraries," *The New Review of Information and Library Research* 6 (2000): 5–23.

16. Valarie A. Zeithaml, A. Parasuraman, and Leonard L. Berry, *Delivering Service Quality: Balancing Customer Perceptions and Expectations* (New York: The Free Press, 1990).

17. Ibid., p. 36.

18. Ibid., p. 52.

19. Rowena Cullen and Philip Calvert, "Organisational Factors Affecting the Delivery of Service Quality in Academic Libraries," in *Library Measures to Fill the Void: Proceedings of the Fifth Northumbria International Conference on Performance Measurement in Libraries and Information Services,* edited by Sandra Parker (Bradford, England: Emerald, 2004), 166–172.

20. See, for instance, Patricia P. Nelson, "Library Services for People with Disabilities: Results of a Survey," *Bulletin of the Medical Library Association* 84, no. 3 (July 1996): 397–401.

21. Katherine J. Miller-Gattenby and Michelle Chittenden, "Reference Service for All: How to Support Reference Service to Clients with Disabilities," in *Reference Services for the Adult Learner: Challenging Issues for the Traditional and Technological Era,* edited by Kwasi Sarkodie-Mensah (New York: Haworth, 2000): 313–326.

22. See Marilyn Graubart, "Serving the Library Needs of Students with Physical Disabilities," *Library Hi Tech* 14 (1996): 37–40.

23. See, for instance, Jill Mendle, "Library Services for Persons with Disabilities, *The Reference Librarian* 49/50 (1995): 105–112.

24. *The Carnegie Classification of Institutions of Higher Education* (Menlo Park, CA: Carnegie Foundation for the Advancement of Teaching, 2001).

25. See, for instance, Suzanne Heaven and Anne Goulding, "Higher Education Libraries and SENDA," *The New Review of Academic Librarianship* 8 (2002): 175–194.

26. North Carolina State University, Center for Universal Design, *Universal Design for Learning* (Raleigh, NC: North Carolina State University, 1997). Available at http://iod.unh.edu/EE/articles/articles_udl.html (accessed November 11, 2004).

27. University of Wisconsin–Stout, Library Learning Center, "Services for Library Users with Disabilities" (Menomonie, WI: University of Wisconsin-Stout, n.d.). Available at http://www.uwstout.edu/lib/services/disabled_2.htm (accessed November 11, 2004).

28. University of Wisconsin–Stout, Center for Assessment and Continuous Improvement, *Welcome* (Menomonie, WI: University of Wisconsin–Stout, n.d.). Available at http://www.uwstout.edu/mba/ (accessed November 11, 2004).

29. Paul T. Jaeger, "Beyond Section 508: The Spectrum of Legal Requirements for Accessible E-government Web Sites in the United States," *Journal of Government Information* 30 (2004), 518. See also Burgstahler, Corrigan, and McCarter, "Making Distance Learning Courses Accessible to Students and Instructors with Disabilities;" Andrew Potter, "Accessibility of Alabama Government Web Sites," *Journal of Government Information* 29 (2002): 303–317.

30. Nelson, "Library Services for People with Disabilities," 400.

BIBLIOGRAPHY

ARTICLES

Abeyta, Kateri, and Mary Mouton. "Know Your Audience: Guidelines to Develop Accessible Web Sites," *Colorado Libraries* 28, no. 4 (Winter 2002): 47–48.

Amtmann, Dagmar, Kurt Johnson, and Debbie Cook, "Making Web-based Tables Accessible for Users of Screen Readers," *Library Hi Tech, 20* (2002): 221–231.

Applin, Mary Beth. "Instructional Services for Students with Disabilities," *The Journal of Academic Librarianship* 25 (March 1999): 139–141.

———. "Providing Quality Library Services for Students with Disabilities," *Mississippi Libraries* 67 (Spring 2003): 6–7.

Bardwell, Catherine. "Users with Disabilities: Barriers in the Electronic Age: Challenges Faced by New Zealand University Libraries," *New Zealand Libraries* 48 (1997): 184–186.

Blackorby, Jose, and Mary Wagner. "Longitudinal Postschool Outcomes of Youth with Disabilities: Findings from the National Longitudinal Transition Study," *Exceptional Children* 62 (1996): 399–413.

Blanchard, R. F., and R. L. Galloway. "Quality in Retail Banking," *International Journal of Service Industry Management* 5, no. 4 (1994): 5–23.

Burgstahler, Sheryl. "Distance Learning: The Library's Role in Ensuring Access to Everyone," *Library Hi Tech* 20 (2002): 420–432.

———, Bill Corrigan, and Joan McCarter. "Making Distance Learning Courses Accessible to Students and Instructors with Disabilities: A Case Study," *The Internet and Higher Education* 7 (2004): 233–246.

Byerley, Suzanne. "Usability Testing and Students with Visual Disabilities: Building Electronic Curb Cuts into a Library Web Site," *Colorado Libraries* 27, no 3 (Fall 2001): 22–24.

———, and Mary Beth Chambers. "Accessibility and Usability of Web-based Library Databases for Non-visual Users," *Library Hi Tech* 20 (2002): 169–178.

Calvert, Philip. "Service Quality in Libraries," *The New Review of Information and Library Research* 6 (2000): 5–23.

———, and Peter Hernon. "Surveying Service Quality within University Libraries," *Journal of Academic Librarianship* 23 (September 1997): 408–415.

Cameron, Kim. "Measuring Organizational Effectiveness in Institutions of Higher Education," *Administrative Science Quarterly* 23 (1978): 604–629.

Carlson, Scott. "Left out Online," *The Chronicle of Higher Education* (June 11, 2004): A23.

Coonin, Bryna. "Establishing Accessibility for E-journals: A Suggested Approach," *Library Hi Tech* 20 (2002): 207–220.

Cory, Rebecca. "Students, DS Providers Often Can View Issues Differently," *Disability Compliance for Higher Education* 9, no. 11 (June 2004): 2.

Couper, Mick B. "Web Surveys: A Review of Issues and Approaches," *Public Opinion Quarterly* 64 (2000): 464–494.

Craven, Jenny. "Good Design Principles for the Library Website: A Study of Accessibility Issues in UK University Libraries," *New Review of Information and Library Research* 6 (2000): 25–51.

Cullen, Rowena J., and Philip J. Calvert, "New Zealand University Libraries Effectiveness Project: Dimensions and Concepts of Organizational Effectiveness," *Library & Information Science Research* 18 (1996): 99–119.

———. "Stakeholder Perceptions of University Library Effectiveness," *Journal of Academic Librarianship* 21(1995): 438–448.

Dunn, Kathleen. "Assessing Information Literacy Skills in the California State University: A Progress Report," *The Journal of Academic Librarianship* 28, no. 1/2 (January/February 2002): 26–35.

Edwards, Eli, and William Fisher, "Trust, Teamwork, and Tokenism: Another Perspective on Diversity in Libraries," *Library Administration & Management* 17 (Winter 2003): 21.

Edwards, Phil, Ian Roberts, Mike Clarke, Carolyn DiGuiseppi, Sarah Pratap, Reinhard Wentz, and Irene Kwan. "Increasing Response Rates to Postal Questionnaires: Systematic Review," *British Medical Journal* 324, issue 7347 (2002): 1183–1187.

Euben, Donna R. "Disabilities and the Academic Workplace," *Academe* 90 (September–October 2004): 86.

Fairweather, James S., and Deborah M. Shaver. "Making the Transition to Postsecondary Education and Training," *Exceptional Children* 57 (1990): 264–270.

Graubart, Marilyn. "Serving the Library Needs of Students with Physical Disabilities," *Library Hi Tech* 14 (1996): 37–40.

Green, Ravonne A., and Diane N. Gillespie. "Assistive Technologies in Academic Libraries: A Preliminary Study," *portal: Libraries and the Academy* 1 (2001): 329–337.

Griebel, Rosemary. "If Helen Keller Lived North of the 49th: Canadian Library Services for People with Disabilities," *Feliciter* 49, no. 3 (2003): 155.

Harris, C., and C. Oppenheim. "The Provision of Library Services for Visually Impaired Students in UK Further Education Libraries in Response to the

Special Educational Needs and Disability Act (SENDA)," *Journal of Librarianship and Information Science* 35 (December 2003): 243–257.

Hayden, Helen, Terry O'Brien, and Maoiliosa O Rathaille. "User Survey at Waterford Institute of Technology Libraries: How a Traditional Approach to Surveys Can Inform Library Service Delivery," *New Library World* 106, no. 1208/1209 (2005): 43–57.

Heath, Fred M., Martha Kyrillidou, and Consuella A. Askew, eds. "Libraries Act on Their LibQUAL+™ Findings: From Data to Action," *Journal of Library Administration™* 40 (3/4) (2004): 1–240.

Heaven, Suzanne, and Anne Goulding. "Higher Education Libraries and SENDA," *The New Review of Academic Librarianship* 8 (2002): 175–194.

Hernon, Peter, and Philip Calvert. "E-Service Quality in Libraries: Its Features and Dimensions." *Library & Information Science Research* 27 (2005): 377–404.

———. "Methods for Measuring Service Quality in University Libraries in New Zealand," *Journal of Academic Librarianship* 22 (September 1996): 387–391.

Horwath, Jennifer. "Evaluating Opportunities for Expanded Information Access: A Study of the Accessibility of Four Online Databases," *Library Hi Tech* 20, no. 2 (2002): 199–206.

"Information Access for People with Disabilities," *Library Technology Reports* 40 (May–June 2004): 10–32.

Jaeger, Paul T. "Beyond Section 508: The Spectrum of Legal Requirements for Accessible E-government Web Sites in the United States," *Journal of Government Information* 30 (2004): 518–533.

Jones, Allison, and Lucy A. Tedd. "Provision of Electronic Information Services for the Visually Impaired: An Overview with Case Studies from Three Institutions within the University of Wales," *Journal of Librarianship and Information Science* 35 (June 2003): 105–113.

Keefer, Jane. "The Hungry Rats Syndrome: Library Anxiety, Information Literacy, and the Academic Reference Process," *RQ* 32 (1993): 333–340.

Kirkpatrick, Cheryl H. "Getting Two for the Price of One: Accessibility and Usability," *Computers in Libraries* 23 (January 2003): 26–29.

Kramer, Howard. "Meeting the Needs of Students at a Large University? At CU Boulder," *Colorado Libraries* 28, no. 4 (Winter 2002): 31–34.

Kypri, Kypros, Stephen J. Gallagher, and Martine L. Cashell-Smith. "An Internet-based Survey Method for College Student Drinking Research," *Drug and Alcohol Dependence* 76 (2004): 45–53.

Leckie, Gloria J. "Desperately Seeking Citations: Uncovering Faculty Assumptions about the Undergraduate Research Process," *The Journal of Academic Librarianship* 22 (May 1996): 201–208.

Lilly, Erica B., and Connie Van Fleet. "Wired but Not Connected: Accessibility of Academic Library Home Pages," *The Reference Librarian™* 67/68 (1999): 5–28.

Loiacono, Eleanor, and Scott McCoy, "Web Site Accessibility: An Online Sector Analysis," *Information Technology & People* 17 (2004): 87–101.

Lynch, James, Robert Carver, Jr., and John Michael Virgo. "Quadrant Analysis as a Strategic Planning Technique in Curriculum Development and Program Marketing," *Journal of Marketing for Higher Education* 7 (1996): 17–32.

Mark, Beth L., and Trudi E Jacobson, "Teaching Anxious Students Skills for the Electronic Library," *College Teaching* 43 (1995): 28–31.

McCasland, Margaret, and Michael Golden, "Improving ADA Access: Critical Planning," *The Reference Librarian*™ 67/68 (1999): 257–269.

McNulty, Michael A. "Dyslexia and the Life Course," *Journal of Learning Disabilities* 36 (2003): 363–381.

Mendle, Jill. "Library Services for Persons with Disabilities," *The Reference Librarian*™ 49/50 (1995): 105–112.

Miller-Gatenby, Katherine J., and Michele Chittenden. "Reference Services for All: How to Support Reference Service to Clients with Disabilities," *The Reference Librarian*™ 69/70 (2000): 313–326.

Nelson, Patricia P. "Library Services for People with Disabilities: Results of a Survey," *Bulletin of the Medical Library Association* 84, no. 3 (July 1996): 397–401.

Nitecki, Danuta, and Peter Hernon. "Measuring Service Quality at Yale University's Libraries," *The Journal of Academic Librarianship* 26, no. 4 (July 2000): 259–273.

Oliver R. L., and W. S. DeSarbo. "Response Determinants in Satisfaction Judgments," *Journal of Consumer Research* 14 (1998): 495–507.

Parasuraman, A., Valarie A. Zeithaml, and Leonard L. Berry. "Alternative Scales for Measuring Service Quality: A Comparative Assessment Based on Psychometric and Diagnostic Criteria," *Journal of Retailing* 70 (1994): 201–230.

———, Leonard L. Berry, and Valarie A. Zeithaml. "Refinement and Reassessment of the SERVQUAL Scale," *Journal of Retailing* 67 (1991): 420–450.

Potter, Andrew. "Accessibility of Alabama Government Web Sites," *Journal of Government Information* 29 (2002): 303–317.

Proctor, Briley S. "Social Policy and Its Application to Students with Learning Disabilities in U.S. Institutes of Higher Education," *International Journal of Sociology and Social Policy* 21 (2001): 38–59.

Read, Katherine. "An Overview of Current Library Support for Readers with Special Needs," *Legal Information Management* 4 (Spring 2004): 54–55.

Reeves, C. A., and D. A. Bednar. "Defining Quality: Alternatives and Implications," *Academy of Management Review* 19 (1994): 419–445.

Riddell, Sheila. "Chipping away at the Mountain: Disabled Students' Experiences of Higher Education," *International Studies in the Sociology of Education* 8 (1998): 203–222.

Roer-Strier, D. "University Students with Learning Disabilities Advocating for Change," *Disability and Rehabilitation* 24 (2002): 914–924.

Rothstein, Laura. "Disabilities and Higher Education: A Crystal Ball?," *Change* 35 (May–June 2003): 39–40.

Salend, Suzanne, and Spencer J. Salend. "Adapting Teacher-Made Tests for Mainstreamed Students," *Journal of Learning Disabilities* 18 (June/July 1985): 373–375.

Sax, Linda J., Shannon K. Gilmartin, and Alyssa N. Bryant. "Assessing Response Rates and Nonresponse Bias in Web and Paper Surveys," *Research in Higher Education* 44 (August 2003): 409–432.

Schnakenberg, Mary A. "Access to Information for the Visually Impaired in New Zealand," *New Zealand Libraries* 46 (1990): 16–18.

Scott, Sally S., Joan M. McGuire, Mary D. Sarver, and Stan F. Shaw. "Universal Design for Instruction: A New Paradigm for Adult Instruction in Postsecondary Education," *Remedial and Special Education* 24 (2003): 369–379.

Singh, Delar K. "Students with Disabilities and Higher Education," *College Student Journal* 37 (September 2003): 367–378.

Spindler Tim. "The Accessibility of Web Pages for Mid-Sized College and University Libraries," *Reference & User Services Quarterly* 42 (Winter 2002): 149–154.

Taylor, Margaret. "Widening Participation into Higher Education for Disabled Students," *Education+ Training* 46 (2004): 40–48.

Tinerella, Vincent P., and Marcia A. Dick, "Academic Reference Service for the Visually Impaired: A Guide for the Non-specialist," *College & Research Libraries* 66 (January 2005): 29–32.

Tucker, Richard N. "Access for All? It Depends Who You Are," *IFLA Journal* 29 (2003): 385–388.

Vaca, Dorothy M. "Confronting the Puzzle of Nonverbal Learning Disabilities," *Educational Leadership* 59, no. 3 (2001): 26–31.

Walling, Linda Lucas. "Educating Students to Serve Information Seekers with Disabilities," *Journal of Education for Library and Information Science* 45 (Spring 2004): 137–148.

Wattenberg, Ted. "Beyond Legal Compliance: Communities of Advocacy That Support Accessible Online Learning," *The Internet and Higher Education* 7 (2004): 123–139.

Weyandt, Lisa L., Wendy Iwaszuk, Katie Fulton, Micha Ollerton, Noelle Beatty, Hillary Fouts, Stephen Schepman, and Corey Greenlaw. "The Internal Restlessness Scale: Performance of College Students with and without ADHD," *Journal of Learning Disabilities* 36 (2003): 382–389.

"What Is the State of Adaptive Technology in Libraries Today?," *Library Technology Reports* 40 (May–June 2004): 81–92.

Wollam, Kathy, and Barbara Wessel. "Recognizing and Effectively Managing Mental Illness in the Library," *Colorado Libraries* 29, no. 4 (Winter 2003): 17.

Yannie, Mark. "Extent of Service: Minnesota Libraries Disability Services and Quality of Websites: Assessing Public and Academic Libraries," *Christian Librarian* 47 (2004): 48–52.

———. "A Survey Can Measure the Accessibility of Your Institution's Library," *Disability Compliance for Higher Education* 87, no. 8 (March 2003): 9.

Yavas, Ugur, and Dogan Eroglu. "Assessing Competitive Edge: Exposition and Illustration of a Diagnostic Tool," *Journal of Consumer Marketing* 12, no. 2 (1995): 47–59.

Zull, James E. "The Art of Changing the Brain," *Educational Leadership* 62 (2004): 68–69.

BOOKS

Anderson, Kristin, and Ron Zemke, *Delivering Knock Your Socks off Service,* rev. ed. New York: American Management Association 1991.

Barkley, Russell. *ADHD and the Nature of Self-control.* New York: Guilford Press, 1997.

Barnes, Colin, and Geof Mercer. *Disability.* Cambridge, UK: Policy Press, 2003.

Berry, Leonard L. *On Great Service: A Framework for Action.* New York: The Free Press, 1995.

The Carnegie Classification of Institutions of Higher Education. Menlo Park, CA: Carnegie Foundation for the Advancement of Teaching, 2001.

Craven, Jenny, and Peter Brophy. *Non-Visual Access to the Digital Library (NoVA): The Use of the Digital Library Interfaces by Blind and Visually Impaired People.* Manchester, England: Manchester Metropolitan University, n.d.

Disend, Jeffrey E. *How to Provide Excellent Service in Any Organization,* Radnor, PA: Chilton Book Co., 1991.

Feden, Preston D., and Robert M. Vogel. *Methods of Teaching: Applying Cognitive Science to Promote Student Learning.* Boston: McGraw Hill, 2003.

Henderson, Cathy, ed. *College Freshmen with Disabilities: A Statistical Profile.* Washington, D.C.: American Council on Education, 1995.

Hernon, Peter, and Ellen Altman. *Assessing Service Quality: Satisfying the Expectations of Library Customers.* Chicago: American Library Association, 1998.

———, and Robert E. Dugan. *An Action Plan for Outcomes Assessment in Your Library.* Chicago: American Library Association, 2002.

———, Harold C. Relyea, Robert E. Dugan, and Joan F. Cheverie. *United States Government Information: Policies and Sources.* Westport, CT: Libraries Unlimited, 2002.

———, and John R. Whitman. *Delivering Satisfaction and Service Quality: A Customer-based Approach for Libraries.* Chicago: American Library Association, 2001.

Heyward, Salome. *Disability and Higher Education: Guidance for Section 504 and ADA Compliance.* Horsham, PA: LRP Publications, 1998.

Hirsch, Jr., Edward D. *Cultural Literacy: What Every American Needs to Know.* Boston: Houghton Mifflin, 1987.

Kuhlthau, Carol C. *Seeking Meaning: A Process Approach to Library and Information Services.* Norwood, NJ: Ablex Publishing Corp., 1993.

Lazzaro, Joseph. *Adaptive Technologies for Learning and Work Environments.* Chicago: American Library Association, 2001.

Line, Maurice B. *Library Surveys: An Introduction to the Use, Planning, Procedure and Presentation of Surveys.* London: Clive Bingley, 1982.

Maki, Peggy L. *Assessing for Learning: Building a Sustainable Commitment across the Institution.* Sterling, VA: Stylus Publishing, 2004.

Middle States Commission on Higher Education, *Developing Research and Communication Skills: Guidelines for Information Literacy in the Curriculum.* Philadelphia, PA: Middle States Commission on Higher Education, 2003.

Moore, Nick. *How to Do Research.* London: Library Association, 1983.

Oliver, R. L. *Satisfaction: A Behavioral Perspective on the Consumer.* New York: McGraw-Hill, 1997.

Oppenheim, A. N. *Questionnaire Design, Interviewing, and Attitude Measurement.* New York: Pinter Publishers, 1992.

Pollak, David. *Dyslexia, the Self and Higher Education.* Sterling, VA: Stylus Publishing, 2005.

Powell, Ronald R., and Lynn Silipigni Connaway. *Basic Research Methods for Librarians,* 4th ed. Westport, CT: Libraries Unlimited, 2004.

Schneider, Benjamin, and Susan S. White. *Service Quality: Research Perspectives.* Thousand Oaks, CA: Sage Publications, 2004.

Shapiro, Janet. *No Pity: People with Disabilities Forging a New Civil Rights Movement.* New York: Random House, Inc., 1993.

Underhill, Paco. *The Science of Shopping.* New York: Simon & Schuster, 1999.

Vavra, Terry G. *Improving Your Measurement of Customer Satisfaction: A Guide to Creating, Conducting, Analyzing, and Reporting Customer Satisfaction Measurement Programs.* Milwaukee, WI: ASQ Quality Press, 1997.

Vygotsky, Lev S. *Mind in Society: The Development of Higher Psychological Processes.* Cambridge, MA: Harvard University Press, 1978.

Wender, Paul H. *ADHD: Attention-Deficit Hyperactivity Disorder in Children and Adults.* Oxford: Oxford University Press, 2000.

Zeithhaml, Valarie A., A. Parasuraman, and Leonard L. Berry. *Delivering Quality Service: Balancing Customer Perceptions and Expectations.* New York: The Free Press, 1990.

BOOK / JOURNAL CHAPTERS

Berninger, Virginia W. "The Reading Brain in Children and Youth: A Systems Approach," in *Learning about Learning Disabilities, Third Edition,* edited by Bernice Wong. San Diego, CA: Elsevier Academic Press, 2004, pp. 197–248.

Cullen, Rowena, and Philip Calvert. "Organisational Factors Affecting the Delivery of Service Quality in Academic Libraries," in *Library Measures to Fill the Void: Proceedings of the Fifth Northumbria International Conference on Performance Measurement in Libraries and Information Services,* edited by Sandra Parker. Bradford, England: Emerald, 2004, pp. 166–172.

Gobbo, Kenneth. "College Student Development Programs and Students with Learning Disabilities," in *Understanding Learning Disabilities at the Postsecondary Level: A Landmark College Guide,* edited by Lynne C. Shea and Stuart W. Strothman. Putney, VT: Landmark College, 2003, pp. 107–132.

Herbert, Christina. "Making College Classrooms Accessible to Students with and without Learning Disabilities," in *Promoting Academic Success for Students with Learning Disabilities: The Landmark College Guide to Practical Instruction,* edited by Stuart Strothman. Putney, VT: Landmark College, 2001, pp. 1–26.

Katz, Lynda J. "Students with ADHD in Higher Education" in *Learning Disabilities in Higher Education and Beyond: International Perspectives,* edited by Susan A. Vogel, Gila Vogel, Varda Sharoni, and Orit Dahan. Baltimore: York Press, 2003, pp. 145–171.

Lenz, B. Keith, and Donald D. Deshler, "Adolescents with Learning Disabilities: Revisiting *The Educator's Enigma,*" in *Learning about Learning Disabilities, Third Edition,* edited by Bernice Wong. San Diego, CA: Elsevier Academic Press, 2004, pp. 535–564.

Miller-Gattenby, Katherine J., and Michelle Chittenden. "Reference Service for All: How to Support Reference Service to Clients with Disabilities," in *Reference Services for the Adult Learner: Challenging Issues for the Traditional and Technological Era,* edited by Kwasi Sarkodie-Mensah. New York: Haworth, 2000, pp. 313–326.

Paris, S., G. B. A. Wasik, and J. C. Turner, "The Development of Strategic Readers," in *Handbook of Reading Research,* Volume II, edited by R. Barr, M. L. Kamil, P. B. Mosenthal, and P. D. Pearson. New York: Longman, 1991, pp. 609–640.

Perry, William G., Jr. "Cognitive and Ethical Growth: The Making of Meaning," in *The Modern American College,* edited by Arthur Chickering. San Francisco: Jossey-Bass, 1981, pp. 76–116.

Porter, Stephen R. "Survey Response Rates: What Works?," *New Directions for Institutional Research* (special issue, *Overcoming Survey Research Problems*) 121 (Spring 2004): 5–21.

———— and Michael E. Whitcomb. "Understanding the Effect of Prizes on Response Rates," *New Directions for Institutional Research* (special issue, *Overcoming Survey Research Problems*) 121 (Spring 2004): 51–62.

Shmulsky, Solvegi S. "Developing Critical Thinking in College," in *Promoting Academic Success for Students with Learning* Disabilities: *The Landmark College Guide to Practical Instruction,* edited by Stuart Strothman. Putney, VT: Landmark College, 2001, pp. 105–126.

Welch, Polly, and Chris Palames. "A Brief History of Disability Rights Legislation in the United States," in Strategies for Teaching Universal Design, edited by Polly Welch. Boston, MA: Adaptive Environments Center, 1995, pp. 5–12.

ERIC DOCUMENTS

Loope, Charlene H. "Academic Library Services for Students with Disabilities: A Survey at the University of South Carolina." Columbia, SC: University of South Carolina, 1996 (ERIC ED396503).

Ommerborn, Rainer, and Rudolf Schuemer. "Using Computers in Distance Study: Results of a Survey amongst Disabled Distance Students." 2001 (ERIC, ED456214).

GOVERNMENT PUBLICATIONS / INTERNATIONAL ORGANIZATIONS (NON-WEB)

Assistive Technology Act of 1998 (P.L. 105–394).

Minnesota Office of the Legislative Auditor. *State Agency Use of Customer Satisfaction Surveys: A Program Evaluation Report.* St. Paul, MI: Minnesota Office of the Legislative Auditor, 1995.

New Zealand. Ministry of Health. *The New Zealand Disability Strategy: Making a World of Difference, Whakanui Oranga.* Wellington: Ministry of Health, 2001.

————. Statistics New Zealand. *Disability Counts.* Wellington: Statistics New Zealand, 2001.

Organisation for Economic Co-operation and Development, *Disability in Higher Education.* Paris: Organisation for Economic Co-operation and Development, 2003.

U.S. Bureau of the Census. *Census Brief,* CNBR-97–5. Washington, D.C.: Bureau of the Census, 1997.

REPORTS

Cullen, Rowena, and Peter Hernon, *Wired for Well-being: Citizens' Response to E-government.* A report. Wellington, New Zealand: New Zealand State Services Commission, E-government Unit, June 2004.

New Zealand Disabilities Resource Centre. *Survey of Information Needs of People with Disabilities.* Wellington, New Zealand: New Zealand Disabilities Resource Centre, 1991.

Victoria University of Wellington. *Student Services Strategic Plan.* Wellington: Victoria University of Wellington, 2004.

WEB PUBLICATIONS

American Library Association. Association of College and Research Libraries. *Objectives for Information Literacy Instruction: A Model Statement for Academic Librarians.* Chicago: Association of College and Research Libraries, 2001. Available at http://www.ala.org/ala/acrl/acrlstandards/objectivesinformation. htm (accessed November 10, 2004).

Amherst College Library. "ADA Accessibility." Amherst, MA: Amherst College Library, 2004. Available at http://www.amherst.edu/library/info/ada.html (accessed September 3, 2004).

Association of Research Libraries. "LibQUAL+™ Survey Results." Washington, D.C.: Association of Research Libraries, 2004. Available at http://www.arl. org/pubscat/libqualpubs.html (accessed August 29, 2004).

———. "Service to Users with Disabilities," *Transforming Libraries: Issues and Innovations in ...,* issue 8. Washington, D.C.: Association of Research Libraries, April 1999. Available at http://www.arl.org/transform/disabilities/ (accessed September 3, 2004).

Australian Library and Information Association. "Guidelines on Library Standards for People with Disabilities." Kingston, Australia: Australian Library and Information Association, 1998. Available at http://alia.org.au/policies/disability. standards.html (accessed January 24, 2005).

Bobby™ Web site. Waltham, NA: The Watchfire Co.. Available at http://bobby. watchfire.com/bobby/html/en/index.jsp (accessed August 27, 2004). See also http://bobby.watchfire.com/bobby/html/en/about.jsp (accessed August 27, 2004).

Bohman, Paul Ryan. "University Web Accessibility Policies: A Bridge Not Quite Far Enough." Logan, UT: WebAIM, 2004. Available at http://www.webaim. org/coordination/articles/policies-pilot (accessed November 5, 2004).

Boston College Library. "Services for Persons with Disabilities." Newton, MA: Boston College, O'Neill Library, 2004. Available at http://www.bx.edu/ libraries/centers/oneill/about/s-disabilities/ (accessed September 4, 2004).

Brewer, Judy, ed. "How People with Disabilities Use the Web: W3C Working Draft." Cambridge, MA: World Wide Web Consortium, 2001. Available at http:// www.w3.org/WAI/EO/Drafts/PWD-Use-Web/Overview.html (accessed August 27, 2004).

Bridgewater State College Library. "Services for Users with Disabilities." Bridgewater, MA: Bridgewater State College, Maxwell Library, 2004. Available at http:// www.bridgew.edu.edu/Library/disability.cfm (accessed September 3, 2004).

Carpenter, Scott A. "Accommodation to Persons with Disabilities: A Census of Ohio College and University Libraries," *The Katherine Sharp Review* 3 (Summer 1996). Available at http://www.lis.uiuc.edu/review/summer1996/carpenter. html (accessed September 3, 2004).

Center for Universal Design. "About the Center." Raleigh, NC: North Carolina State University, 1997. Available at http://www.design.ncsu.edu/cud/center/ aboutus.htm (accessed June 1, 2005).

———. "What Is Universal Design?" Raleigh, NC: North Carolina State University, 1997. Available at http://www.design.ncsu.edu/cud/univ_design/princ_ overview.htm (accessed June 1, 2005).

Challacombe-King, Brett, and Katie Taylor, "At the Mighty Steps of Academia: What Foils the Young Disabled Person?" Paper presented at the Standards Plus conference on Exploring the Pathways to Tertiary Education, Auckland, New Zealand, 2004. Available at http://www.imaginebetter.co.nz/coa2004_ proceedings.shtml (accessed May 10, 2005).

Church, Jennifer, Sharon Drouin, and Katherine Rankin. "Electronic Resources on Disabilities: A Wealth of Information on Topics from Jobs to Recreation," *College & Research Libraries News* 61, no. 2 (February 2000). Available at http://www.ala.org/ala/acrl/acrlpubs/crlnews/backissues2000/february3/ electronicresources.htm (accessed November 5, 2004).

Council on Access to Information for Print-Disabled Canadians. Homepage. Ottawa, CA: Council on Access to Information for Print-Disabled Canadians. Available at http://www.collectionscanada.ca/accessinfo/index-e.html (accessed September 4, 2004).

Craven, Jenny. "Understanding the Searching Process for Visually Impaired Users of the Web." Available http://www.ariadne.ac.uk/issue26/craven/intro.html (accessed April 4, 2005).

Curry College. *Curry College Disability Services.* Milton, MA: Curry College. Available at http://www.curry.edu/hr/files/disability_serv.html (accessed July 7, 2004).

Earlham College Libraries. "Library Services for Persons with Disabilities." Richmond, IN: Earlham College Libraries, 2004. Available at http://www.earlham,edu/ ~libr/library/access.htm ((accessed September 3, 2004).

European Union. *Data Protection in the European Union.* (Brussels: European Union, n.d.). Available at http://europa.eu.int/comm/internal_market/privacy/ docs/guide/guide-ukingdom_en.pdf (accessed November 28, 2004).

Forsyth, Elizabeth M. *Measuring and Delivering Quality in Open Employment Services for People with Disability: Is a System of Compliance to Performance Standards in Conflict with Furthering Quality in Service Delivery for Customers?* Adelaide: South Australia: Adelaide University, Graduate School of Management, n.d.). Available at http://www.workable.org/au/archive/measuring_ and_delivering_quality.htm (accessed August 31, 2004).

Gallaudet University. "The Gallaudet Mission, Vision and Communication Statements." Washington, D.C.: Gallaudet University, n.d. Available at http:// www.gallaudet.edu/mission.htm (accessed September 14, 2004).

Graves, Rebecca S. "Re: Sequencing Info. Lit. in College?," Information Literacy Instruction Listserv (ILI-L) listserv (August 23, 2004). Available at http:// lp-web.ala.org:8000/ (accessed November 30, 2004).

Greene, Gary. "A Spelling Test for Teachers of Students with Learning Disabilities," *LD Forum* 20, no. 3 (1995). Available at http://www.ldonline.org/ ld_indepth/teaching_techniques/spelling_test.html (accessed November 8, 2004).

Griffith University. "Students with Disabilities Policy." Queensland, Australia: Griffith University, n.d. Available at http://www62.gu.edu/au/policy/librry.nsf/mainsearcgh/c5572a3154e0fefda256bba0063129f (accessed September 4, 2004).

Henderson, Cathy. *College Freshmen with Disabilities: A Biennial Statistical Profile.* Washington, D.C.: The George Washington University HEATH Resource Center, 2001. Available at http://www.heath.gwu.edu/PDFs/collegefreshmen.pdf (accessed November 22, 2004).

Horn, Laura, and Jennifer Berktold. "Students with Disabilities in Postsecondary Education: A Profile of Preparation, Participation, and Outcomes," *Education Statistics Quarterly* 1, no. 3 (1999). Available at http://nces.ed.gov/programs/quarterly/vol_1/1_3/4-esq13-a.asp (accessed May 22, 2005).

ICF Australian User Guide V1.0. Canberra: Australian Institute of Health and Welfare, 2003. Available at http://www.aihw.gov.au/publications/dis/icfaugv1/icfugv1.pdf (accessed October 3, 2004).

Jiwnani, Kanta. "Designing for Users with Cognitive Disabilities." College Park, MD: University of Maryland, April 2001. Available at the University of Maryland Universal Usability in Practice Web site, http://www.otal.umd.edu/uupractice/cognition/ (accessed December 3, 2004).

Kuhlthau, Carol C. "Kuhlthau's Model of the Stages of the Information Process." Arcata, CA: Humboldt State University Library, 1999. Available at http://library.humboldt.edu/~ccm/fingertips/kuhlthau.html (accessed September 28, 2004).

Landmark College. "About Landmark." Putney, VT: Landmark College, 2005. Available at http://www.landmark.edu (accessed March 11, 2005).

———. "National Institute at Landmark College." Putney, VT: Landmark College, 2003. Available at http://www.landmarkcollege.org/institute/index.html (accessed September 7, 2004).

———. Library. "Welcome to the Library." Putney, VT: Landmark College, 2005. Available at http://www.landmark.edu/Library/index.html (accessed March 11, 2005).

LD Online. "Types of LD." Washington, D.C.: WETA , n.d. Available at http://www.ldonline.org/abcs_info/ld_types.html (accessed November 27, 2004).

Library and Information Commission. "REVEAL: The National Database of Resources in Accessible Formats." London: Library and Information Commission, 2000. Available at http://www.ukoln.ac.uk/services/lic/sharethevision/ (accessed October 12, 2004).

Memorial Hall Library. "User and Non-User Survey: Planning for Library Services for People with Disabilities." Andover, MA: Memorial Hall Library, n.d. Available at http://www.mhl.org/disabilties/ (accessed September 3, 2004).

Montgomery College Libraries. "Library Services for Patrons with Disabilities." Montgomery County, MD: Montgomery College Libraries, 2004. Available at http://www.montgomerycollege.edu/library/library_services-for_disabilities.htm (accessed September 3, 2004).

National Joint Committee on Learning Disabilities, "The ABCs of LD and ADHD." Rockville, MD: National Joint Committee on Learning Disabilities, 2004. Available at http://www.ldonline.org/abcs_info/articles-info.html (accessed September 8, 2004).

National Library of Australia. Forum on Library Services for People with Disabilities. Homepage. Canberra, Australia: National Library of Australia, 2002. Available at http://www.nla.gov.au/initiatives/meetings/disabilities/index2002. html (accessed January 24, 2005).

———. Papers. Canberra, Australia: National Library of Australia, 2005. Available http://www.nla.gov.au/initiatives/meetings/disabilities/papers.html(accessed January 24, 2005).

National Organization on Disability. "Education Levels of People with Disabilities." Washington, D.C.: National Organization on Disability, 2001. Available at http://www.nod.org/content.cfm?id = 130 (accessed September 8, 2004).

New Zealand. Ministry of Economic Development. *Digital Strategy: A Draft New Zealand Digital Strategy for Consultation.* Wellington, NZ: The Ministry, 2004. Available at http://www.med.govt.nz/pbt/infotech/digital-strategy/draft/draft.pdf (Accessed September 15, 2004).

———. Ministry of Education. *Participation in Tertiary Education 2003.* Wellington, NZ: Ministry of Education, 2003. Available at http://www.minedu.govt.nz/index. cfm?layout = document&documentid = 8811&indexid = 8655&indexparentid = 8654 (accessed September 5, 2004).

———. Ministry of Social Development. Office for Disability Issues. NZ Disability Strategy. Wellington: Ministry of Social Development, n.d. Available at http://www.odi.govt.nz/nzds/index.html (accessed April 20, 2005).

———. *New Zealand Disability Strategy—Education's Implementation Work Plan.* Wellington, NZ: Ministry of Education, 2004. Available at http://www. minedu.govt.nz/index.cfm?layout = document&documentid = 7356&data = 1 (accessed September 4, 2004).

———. Office for Disability Issues. *Publications: NZ Disability Strategy Publications.* Wellington: Ministry of Social Development, Office for Disability Issues, 2004. Available at http://www.odi.govt.nz/publications/publications.html (accessed September 5, 2004).

———. Office of the Privacy Commissioner. Fact Sheet No. 3: "Information Privacy Principles." Wellington, New Zealand: Office of the Privacy Commissioner, 2004. Available at http://www.privacy.org.nz/people/peotop.html (accessed November 28, 2004).

———. Public Access to Legislation Project. Wellington, New Zealand: Parliamentary Counsel Office, 2005. Available at http://www.legislation.govt.nz/ (accessed January 24, 2005).

———. Statistics New Zealand. *Disability.* Wellington: Statistics New Zealand, 2002. Available at http://www.stats.govt.nz/domino/external/web/Prod_Serv. nsf/htmldocs/Disability (accessed September 5, 2004)

———. Statistics New Zealand. *New Zealand Disability Survey Snapshot 1: Key Facts.* Wellington: Statistics New Zealand, 2002. Available at http://www.stats. govt.nz/domino/external/pasfull/pasfull.nsf/web/Media+Release+2001+ Disability+Survey+Snapshot+1+Key+Facts?open (accessed September 5, 2004).

Noble, Steve. "Delivering Accessible Library Services in a Distance Learning Environment," *Information Technology and Disabilities* 6, no. 1/2 (April 1999). Available at http://www.rit.edu/~easi/itd/itdv06n1/artricle5.html (accessed January 7, 2005).

North Carolina State University. Center for Universal Design. *Universal Design for Learning*. Raleigh, NC: North Carolina State University, 1997. Available at http://iod.unh.edu/EE/articles/articles_udl.html (accessed November 11, 2004).

———. "What Is Universal Design?" Raleigh, NC: North Carolina State University, Center for Universal Design, 1997. Available at http://www.design.ncsu.edu/cud/univ_design/ud.htm (accessed November 22, 2004).

North Lindsey College. "Disability Statement." Scunthorpe, UK: North Lindsey College. Available at http://www.northlindsey.ac.uk/nlcds.htm (accessed September 3, 2004).

Paul, Stanley. "Students with Disabilities in Higher Education: A Review of the Literature," *College Student Journal* 34 (June 2000). [Electronic Version from Infotrac].

Postsecondary Students with Disabilities. Recent Data from the 2000 National Postsecondary Student Aid Survey (n.d.). Available at The George Washington University, HEATH Resource Center Web site, http://www.heath.gwu.edu/PDFs/Recent%20Data.pdf (accessed November 24, 2004).

Providenti, Michael. "Library Web Accessibility at Kentucky's 4-Year Degree Granting Colleges and Universities," *D-Lib Magazine* 10, no. 9 (September 2004). Available at http://www.dlib.org/dlib/september04/providenti/09/providenti.html (accessed January 21, 2005).

Quality Assurance Agency for Higher Education. *Code of Practice for the Assurance of Academic Quality and Standards in Higher Education. Section 3: Students with Disabilities*. Gloucester, UK: Quality Assurance Agency for Higher Education, October 1999. Available at http://www.qaa.ac.uk/public/COP/COPswd/contents.htm (accessed November 24, 2004).

Rao, Shaila. "Faculty Attitudes and Students with Disabilities in Higher Education: A Literature Review," *College Student Journal* 38 (June 2004): 191–197. [Electronic Version available through Infotrac].

Roanoke College. "Services for Students with Disabilities. Salem, VA: Roanoke College Library, 2004. Available http://www.roanoke.edu/library/disability.htm (accessed September 3, 2004).

Rutgers University Libraries. "Library Services for Persons with Disabilities." New Brunswick, NJ: Rutgers University Libraries, 2004. Available http://www.libraries.rutgers.edu/rul/lib_servs/disabil.shmtl (accessed September 3, 2004).

Santa Monica College Library. "Learning Disabilities." Santa Monica, CA: Santa Monica College, n.d. Available at http://library.smc.edu/research/topics/learning_disabilities.htm (accessed November 27, 2004).

Schmetzke, Axel. "Web Accessibility Survey Homepage." Stevens Point, WI: University of Wisconsin Library, 2004. Available at http://library.uwsp.edu/aschmetz/Accessible/websurveys.htm (accessed September 3, 2004).

Shaw, Stan F., Sally S. Scott, and Joan M. McGuire. "Teaching College Students with Learning Disabilities," *ERIC Digest* (ED459548). Available at http://www.ericfacility.net/ericdigests/ed459548.html (June 1, 2005).

Stanford University. Archimedes Project. Palo Alto, CA: Stanford University. Available at http://archimedes.stanford.edu/ (accessed November 5, 2004).

"Task Force on Access to Information for Print Disabled Canadians Formed." Fredericton, NB, CA: National Adult Literacy Database Inc., 2000. Available at http://www.nald.ca/WHATNEW/hnews/2000cnib.htm (accessed September 4, 2004).

Texas Tech University Libraries. "University Libraries Strategic Plan." Lubbock, TX: Texas Tech University Libraries, 2004. Available at http://library.ttu.edu/sp/ulsp_text.php (accessed August 24, 2004).

United Kingdom. Her Majesty's Stationery Office. *Copyright (Visually Impaired Persons) Act 2002.* London: Her Majesty's Stationery Office, 2002. Available at http://www.legislation.hmso.gov.uk/acts/acts2002/20020033.htm (accessed January 24, 2005).

———. Office of the Information Commissioner. Homepage. London: Office of the Information Commission International, 2004. Available at http://www.informationcommissioner.gov.uk/ (accessed November 28, 2004).

Universal Design Education Online. Homepage. Center for Universal Design, North Carolina State University; IDEA Center, University at Buffalo; Global Universal Design Educator's Network, 2004). Available at http://www.udeducation.org/learn/aboutud.asp (accessed June 1, 2005).

University of Arkansas Libraries. "StaffWeb: Initiative Review Group I: Final Report, June 30, 2001." Little Rock, AR: University of Arkansas Libraries, 2001. Available at http://libinfo.uark.edu/Strategic Planning/irglfinal.asp (accessed August 24, 2004).

University of Canterbury. "Facilities for Users with Disabilities." Christchurch, New Zealand: University of Canterbury, 2004. Available at http://library.canterbury.ac.nz/services/disabled.shtml (accessed October 5, 2004).

University of Colorado, Colorado Springs. "Policies for Students with Disabilities." Colorado Springs, CO: University of Colorado, 2004. Available at http://web.uccs.edu/library/Library%20Information%20and%20Services/disabil.htm (accessed September 29, 2004).

University of Kentucky. "Self-study: Section V, Educational Support Services." Lexington, KY: University of Kentucky, n.d. Available at http://www.uky.edu/SelfStudy/VCOMMREPORT/SectionV.pdf (accessed August 31, 2004).

University of Manitoba. "Information for Library Users with Disabilities." Winnipeg, CA: University of Manitoba Libraries, 2004. Available at http://www.umanitoba.ca/libraries/get_it/disability_services.shmtl (accessed September 3, 2004).

University of Maryland Medicine. "Learning Disabilities—Types" (A partnership of the University of Maryland Medical Center and the University of Maryland School of Medicine). Baltimore, MD: University of Maryland Medicine, n.d. Available at http://www.umm.edu/mcadd/ld_types.html (accessed November 27, 2004).

University of Massachusetts, Boston, Healey Library. "LibQUAL+™ Results: Library as Place (by Patron Group)." Available at http://www.lib.umb.edu/libqual/4a/cfm (accessed August 30, 2004).

University of Notre Dame. "University Libraries: Services for Students with Disabilities." Notre Dame, IN: University of Notre Dame Libraries, 2004. Available at http://www.library.nd.edu/services/disabilities/index.shtml (accessed November 5, 2004.)

University of Washington. Disabilities. Opportunities, Internetworking, and Technology (DO-IT). Seattle, WA: University of Washington. Available at http://www.washington.edu/doit/ (accessed November 5, 2004).

————. National Center on Accessible Information Technology at the University. AccessIT. Seattle,WA: University of Washington. Available at http://www. washington.edu/accessit/index.php (accessed November 5, 2004).

University of Wisconsin–Madison. College of Engineering. Trace Research & Development Center. Homepage. Madison, WI: University of Wisconsin. Available at http://trace.wisc.edu/ (accessed November 5, 2004).

University of Wisconsin–Stout. Center for Assessment and Continuous Improvement. *Welcome*. Menomonie, WI: University of Wisconsin–Stout, n.d. Available at http://www.uwstout.edu/mba/ (accessed November 11, 2004).

————. Library Learning Center, "Services for Library Users with Disabilities." Menomonie, WI: University of Wisconsin–Stout, n.d. Available at http:// www.uwstout.edu/lib/services/disabled_2.htm (accessed November 11, 2004).

U.S. Bureau of the Census. "Disability Status: 2000—Census 2000: Table 1. Characteristics of the Civilian Noninstitutionalized Population by Age, Disability Status, and Type of Disability: 2000." Washington, D.C.: Bureau of the Census, 1997. Available at http://www.census.gov/hhes/www/disable/disabstat2k/ table1.html (accessed September 5, 2004).

————. "Facts for Features." Washington, D.C.: Bureau of the Census, 2002. Available at http://www.census.gov/Press-Release/www/2002/cb02ff11.html (accessed September 7, 2004).

U.S. Department of Education, National Center for Education Statistics. *The Condition of Education 2003: Services and Accommodations for Students with Disabilities*. Washington, D.C.: National Center for Education Statistics, 2003. Available at http://nces.ed.gov/programs/coe/2003/section5/indicator34. asp (accessed September 4, 2004).

————. Office for Civil Rights. "Auxiliary Aids and Services for Postsecondary Students with Disabilities." Washington, D.C.: Office for Civil Rights, 1998. Available at http://www.ed.gov/about/offices/list/ocr/docs/auxaids.html (accessed July 7, 2004; June 8, 2005).

————. "The Civil Rights of Students with Hidden Disabilities under Section 504 of the Rehabilitation Act of 1973." Washington, D.C.: Office for Civil Rights, n.d. Available at http://www.ed.gov/about/offices/list/ocr/docs/hq5269. html (accessed July 7, 2004).

U.S. Department of Health and Human Services, National Institute of Mental Health. *Teenage Brain: A Work in Progress*. Bethesda, MD: National Institute of Mental Health, 2001. Available at http://www.nimh.nih.gov/publicat/teenbrain. cfm (accessed December 3, 2004).

Valle Verde Library. "Designing Web Pages for People with Disabilities." El Paso, TX: El Paso Community College, Valle Verde Library, 2004). Available at http:// www.epcc.edu/vvlib/webada.html (accessed September 4, 2004).

Washington State University Libraries. "WSU Library Services for Users with Disabilities." Pullman, WA: University of Washington Libraries, 2004. Available at http://www.wsulibs.wsu.edu/govdoc/disabilities.htm (accessed September 5, 2004).

Wiler, Linda Lou, and Eleanor Lomax, "The Americans with Disabilities Act Compliance and Academic Libraries in the Southeastern United States," *Journal of Southern Academic and Special Librarianship* 2, no. 1/2 (2000). Available at http://southernlibrarianship.icaap.org/content/v02n01/wiler_l01.html (accessed November 5, 2004).

Wisconsin Association of Academic Librarians, Information Library Committee. "Information Literacy Competencies and Criteria for Academic Libraries in Wisconsin" (October 1998). Available at http://www.wla.lib.wi.us/waal/infolit/ilcc.html (accessed November 10, 2004).

Wolanin, Thomas R., and Patricia E. Steele. *Higher Education Opportunities for Students with Disabilities: A Primer for Policymakers.* Washington, D.C.: The Institute for Higher Education Policy, June 2004. Available at http://www.ihep.com/Pubs/PDF/DisabilitiesReport2004.pdf (accessed September 4, 2004).

World Health Organization. *Towards a Common Language for Functioning, Disability and Health: ICF.* Geneva: World Health Organization, 2002. Available at http://www3.who.int/icf/beginners/bg.pdf (accessed October 2, 2004).

W3C®. "List of Checkpoints for Web Content Accessibility Guidelines." Cambridge, MA: World Wide Web Consortium, 2004. Available at http://www.w3.org/TR/WAI-WEBCONTENT/checkpoint-list.html (accessed November 30, 2004).

OTHER

Association of Research Libraries. *LibQUAL+: Policies and Procedures Manual.* Draft. Washington, D.C.: Association of Research Libraries, 2002, 2003.

Betts v. Rector & Visitors, 18 Fed Appx. 114 (4th Cir. 2001).

Davis v. University of North Carolina, 263 F.3d 95 (4th Cir. 2001).

Dean College. "The Institute for Students with Disabilities at Dean College: Summary of Results and Findings, 2001–2003." Franklin, MA: Dean College, 2004.

Marlon v. Western New England College, 2003 U.S. Dist. LEXIS 22095 (D. Mass. 2003), *aff'd* 2005 U.S. App. LEXIS 407 (1st Cir. 2005).

Middle States Commission on Higher Education. *Characteristics of Excellence in Higher Education: Eligibility Requirements and Standards for Accreditation.* Philadelphia, PA: Middle States Commission on Higher Education, 2002.

Pacella v. Tufts University School of Dental Medicine, 66 F. Supp. 2d 234 (D. Mass. 1999).

Price v. National Board of Medical Examiners, 966 F. Supp. 419 (S.D.W.V., 1997).

Wong v. Regents of the University of California, 379 F.3d 1097 (9th Cir. 2004).

INDEX

Academic freedom, ADA, 42
Academic Librarians Assisting the
    Disabled, 71
Access Board, 22
Accessibility, universal design, 53
ADA, 2, 33; academic freedom, 42;
    application, 31; civil rights law, 47;
    compliance, 96; court cases, 36, 43
    n.6; disabilities covered by, 3, 34–35;
    excluding students, 41; impairment,
    37; implementation, 71; major life
    activity, 36; prohibitions and require-
    ments, 18, 34; reasonable accommo-
    dation, 38–42; substantially limiting
    impairment, 35–36, 43 n.5; Title II,
    15; unreasonable exemptions, 39–40
Adaptive technology (New Zealand), 63
Adaptive technology (USA), 93, 97
American Foundation for the Blind, 22
American Library Association, Associa-
    tion of Specialized and Cooperative
    Library Agencies, 22
Americans with Disabilities, Department
    of Justice, 23
Americans with Disabilities Act (1990).
    See ADA

Applin, Beth, 94–95
Archimedes Project, 21
Architectural and Transportation
    Barriers Compliance Board (Access
    Board), 47
Architectural Barriers Act (1968), 46
Arkansas, University of, 100
Assistive Devices Industry Office
    (Canada), 22
Association for Higher Education Access
    and Disability (Ireland), 23
Association of College and Research
    Libraries, 189
Association of Research Libraries, 96
Association on Higher Education and
    Disability (AHEAD), guidelines, 20,
    23
Attention-deficit hyperactivity disorder
    (ADHD), 72–74; survey response,
    143, 145
Auckland, University of (New Zealand),
    Disability Services, 80–81
Australia: applying service quality survey
    results, 160; Guidelines on Library
    Standards for People with Disabilities,
    20; National Information Library

Service, 25; The Open Road, 25–26;
    Workable Electronic Network, 26
Australian Human Rights & Equal
    Rights Commission, 23
Australian Library and Information
    Association, 20

Background knowledge, 74
Berry, Leonard L., 104–5
Blind students, 31; surveying, 166
Bobby compliance, 98
Bohman, Paul Ryan, 98
Braille resources, 18
Budgetary concerns: New Zealand, 64;
    USA, 53
Burgstahler, Sheryl, 191

California State University, Long Beach,
    21
Calvert, Philip, 96–97
Canada, Assistive Devices Industry
    Office, 22
CAN-DO (New Zealand), 60
Canterbury, University of (New
    Zealand): Disability Support Services,
    81; library services, 82; policy on
    seeing-eye dogs, 91 n.42, 82
Carpenter, Scott A., 96
Center for Accessible Housing. See
    Center for Universal Design
Center for Universal Design, 50–51, 73
Chronicle of Higher Education, 97
Civil rights: Department of Education:
    Office of Civil Rights (OCR), 9, 18;
    Disabled People's International, 49;
    law, 46; social construction move-
    ment, 48
Clark, Helen (New Zealand Prime
    Minister), 6
Classroom instruction, students with
    disabilities, 187
Coleman, Diane, 54
Colorado at Colorado Springs, Univer-
    sity of, 99
Comfort animal, 82
Communications, 65
Communication technologies, 6

Computer equipment and service,
    service quality survey statements,
    135, 152, 193, 197–99
Confidentiality rules, Gallaudet Univer-
    sity, Washington, D.C., 87
Confidentiality statements, 144
Confirmation/disconfirmation theory,
    104
Consortium for Libraries in Higher
    Education Networking to Improve
    Library Access for Disabled User
    (UK), 23; guidelines, 20
Coordinator of Students with Disabili-
    ties (VUW), 60
Copyrighted material, 9
Copyright (Visually Impaired Persons)
    Act 2002 (U.K.), 9
Corrigan, Bill, 191
Court cases, students with disabilities,
    36, 43 n.6
Craven, Jenny, 99
Critical thinking, 75; strategy routines,
    76
Cronin, Bryna, 99
Cullen, Rowena, 96–97, 101–2
Curry College, Massachusetts, 15–16

Data collection, 160, 170; focus groups,
    169; privacy legislation (New
    Zealand), 161
Data presentation. See Gaps model of
    service quality; Gap analysis
Deaf Student (New Zealand), 59, 66
    n.8
Dean College, Massachusetts, 27 n.7;
    service statement, 17
Department of Education: Office of
    Civil Rights (OCR): academic
    freedom, 9; required library services,
    18
Department of Justice, Americans with
    Disabilities, 23
Design modification: Universal Design,
    52
Dick, Marcia A., 95
Digital Text Library, Landmark College
    Library, 78–79

Disabilities, Opportunities, Internet-
working, and Technology (DO-IT),
21, 191
*Disabilities Compliance for Higher
Education*, 19
Disability: defined by World Health
Organization, 4; defined by 1973
Rehabilitation Act (Section 504), 3;
hidden, 18; print, 20–21; psychologi-
cal, 10, 38–39; social model, 4, 7; vs.
impairment, 49
Disability coordinator, 83
Disability Equity Training (VUW), 61
Disability in Higher Education, 5
Disability Liaison Person (VUW), 61
Disability literature; overview, 93–94
Disability Services: Auckland, University
of (New Zealand), 80–81; individual
needs, 49–50
Disability statistics: American, 1–2, 72;
New Zealand, 5–6
Disability Strategy (New Zealand), 6,
57–58
Disability Support Services, Canterbury,
University of (New Zealand), 81
Disability Support Services (DSS),
VUW, 57; equity in action card, 66
n.11; library staff, 65; statistics, 59;
student advocates, 58; student
database, 161; student feedback, 64;
survey development, 118
Disability vs. impairment, 4, 49
Disabled People's Association (Singa-
pore), 24
Disabled People's International, 49
Diversity, 45

E-government, *Wired for Well-being:
Citizens' Response to E-government*
(New Zealand), 101
E-mailing surveys, 166
E-service quality, dimensions, 106
East Carolina University library, 99
Education for Handicapped Children
Act of 1975. *See* Individuals with
Disabilities Education Act (IDEA)
Edwards, Eli, 93

Enable New Zealand, 24
Equal access, 19
Equal Access to Software and Informa-
tion (EASI), 24
Equal opportunities, 33
Ethical approval of survey, 160
Euben, Donna R., 117
Expectation and performance, 176;
hypothetical data, 177–78, 180; mean
scores, 179, 181

Facilities and equipment access (New
Zealand), 63
Factor analysis, 129
Faculty, attitude, 7–9
Fisher, William, 93
Flexible assessment, 78
Forsyth, Elizabeth M., 107, 160, 164

Gallaudet University, Washington, D.C.,
16–17, 71; confidentiality rules, 87;
library policy, 86; Office for Students
with Disabilities, 70
Gap analysis, 175–76, 179, 200;
application, 201; critical assessment,
181; hypothetical data, 177–78, 180;
mean scores, 121, 123–24; Victoria
University of Wellington (New
Zealand), 120
Gaps model of service quality, 103–4
Golden, Michael, 94
Government policies, response of
university, 187
Government regulations, compliance
with (UK), 100
Grand Mean, 183
Greene, Gary, 21
Guidelines on Library Standards for
People with Disabilities (Australia),
20

Handicapped access, 49
Harris, Clare, 100
Henderson, Cathy, 2
Hernon, Peter, 101–2, 110
Heyward, Salome, 8
Hidden disability, 18, 19

Higher education: disability service statements, 16; students with disabilities, 2, 72
Horwath, Jennifer, 166

Ideal library, use in survey, 133–34, 151
Impairment, 35; vs. disability, 4, 49; regarded as having, 37
Individuals with Disabilities Education Act (IDEA), 47
Information literacy: definition, 188; library program, 190; research process, 189
Information technologies, 6; Universal design, 74
Intercept survey, 167
International Classification of Functioning, Disability, and Health (ICF), disability defined, 4
Ireland, Association for Higher Education Access and Disability, 23

Journal of Learning Disabilities, 148
Journal of Library Administration, 108

Kearney State University Library, Nebraska: library services, 68; special challenges, 69
Kentucky, University of, 19
Kirkpatrick, Cheryl H., 111
Kirwan, William, 45

Landmark College Library, Putney, Vermont, 72–73; Digital Text Library, 78, 146; layout, 79; level of use, 149; service philosophy, 139; Universal design, 73; web site, 80
Landmark College Library, service quality survey: cover letter, 141; insights, 150; low response, 143–45; promotion, 142–43; quadrant analysis, 145–47; revision, 139–40, 149; text of, 151–55
Learning differences, 89 n.4, 190
Learning disabilities: critical thinking, 75; defined, 3, 35
Learning Disabilities Worldwide, 24

Learning strategy routines: critical thinking, 76; research process, 77
Level of service, 111; Gallaudet University, 70; Kearney State University Library, 68; University of Pittsburgh, 69
LibQUAL, 108–10, 118, 166. *See also* SERVQUAL
Library, access to, 52
Library and Information Commission (UK), 111
Library database, ethical use, 161
Library Learning Center, 203–4
Library of Congress, 24
Library service policies, 61; Gallaudet University, 86–87; Massey University, 88–89; seeing-eye-dogs, 91 n.42, 82
Library services, 94–95; additional research, 110; Canterbury, University of (New Zealand), 82; compliance with government regulations (UK), 100; disability staff training, 62, 84; Disability Support Services (VUW), 65; efficacy, 52; faculty, 190; improving and retaining, 146; level of use, 149; Massey University, 83; proxy borrowing, 81, 82; quality assessment and dimensions, 80, 106; required by law, 18; separate facilities, 60; surveys, 96–97, 100. *See also* Web site
Library staff: disability specialists, 203–4; participation in survey, 150; training, 202
Library staff service quality survey statements, 123–24, 136, 154–55, 194
Library Technology Reports, 95
Lomax, Eleanor, 96
Long-term strategizing, universal design, 53
Loope, Charlene H., 100

Mace, Ron, 73
Major life activity, ADA, 36
Maki, Peggy L., 190
Massey University (New Zealand): disability coordinator, 83; library

policy, 88–89; library services, 84; special accommodation, 192

McCarter, Joan, 191

McCasland, Margaret, 94

National Center for Education Statistics, 2, 8, 24

National Center on Accessible Information Technology, 21

National Council on Disability, 24

National Information Library Service (Australia), 25

National Organization on Disability, 8

New Zealand: accessibility, 63; adaptive technology, 63; budgetary concerns, 64; CAN-DO, 60; Clark, Helen (Prime Minister), 6; data collection, 161, 169–70; Deaf Students, 59, 66 n.8; Disability Services, 80–81; Disability Strategy, 6, 57–58; Enable New Zealand, 24; facilities and equipment access, 63; Office for Disability Issues, 25; Privacy Act of 1993, 161; Royal New Zealand Foundation of the Blind, 118; Special Supplementary Grant, 65 n.2, 66 n.12; statistics for students with disabilities, 5–6, 58–59; Tertiary Education Commission, 65 n.5, 66 n.12; *Wired for Well-being: Citizens' Response to E-government*, 101

New Zealand Universities: Auckland, University of, 80–81; Canterbury, University of, 81–82, 91 n.42, 82; librarians, 118; Massey University, 83–84, 88–89, 192; Victoria University of Wellington (VUW)

Nitecki, Danuta, 110

North Carolina State University, 51

Northern Illinois University, 95

Nursing students, disabled, 32

Office for Civil Rights (OCR), Department of Education: academic freedom, 9; Annual Report, 19; required library services, 18

Office for Disability Issues (New Zealand), 25

Office for Students with Disabilities (Gallaudet University Library), 70

Office of Disability Services (University of Pittsburgh), 69–70

Online catalog, service quality survey statements, 135, 152, 193, 196–97

Online resources, accessibility, 97–98, 191

Open Road (Australia), 25–26

Oppenheim, A. N., 160, 165

Oppenheim, Charles, 100

Otherwise qualified, 9, 32; Section, 504, 34–35

Parasuraman, A., 104–5

Paul, Stanley, 8

PDF (portable document format) files, 166

Performance and expectation. *See* Expectation and performance

Pittsburgh, University of: library services, 69; special challenges, 70

Print disability, 20–21

Print format, service quality surveys, 165

Privacy Act of 1993 (New Zealand), 161

Privacy issue: students with disabilities, 161; Web-based survey, 168

Proctor, Briley S., 8

Providenti, Michael, 99

Proxy borrowing, library services, 81, 82

Psychology of survey response, 164

Quadrant analysis: quadrant determination, 183; Service quality surveys, 125–29, 145–47, 182

Quality assessment, Landmark College Library, 80

Quality Assurance Agency (UK), 20

Quality of education, students with disabilities, 188

Quality of Service. *See* Service Quality

Rao, Shaila, 8
Reasonable accommodation, 37–38, 43 n.3
Regarded as having impairment, 37
Rehabilitation Act (1973). *See* Section 504; Sections, 508
Research agenda, 202
Research process for service quality, case studies, 203
Research process for students: ADHD, 73; flexible assessment, 78; information literacy, 189; learning strategy routines, 77; skill deficits, 75; skill development, 76; universal design, 74
Riddell, Sheila, 9
Royal New Zealand Foundation of the Blind, 118

Schmetzke, Axel, 95
Schneider, Benjamin, 105
Section 504: civil rights law, 46; disability defined, 3; excluding students, 41; general, 2, 15, 33, 46; otherwise qualified, 34–35; prohibitions and requirements, 18, 34; reasonable accommodation, 38; substantially limiting impairment, 35–36, 43 n.5; unreasonable exemptions, 39–40
Sections, 508, 19, 26, 47–48
Seeing-eye dogs, 91 n.42, 82
Self-identification, students with disabilities, 71, 73
Separate facilities, library services, 60
Service quality survey design, 164, 167, 169, 174
Service quality: dimensions, 106; research tools, 202–3; SERVQUAL program, 105, 110, 118, 164. *See also* Gaps model of service quality; Victoria University of Wellington (New Zealand)
Service quality survey evaluation, 173; data-processing software, 174; grand mean, 185; hypothetical data, 177–78, 180; integrated software, 175; mean scores, 179, 181; non-response, 176; quadrant determination, 183; verifying and analyzing data, 176, 179, 181
Service quality survey evaluation, quadrant analysis, 125–29, 145–47, 182
Service quality survey report format, 185
Service quality survey reports: feedback to participants, 184; graphs, 181–82; survey partners, 185; wider public, 186
Service quality surveys: applying results, 122, 126; Australia, 160; blind or visually impaired students, 166; development of, 119–20, 159; e-mailing, 166; explanatory material, 165; factor analysis, 129; finding respondents, 162; gap analysis, 175; incentives for taking, 162–63; insights, 148; intercept, 167; low response, 144; PDF files, 166; pilot, 173; print format, 165; role of, 109; target population, 119, 170; testing, 168; timeline, 161; Web-based, 167
Service quality survey statements, 130; access, 134; electronic resources, 198; facility, 135–37; general, 153; materials, 194, 198; planning issues, 160–61; revision of, 131–32; selection, 163, 192
Service quality survey statements about computers, 135, 152, 193, 197–99
Service quality survey statements about online catalog, 135, 154, 193, 196–97
Service quality survey statements about staff, 123–24, 136, 154–55, 194
Service quality survey statements about Web site, 134, 152, 193, 195–96
Service quality survey statements, ranking importance, 127–29, 137, 147–48
Service quality surveys, revision, 131–32, 140–41, 149
Service satisfaction vs. quality, 107–8
Service statements, 16; Dean College, Massachusetts, 17

SERVQUAL (program), 105, 110, 118, 164. *See also* LibQUAL

Singapore, Disabled People's Association, 24

Skill deficits: information literacy, 188–91; nonacademic, 76; research process, 74–75

Snap Survey, 174

Social construction, 48–49

South Carolina, University of, 100

Special challenges: Gallaudet University, D.C., 70; Kearney State University Library, 69; research projects, 73; University of Pittsburgh, 70

Special Educational Needs and Disabilities Act of 2001 (SENDA) (UK), 100

Special equipment and service: Kearney State University Library, 68; University of Pittsburgh, 69

Special Supplementary Grant (New Zealand), 65 n.2, 66 n.12

Spindler, Tim, 98

Spreadsheets, 175

Staff training, 72; Gallaudet University, D.C., 70, 71; Kearney State University Library, 68; University of Pittsburgh, 69–70

Stanford University, 21

Steele, Patricia E., 1–2; disability issues, 7

Strategizing, long-term, universal design, 53

Student advocates; Disability Support Services, 58

Students with disabilities: background knowledge, 74; challenges to library services, 45–46, 84; classroom instruction, 187, 190; court cases, 36; discrimination, 3, 33; dismissal, 44 n.15; excluding, 41; guidelines, 20; higher education, 47; issues, 7, 9; library contact people, 62; library orientation, 191; library, use of, 149; online resources, 97–98, 191; privacy of personal information, 161; quality of education, 188; registered, 162; research projects, 73–74; responsibility for service, 85; self-identification, 71; service statements, 16; significant threat, 40–41; social interaction, 78; special accommodation, 192; survey response, 145; undocumented, 170; use of services, 19; Web-site preferences, 101, 102

Students with disabilities, service expectations, 117, 122–25, 130

Students with disabilities statistics: New Zealand, 5–6, 58–59; USA, 1–2, 48, 72

Substantially limiting impairment, 35–36, 43 n.5

Survey, budget concerns (Australia), 160

Survey partners, service quality survey reports, 184–85

Sutherland Room (VUW), 60

Taylor, Margaret, 8

Telecommunications Act of 1996, 47

Tertiary Education Commission (New Zealand), 65 n.5, 66 n.12

Texas Tech University, 17

Texas Tech University Libraries, 94

Tinerella, Vincent P., 95

Trace Research and Development Center, 21

United Kingdom: compliance with government regulations, 100; Consortium for Libraries in Higher Education Networking to Improve Library Access for Disabled User, 20, 23; Copyright (Visually Impaired Persons) Act, 2002, 9; Library and Information Commission, 111; Quality Assurance Agency, 20; Special Educational Needs and Disabilities Act of 2001 (SENDA), 100

Universal design, 53; design modification, 52; flexible assessment, 78; information technologies, 74–75; Landmark College Library, 73; principles of, 51, 203; research process, 77

U.S. Bureau of the Census (1997), 1
U.S Supreme Court; disability services,
    50

Valle Verde Library, El Paso, Texas, 17
Vavra, Terry, 104, 109
Victoria University of Wellington (New
    Zealand): applying survey results,
    122; disability staff training, 62;
    Disability Equity Training, 61;
    Disability Support Services (DSS),
    57–58, 118; Special Supplementary
    Grant, 65 n.2, 66 n.12; Sutherland
    Room, 60; target population, 119
Victoria University of Wellington
    (VUW), service quality survey:
    development of, 119; factor analysis,
    129; gap analysis, 120; 129–30;
    quadrant analysis, 125–29; results,
    120–21, 123–25; revision, 131–32;
    selection of statements, 163–64

Walling, Linda L., 19
Washington, University of: Disabilities,
    Opportunities, Internetworking, and
    Technology (DO-IT), 21, 191; Web-
    site accessibility, 99–100
Web Accessibility in Mind (WebAIM),
    26
Web-based survey, 167; privacy issue,
    168
Web Design, 101

Web site: accessibility, 98–99, 101;
    Bobby compliance, 98–99; Landmark
    College Library, 80; Wisconsin-
    Stevens Point, 95
Web site, service quality survey state-
    ments, 134, 152, 193, 195–96
White, Susan S. 105
Wiler, Linda Lou, 96
*Wired for Well-being: Citizens' Response
    to E-government* (New Zealand), 101
Wisconsin Association of Academic
    Librarians, 189
Wisconsin–Madison, University of, 21
Wisconsin–Stevens Point, University of,
    95
Wisconsin–Stout, University of, 203–4
Wolanin, Thomas R., 1–2; disability
    issues, 7
Workable Electronic Network (Austra-
    lia), 26
Workforce Investment Act 1998
    (Section 508), 19, 26
World Health Organization, 4
Worldwide Wide Web Consortium
    (W3C), 26

Yannie, Mark, 99

Zeithaml, Valarie A., 104–5

ABOUT THE EDITORS AND CONTRIBUTORS

PHILIP CALVERT (Philip.Calvert@vuw.ac.nz) is Senior Lecturer at Victoria University of Wellington (New Zealand). He has been there since 1990. Prior to then, he worked in a variety of academic and public libraries in the United Kingdom, Fiji, and Papua New Guinea, and in the computer industry as a programmer and marketing manager. He has also taught programs and workshops in Singapore, Thailand, and Vietnam. His research interests relate to performance measurement and library effectiveness, assessing service quality, journal quality, misconduct and misinformation, social inclusion and public libraries, and library funding. He has edited library journals and is currently involved with four journals in various capacities.

AVA GIBSON (ava.gibson@vuw.ac.nz) is Manager of the Disability Support Services at Victoria University of Wellington. She is responsible for the development of services for students with impairments within the university, being the first appointed staff member in the area as a half-time Coordinator for Students with Disabilities in 1994. The service now has 10 full-time office staff, approximately 15 part-time staff, and 110 volunteers. She has extensive experience in the sector and has been actively involved on a national level, as the former Vice President of ACHIEVE (The National Post-Secondary Education Disability Network, Inc.). She chaired the development of Kia Orite—Achieving Equity: The New Zealand Code of Practice for Creating an Inclusive Environment for Students with Impairment, for ACHIEVE. Ms. Gibson has a BSW (with honors) from Massey University and before working in the tertiary sector worked as a community social worker and counselor.

TODD K. HERRIOTT (todd.herriott@simmons.edu) is the ADA Compliance Officer/Director of Disability Services at Simmons College. He previously worked for Iowa State University in Ames, Iowa, as the Coordinator for Disability Services. With experience at a large public institution and a small private institution, Mr. Herriott has a broad perspective of issues surrounding disability within post-secondary education.

Mr. Herriott completed his undergraduate degrees in sociology and political science from Drake University in Des Moines, Iowa, and his MS in education, specializing in educational leadership and policy studies. Prior to coming into higher education he worked as a psychiatric rehabilitation counselor for a mental health agency in central Iowa. Mr. Herriott has written a number of articles and book chapters focusing on issues of disability and identity development among minority status populations within higher education.

PETER HERNON (peter.hernon@simmons.edu) is a professor at Simmons College, Graduate School of Library and Information Science, where he teaches courses on government information policy and resources, evaluation of information services, research methods, and academic librarianship. He received his Ph.D. from Indiana University in 1978 and has taught at Simmons College, the University of Arizona, and Victoria University of Wellington (New Zealand). He is the coeditor of *Library & Information Science Research,* founding editor of *Government Information Quarterly,* and past editor of *The Journal of Academic Librarianship.* He is the author of approximately 250 publications, 41 of which are books. Among these are *Outcomes Assessment in Higher Education* (Libraries Unlimited, 2004), *The Next Library Leadership* (Libraries Unlimited, 2003), and *Assessing Service Quality* (1998).

JENNIFER LANN (JLann@landmark.edu) is Director of Library Services at Landmark College. She received her MLIS from the University of Pittsburgh in 1997 and then became the Research Services Librarian at the Landmark College Library in 1998. She is the coauthor of the chapter "Learning Disabilities, AD/HD, and the Research Process" for the Title VII-funded guide *Promoting Academic Success for Students with Learning Disabilities* (2001). She has also taught workshops for librarians and educators about research instruction for students with learning differences.

KATHLEEN ROGERS (kathleen.rogers@simmons.edu) is the General Counsel for Simmons College. For more than a decade, she has advised and represented numerous Boston area colleges and universities and their faculty and deans in litigation and risk management, particularly in cases involving disability and employment law issues. Ms. Rogers is a graduate of Regis College and Northeastern University School of Law. She is a frequent speaker on employment and disability law issues.